D1756222

Work and Welfare in Europe

Series Editors: **Denis Bouget**, University of Nantes, France, **Jochen Clasen**, University of Edinburgh, UK, **Ana Guillén Rodriguez**, University of Oviedo, Spain, **Jane Lewis**, London School of Economics and Political Science, UK and **Bruno Palier**, Sciences-po Paris, France

Titles include:

Lorenza Antonucci, Myra Hamilton and Steven Roberts
YOUNG PEOPLE AND SOCIAL POLICY IN EUROPE
Dealing with Risk, Inequality and Precarity in Times of Crisis

Simone Baglioni and Marco Giugni
CIVIL SOCIETY ORGANIZATIONS, UNEMPLOYMENT, AND PRECARITY
IN EUROPE
Between Service and Policy

Egidijus Barcevicius, Timo Weishaupt and Jonathan Zeitlin
ASSESSING THE OPEN METHOD OF COORDINATION
Institutional Design and National Influence of EU Social Policy Coordination

Sigrid Betzelt and Silke Bothfeld
ACTIVATION AND LABOUR MARKET REFORMS IN EUROPE
Challenges to Social Citizenship

Sonja Drobnic and Ana Guillén Rodriguez
WORK-LIFE BALANCE IN EUROPE
The Role of Job Quality

Colette Fagan, Maria Gonzalez Menendez and Silvia Gomez Anson
WOMEN IN MANAGEMENT
European Employment Policy

Neil Fraser, Rodolfo Gutierrez and Ramon Pena-Cassas
WORKING POVERTY IN EUROPE

Paolo Graziano, Sophie Jacquot and Bruno Palier
THE EU AND THE DOMESTIC POLITICS OF WELFARE STATE REFORMS
Europa, Europae

Karl Hinrichs and Matteo Jessoula
LABOUR MARKET FLEXIBILITY AND PENSION REFORMS
Flexible Today, Secure Tomorrow?

Trudie Knijn
WORK, FAMILY POLICIES AND TRANSITIONS TO ADULTHOOD IN EUROPE

Max Koch and Martin Fritz
NON-STANDARD EMPLOYMENT IN EUROPE
Paradigms, Prevalence and Policy Responses

Colin Lindsay and Donald Houston
DISABILITY BENEFITS, WELFARE REFORM AND EMPLOYMENT POLICY

Ive Marx and Kenneth Nelson
MINIMUM INCOME PROTECTION IN FLUX

Livia Sz. Oláh and Ewa Fratczak
CHILDBEARING, WOMEN'S EMPLOYMENT AND WORK-LIFE BALANCE
POLICIES IN CONTEMPORARY EUROPE

Emmanuele Pavolini and Ana M. Guillén
HEALTH CARE SYSTEMS IN EUROPE UNDER AUSTERITY
Institutional Reforms and Performance

Birgit Pfau-Effinger and Tine Rostgaard
CARE, WORK AND WELFARE IN EUROPE

Martin Schröder
INTEGRATING VARIETIES OF CAPITALISM AND WELFARE STATE RESEARCH
A Unified Typology of Capitalisms

Costanzo Ranci, Taco Brandsen and Stefania Sabatinelli
SOCIAL VULNERABILITY IN EUROPEAN CITIES
The Role of Local Welfare in Times of Crisis

Rik van Berkel, Willibrord de Graaf and Tomáš Sirovátka
THE GOVERNANCE OF ACTIVE WELFARE STATES IN EUROPE

Work and Welfare in Europe
Series Standing Order ISBN 978–0–230–28026–7
(*outside North America only*)

You can receive future titles in this series as they are published by placing a
standing order. Please contact your bookseller or, in case of difficulty, write to
us at the address below with your name and address, the title of the series and
the ISBN quoted above.

Customer Services Department, Macmillan Distribution Ltd, Houndmills,
Basingstoke, Hampshire RG21 6XS, England

Young People and Social Policy in Europe

Dealing with Risk, Inequality and Precarity in Times of Crisis

Edited by

Lorenza Antonucci
University of the West of Scotland, UK

Myra Hamilton
University of New South Wales, Australia

Steven Roberts
University of Kent, UK

palgrave
macmillan

First published 2014 by
PALGRAVE MACMILLAN

Palgrave Macmillan in the UK is an imprint of Macmillan Publishers Limited, registered in England, company number 785998, of Houndmills, Basingstoke, Hampshire RG21 6XS.

Palgrave Macmillan in the US is a division of St Martin's Press LLC, 175 Fifth Avenue, New York, NY 10010.

Palgrave Macmillan is the global academic imprint of the above companies and has companies and representatives throughout the world.

Palgrave® and Macmillan® are registered trademarks in the United States, the United Kingdom, Europe and other countries.

ISBN 978–1–137–37051–8

This book is printed on paper suitable for recycling and made from fully managed and sustained forest sources. Logging, pulping and manufacturing processes are expected to conform to the environmental regulations of the country of origin.

A catalogue record for this book is available from the British Library.

A catalog record for this book is available from the Library of Congress.

Contents

List of Tables   vii

List of Figures   ix

Foreword by Andy Furlong   x

Acknowledgements   xii

Notes on Contributors   xiii

1   Introduction: Young People and Social Policy in Europe:
    Past and Present   1
    Myra Hamilton, Lorenza Antonucci and Steven Roberts

2   Constructing a Theory of Youth and Social Policy   13
    Lorenza Antonucci, Myra Hamilton and Steven Roberts

Part I   Precarity, Social Exclusion and Youth Policy in Europe

3   The Complex Nature of Youth Poverty and Deprivation
    in Europe   37
    Eldin Fahmy

4   At Risk of Deskilling and Trapped by Passion: A Picture of
    Precarious Highly Educated Young Workers in Italy, Spain
    and the United Kingdom   62
    Annalisa Murgia and Barbara Poggio

5   Social Exclusion, Risk and the UK Youth Labour Market   87
    Clive Sealey

6   Young People at Work in Greece before and after
    the Crisis   106
    Lefteris Kretsos

7   The Impacts of Employment Instability on Transitions to
    Adulthood: The *Mileuristas* Young Adults in Spain   125
    Alessandro Gentile

Part II Changing Transitions, Welfare Sources and Social Policies

8 Labour Market Risks and Sources of Welfare among
   European Youth in Times of Crisis   147
   Lara Maestripieri and Stefania Sabatinelli

9 Have Nordic Welfare Regimes Adapted to Changes
   in Transitions to Adulthood? Unemployment Insurance
   and Social Assistance among Young People in the Nordic
   Welfare States   169
   Anna Angelin, Timo Kauppinen, Thomas Lorentzen,
      Olof Bäckman, Pasi Moisio, Espen Dahl and Tapio Salonen

10 The Dualisation of Social Policies towards Young People
   in France: Between Familism and Activation   189
   Tom Chevalier and Bruno Palier

11 Young Adults' Transitions to Residential Independence in
   the UK: The Role of Social and Housing Policy   210
   Ann Berrington and Juliet Stone

12 Life-Course Policy and the Transition from School
   to Work in Germany   236
   Walter R. Heinz

13 Youth Transitions, Precarity and Inequality and the Future
   of Social Policy in Europe   256
   Lorenza Antonucci and Myra Hamilton

Index   266

Tables

3.1 Poverty amongst young Europeans aged 16–24 (% and 16–24/25+ ratios), 2009   46

3.2 Young Europeans aged 16–24 experiencing poverty: totals (in thousands) and as a percentage of total youth poverty by country and region, 2009   48

3.3 Poverty amongst young Europeans aged 16–24: multidimensional classification by region (column %), 2009   49

3.4 Low income, deprivation and subjective poverty in Europe by selected respondent characteristics: frequencies and multivariate odds ratios, 2009   51

A.1 Sample sizes: persons in households (unweighted)   57

A.2 Youth income poverty based on 60 per cent national median threshold and 60 per cent Europe-wide median threshold, 2009 (percentage poor)   57

5.1 'At Risk' social exclusion profile of research participants (names have been changed to protect anonymity)   94

5.2 Changes in participants' labour market circumstances between diary interviews and follow-up interviews (eight weeks)   95

6.1 Demographic characteristics of young people (15–29 years old), 1980–2007   112

6.2 Part-time employment for selected age groups, 1987–2007   113

6.3 Percentage of involuntary part-time employment by age group (2007)   113

6.4 Temporary employment for selected age groups   113

6.5 Percentage of involuntary temporary employment by age group (2007)   113

6.6 Employment changes in Greece, 2009–12   117

6.7 Unemployment rate by age group, 2007–12   117

7.1 A typology of *mileuristas* young adults   131

9.1 Distribution of the months of social assistance receipt by country   180

9.2   Social assistance receipt (%) by selected social
background life-course variables   181
11.1a Changing distribution of living arrangements of young
men in the UK by age group in 1998, 2008 and 2012   221
11.1b Changing distribution of living arrangements of young
women in the UK by age group in 1998, 2008 and 2012   222
11.2   Housing tenure of young adults living outside the
parental home by age group, sex and living
arrangements, UK, 2012   225
11.3   Prevalence of non-resident fatherhood in the UK   227

Figures

4.1 Incidence of temporary work in Europe on total
dependent employment by age in 2010   66

4.2 Transition rates from temporary to permanent contracts,
by education level (2005–07)   66

5.1 Sources of employment – Formal vs Informal
Information Networks (designed with NVivo)   99

7.1 The analytical model   131

7.2 The representation of employment instability by each
type of *mileuristas*   132

9.1 Unemployment benefits coverage for unemployed
persons aged less than 25, Finland, 1988–2008   176

9.2 Unemployment benefits coverage for unemployed
persons aged less than 25, Norway, 1989–2010   177

9.3 Unemployment benefits coverage for unemployed
persons aged less than 25, Sweden, 1999–2009   178

10.1 Distribution of student support, 2011 (per cent)   197

10.2 Unemployment rate by age, 1975–2012 (per cent)   198

10.3 Young people in subsidised non-standard jobs,
1990–2010 (per cent)   200

10.4 Part-time jobs (civil service excluded) by age and sex in
2011 (per cent)   201

11.1 Percentage of young adults aged 25–34 living with their
parents, 2011   213

11.2 UK HE enrolment rate, 1970–2010   214

11.3 Number of dwellings that are privately rented dwellings
and number of housing benefit recipients, 1996–2011,
Great Britain   217

11.4 Percentage of men and women living outside a family
who are in receipt of housing benefit, by living
arrangements and age group, 2012   226

11.5 Distribution of living arrangements among UK
non-resident fathers by age group   228

Foreword

Social scientists are currently coming to terms with ways in which young people's lives have changed in the aftermath of the Great Recession. This is complex because the repercussions of recession are still being felt and it can be difficult to separate established longer-term trends from the more temporary impact of global economic upheaval. What is becoming clear is that the post-recession landscape will have features that were far less pronounced in the pre-recession world. Moreover, young people, who bore the brunt of the recession, suffering from rates of unemployment and job insecurity that were far more severe than among older people, will experience these new realities more intensely than their fellow citizens of more advanced years.

Terms such as 'lost generation', which are frequently used to describe the long-term impact of recession, are misleading because they imply that those who left education during the recession and in its immediate aftermath will be scarred by the experience, while those who follow shortly afterwards will be able to access the sorts of opportunities that defined the economy pre-recession. The evidence from social science increasingly points towards a hostile new landscape: one in which opportunities are precarious and one marked by polarisation. This new terrain is described in some detail in this collection.

The implications for young people entering the new economy are far-reaching, and this book provides a rich illustration of the impact of precarity on young people across Europe, highlighting the inadequacies of policy in states that have abdicated responsibility for providing equally for all their citizens. The comparative analyses and country case studies within each of the major sections of the book help us to stand back to survey the bigger picture, while also providing detailed discussions of the impact of the changes on sub-groups as diverse as precarious workers in Spain and Greece and 'troublesome' youth in the UK.

From a policy perspective, much emphasis has been placed on encouraging participation in education (especially at the tertiary level), partly through discouraging early labour market entry and applying sanctions to those unfortunate enough to require welfare support. While education is frequently seen as a means of reducing the risks of unemployment on an individual level, there are highly educated young people across Europe who are unemployed or working in low-skill, low-pay jobs. Indeed, Spain and Greece, countries with the highest unemployment rates in Europe, also have the most highly educated young people in Europe. Unemployment and underemployment must be understood as problems of demand, not of supply.

In order to develop effective and socially just policy we need a better understanding of the lives of young people under the conditions that they face in the post-recession environment. In many countries policy is framed by assumptions of linear, unbroken, transitions, by traditional notions of independence and with confidence that most employment is relatively stable and provides an acceptable standard of living. Such assumptions are challenged in the post-recession economy where many of those fortunate enough to have jobs work under conditions of uncertainty and are unable to work sufficient hours to secure a decent living. Inequality is rising and new divisions are opening up as social policy is framed in ways that marginalise those most affected by contemporary conditions, many of whom are young.

While young people are resourceful and often develop imaginative solutions to create fulfilling lives under trying circumstances, there is clear evidence that their lack of control over key aspects of their lives results in anxiety and stress and impacts on their psychological health. There is also evidence that policies that respect and facilitate personal choice and autonomy, which avoid the temptation to penalise young people who are unsuccessfully negotiating difficult circumstances, help increase well-being among young people. Indeed, many of the policy changes introduced during the recession with the express purpose of reducing expenditure may represent false economies because there will be an increased pressure on health services from those most affected. One of the important achievements of this book is to make linkages between the changing experiences of young people across a wide range of policy domains while simultaneously exploring the implications for policy.

Andy Furlong

Andy Furlong is Professor of Social Inclusion and Education and Dean of Research at the University of Glasgow and is Editor-in-Chief of the *Journal of Youth Studies*.

Acknowledgements

The editors would like to thank all the authors for contributing to this publication. We also thank the organisers of the European Network for Social Policy Analysis (ESPAnet) Conference (University of Edinburgh, 2012) for hosting our stream 'Young People and Social Policy in Europe: New Risks and Emerging Challenges' and the organisers of the inaugural Journal of Youth Studies Conference (University of Glasgow, 2013) for hosting our panel on 'Young People and Social Policy in Europe'. In particular we would like to thank Tracy Shildrick and Rob MacDonald for their inputs. We are very thankful to Andy Furlong for writing the Foreword of this publication. Finally, we would like to thank our respective organisations for their support.

Contributors

Anna Angelin holds a post-doctoral position at the School of Social Work, Lund University, Sweden. Her main research interests and areas of publication are marginalisation, social assistance and youth-child poverty. Her doctoral dissertation was on the subject of long-term unemployment and benefit receipt among young adults.

Lorenza Antonucci is Lecturer in Social Policy of the School of Social Sciences at the University of the West of Scotland (UWS). In 2010 she won the first Policy Press award for her doctoral research on young people in university in Europe. This research is to be presented in *University Lives in Crisis* (forthcoming). She has researched and published in the areas of higher education studies, social policy and youth studies. She collaborates with several European think tanks (e.g., Foundation of European Progressive Studies, Policy Network) and European organisations (e.g., Youth Partnership of the Council of Europe/European Commission) and sits on the Executive Committee of the Social Policy Association (SPA).

Olof Bäckman is an Associate Professor of Sociology at the Swedish Institute for Social Research (SOFI), Stockholm University, Sweden. His research has mainly concerned poverty, unemployment and social exclusion in a life-course perspective. How structural factors such as social policy, educational policy and the economic cycle intervene in processes of cumulative disadvantage is an important theme in his research. He has also been involved in several research projects dealing with the dynamics of means-tested social assistance benefit receipt.

Ann Berrington is Professor of Demography and Social Statistics at the University of Southampton, UK. Her primary areas of research relate to the analysis of the life-course using longitudinal methods. She has published work in a variety of substantive and methodological areas including transitions to adulthood in Britain and Europe; timing of parenthood in the UK; cohabitation, marriage and divorce in developed countries; modelling relationships between attitudes and demographic behaviour using longitudinal repeated measures data; and methods dealing with attrition and item non-response in longitudinal surveys.

Tom Chevalier is a PhD student at the Centre d'Etudes Européennes (CEE), Sciences Po Paris, and works on the place of young people in European welfare states. He has an MPhil in Public Affairs and an MPhil in Philosophy, and was Visiting Scholar at Oxford University (academic year 2012–13). In 2012 he published *L'Etat-providence et les jeunes* (Young people and the welfare state in France), after having won the award for the best MPhil dissertation in Political Science (organised by the publisher l'Harmattan).

Espen Dahl is a Professor at Oslo and Akershus University College, the Social Welfare Research Centre in Norway. Research interests and areas of publication are health inequalities, comparative welfare state research, social and health policy.

Eldin Fahmy is Senior Lecturer in the School for Policy Studies at the University of Bristol, UK. His research interests focus on the analysis of poverty, inequality and social exclusion, with a specific interest in youth inclusion and social policy. He has published more than 30 articles, books and research reports on related topics including the spatial analysis of poverty and wealth, the applications of multi-method approaches in poverty research, youth poverty and inclusion, fuel poverty, and rural poverty. He was Co-Investigator on the ESRC-funded 2012 UK Survey of Poverty and Social Exclusion, the largest survey of its kind ever commissioned in the UK.

Alessandro Gentile is Assistant Professor of Sociology at the Faculty of Social Sciences and Labour, University of Zaragoza, and a member of the POSEB research group (Social Policy and Welfare State) in the Institute of Public Goods and Policies of the Spanish National Research Council (IPP-CSIC). His main topics of study and research are new social risks, welfare reform and societal change, with a special focus on the sociology of labour and sociology of the family. He has published several articles and book chapters related to these topics and, more specifically, to employment instability, young people's transitions to adulthood, intergenerational solidarity and family policies from a comparative perspective.

Myra Hamilton is a Research Fellow at the Social Policy Research Centre at the University of New South Wales in Australia. Her research focuses on the perceptions and management of social risks over the life-course. Her areas of publication include youth transitions, activation policies, the service needs and experiences of people with caring responsibilities, especially young carers, and pensions policy.

Walter R. Heinz is Professor Emeritus of Sociology and Psychology and Senior Faculty member of the Bremen International Graduate School of Social Sciences (BIGSSS), University of Bremen, Germany. His research interests and areas of publication are sociology of youth, transitions from education to work in cross-national perspective, biography and life-course studies.

Timo Kauppinen is a Senior Researcher at the Minimum Income Unit of the National Institute for Health and Welfare in Finland. His research interests and main areas of publication include social assistance receipt and educational outcomes among young people, and urban and housing research.

Lefteris Kretsos is a Senior Lecturer of Industrial Relations at University of Greenwich. His research is focused on the rising trends and patterns of precarious employment, especially among young workers.

Thomas Lorentzen is an Associate Professor at the Department of Sociology at the University of Bergen, Norway. He works with longitudinal analyses of register data focusing on labour market outcomes and welfare receipt. He also teaches quantitative methods for the social sciences. He is currently involved in several comparative register-data-based analyses of social security and working life in the Nordic welfare states.

Lara Maestripieri is post-doctoral fellow at the Polytechnic of Milan, Department of Architecture and Urban Studies. Her main research interests deal with narrative and biographical methods in the social research and investigation of post-industrial societies, with a focus on analysis of female participation in the labour market, precarity and professional identity among knowledge workers.

Pasi Moisio is a Research Professor at the Minimum Income Unit, National Institute for Health and Welfare in Finland. His research interests and main areas of publication are poverty, intergenerational inequality and minimum income protection.

Annalisa Murgia is a member of the Research Unit on Communication, Organizational Learning and Aesthetics and of the Centre of Interdisciplinary Gender Studies of the University of Trento (Italy), where she teaches Human Resources Management. Her research focuses on work trajectories, with a special focus on knowledge workers, workers with temporary and precarious jobs, and the social construction of gender in professional careers. She has authored and co-authored several articles and books on these topics.

Bruno Palier is CNRS Research Director at Sciences Po Paris, Centre d'études européennes, France. Trained in social science, he is studying welfare reforms in Europe. He has published numerous articles in journals such as *Politics and Society, Journal of European Social Policy, West European Politics, Governance, Socio-Economic Review, Global Social Policy* and *Social Politics*. In 2012 he co-edited *The Age of Dualization: The Changing Face of Inequality in Deindustrializing Societies* and *Towards a Social Investment Welfare State? Ideas, Policies and Challenges*.

Barbara Poggio is Assistant Professor of Sociology of Organization and coordinator of the Centre of Interdisciplinary Gender Studies of the University of Trento. She has carried out several studies on the social construction of gender in organisations, with a special focus on methodological issues. Her research interests mainly deal with gender policies in organisations and with gender and scientific careers. She has published in international journals and with different international publishers.

Steven Roberts is Senior Lecturer in Social Policy and Sociology at the University of Kent's School of Social Policy, Sociology and Social Research (SSPSSR). He is convenor of the British Sociological Association Youth Study Group, Vice Chair of the European Sociological Association Youth and Generation Research Network, and sits on the editorial boards of *Journal of Youth Studies* and *Sociological Research Online*. He has a diverse range of research interests, which all centre on the youth stage of the life-course. His published work, which appears in a number of internationally recognised academic journals, includes explorations of how social class and gender shape, influence and constrain young people's transitions to adulthood independence and their experiences of education, employment, consumption and the domestic sphere.

Stefania Sabatinelli teaches Social Policies at the Polytechnic of Milan, Department of Architecture and Urban Studies. Her research mainly deals with comparative welfare analysis, particularly of activation and care policies. Among her publications: 'Activation and rescaling: inter-related questions in social policy?', in Y. Kazepov (ed.), *Rescaling Social Policies Towards Multilevel Governance in Europe* (2010); 'Nothing on the move or just going private? Understanding the freeze on care policies in Italy' (with B. Da Roit) in *Social Politics* (2012).

Tapio Salonen is Professor in Social Work and Dean at Faculty of Health and Sciences, Malmö University in Sweden. His main research interests include poverty, marginality, participatory strategies and social policy.

Clive Sealey is a Senior Lecturer in Social Policy and Theory at the University of Worcester, UK. Prior to this he completed his PhD at the University of Birmingham. His research interests are poverty and social exclusion, and issues related to ideology and social policy.

Juliet Stone is a Research Fellow at the ESRC Centre for Population Change, University of Southampton. Her research is based primarily around an interest in life-course processes and associated method-ological challenges. Specific areas of research include changing living arrangements in young adulthood, life-course determinants of health in later life and fertility dynamics in the context of economic recession.

1
Introduction: Young People and Social Policy in Europe
Past and Present

Myra Hamilton, Lorenza Antonucci and Steven Roberts

Young people in contemporary Europe face not only a heightened sense of risk (Beck, 1992; Furlong and Cartmel, 2007; Taylor-Gooby, 2004), but also the looming prospect of becoming 'the first generation to do worse than their parents'. The challenges facing young people as they navigate transitions to adulthood are therefore unprecedented in European societies. Their experiences of risks, such as labour market insecurity and social exclusion across a range of domains, have become increasingly relevant in the media and in policy debates. Since 2008, the economic crisis has intensified the risks experienced by young people in Europe and created new forms of insecurity and exclusion. The austerity measures implemented in several European countries, such as labour market reforms aimed at promoting flexible labour markets (Jessoula et al., 2010; Madsen et al., 2013) and cuts in state support for students in higher education (Callender, 2012), have contributed to this insecurity. Recent studies have shown that young people are a group that is feeling the effects of the crisis and associated austerity measures most strongly (Busch et al., 2013; Dietrich, 2013; McKee, 2012; Theodoropoulou and Watt, 2011). There is therefore a compelling need for reflection upon the efficacy of social policies for young people in times of crisis and the assumptions that underpin them, and for identifying policies that can mitigate, and indeed reverse, the effects of these new risks. This book sets out to address the changed policy landscape and consequent heightened complexity and urgency of young people's needs.

1.1 Young people in the crisis: new or old transitions?

The need for 'youth policies' is not a new focus in European policy-making. Indeed, the 1990s and early 2000s saw youth policy become a burgeoning area of policy formation, with a focus on activation policies, tertiary education (such as the European Commission's Europe 2020 initiatives), social inclusion (such as the European Commission's EU Youth Strategy 2010–18) and youth unemployment (the Youth Guarantee, endorsed in 2013). However, while the early focus of youth policy was specifically on young people Not in Education, Employment or Training (NEETs) (Yates and Paine, 2006), there is now increasing interest in 'young people' as a whole cohort at risk of precariousness (Standing, 2011) and in young adulthood as a new age group in need of specifically targeted social policies.

In the broad literature concerning young people, there is still an emphasis on situating the current crisis within longer-term changes in youth biographies. In particular, it is still unclear whether the challenges faced by young Europeans in the crisis represent a period effect, and could be considered a repeat of the crisis in the 1980s, or if the processes emerging from the crisis at the start of the 21st century point to new and unprecedented challenges. In other words, there is a need to clarify whether we can really identify a new generation (the Millennial or the Y generation) that faces specific cohort challenges that are different from the ones young people have faced before. In many respects, scholarly debate on the 'new' risks faced by young people and the 'extraordinary' nature of current transitions has been in place for some time, and has been linked to epochal changes, such as the presence of fragmented transitions in late modernity (Furlong and Cartmel, 2007). We need to be aware that 'youth studies [...] has a tendency to highlight change over continuity', and this derives from the fact that in academia '"the shock of the new" grabs more headlines than "same as it ever was"' (MacDonald, 2011, p. 428). Even if we consider the current challenges faced by young people in Europe to be the effect of longer-term changes associated with the passage to late modernism (Furlong and Cartmel, 2007; Heinz, 2009), there is no agreement on their effects. While some youth scholars have argued that the shift towards uncertain and fragmented transitions creates greater choice and opportunity for young people (Arnett, 2006; Patterson et al., 2009), others have suggested that for many these transitions continue to be shaped by pervasive structural factors, creating vastly different experiences and outcomes (Bynner, 2005; Evans, 2002; Schoon and Bynner, 2003).

There seems, however, to be a consensus on the detrimental short-term effects of the crisis on young Europeans. For Bell and Blanchflower (2011), the effects of the 'Great Recession' on the transitions of young people in the labour market are unprecedented, involving underemployment on a new scale. Comparing the effects of the current economic crisis and the 1980s crisis on young people, MacDonald (2011) finds that there are new elements to consider, such as the importance of focusing on young people in the 'missing middle' (Roberts, 2011), who are 'not-NEETs' and 'not-troubled', but who are now also exposed to precarious conditions. This also points to a need to consider university-to-work transitions, rather than just school-to-work transitions (Macdonald, 2011). Similarly, Furlong, Woodman and Wyn (2011) believe that the contemporary reconfiguration, both culturally and structurally, of educational and labour market conditions has created a generational problem that affects all young people, not just those at the bottom. This book is positioned both within the short-term changes deriving from the economic crisis in Europe and the longer-term changes associated with individualisation and exposure to risk in late modernity.

1.2 The contribution of social policy theory

There is no doubt that youth policy is of growing importance, but the application of the tools and concepts of social policy theory or policy studies to research on young people is curiously underdeveloped in the existing social policy literature. A coherent conceptual approach to youth policy is made all the more urgent because youth is a phase of the life-course that presents several challenges to the traditional paradigm of social policy. First, the phase of 'youth' challenges the assumption underpinning the traditional welfare state that there is an age-related division between dependent individuals and independent individuals, instead creating a complex period of semi-dependence or fluctuating dependency status (Coles, 1995). Second, while there has been a large body of literature on older people (Bovenberg et al., 2010; Walker and Naegele, 2009), and children and the family (Bradshaw, 2012; Kjorholt and Qvortrup, 2012; Saunders, 2009), less attention has been devoted to the specific social policy needs of young people. However, the period of youth, rather than a phase between two dominant stages of the life-course relevant for social policy – childhood and adulthood – is a vital life-course stage in its own right, and one that generates specific policy needs.

In addition, evidence suggests that youth has become a more discrete and protracted phase of the life-course owing to a number of contemporary challenges to the traditional life trajectory, such as delays in marriage and family formation and later labour market entry thanks to higher levels of youth unemployment and participation in higher education (Laaksonen, 2000; Vickerstaff, 2006; Walther, 2006). Finally, young people undergo transitions that are specific to their life-course stage, such as moving out of the family home, moving in and out of education and training, and entering the labour market for the first time. These transitions have become more fragmented owing to contemporary changes (Furlong and Cartmel, 2007), and are shaped by structural inequalities, as will be discussed in Chapter 2. The policy context is struggling to keep pace with the rapidly changing and increasingly differentiated needs associated with these important transitions.

Recent European initiatives (for example, the Youth Guarantee, 2013) suggest that greater attention is being placed on adapting policies to the new conditions and transitions facing young people. Simultaneously, students and analysts of social policy must also pay heed to the ways in which economic and social policies shape opportunity structures, and play a role in constructing the youth phase more broadly. For example, from October 2013, the UK introduced different rates of the National Minimum Wage for people of different ages (£6.31 per hour for adults aged 21 and over; a 'development rate' of £5.03 per hour for workers aged 18–20 years; a rate of £3.72 per hour for 16–17-year-olds; and an apprentice minimum wage rate of £2.68 per hour). This policy forms part of a wider institutionalised discourse across Europe that positions young people as 'deficient' (perceived and constructed as lacking in value and skills), creates a 'second-class' labour market for young people and has the potential to further entrench youth disadvantage and precariousness. It is possible to find a correspondence between the European discourse and the three new dominating policy paradigms in the European labour market that Knijn (2012) has identified: the social investment approach, the transitional labour market model and the individual life-course model, which 'propose, respectively, *investing in, facilitating, and individualising* the new social risks of newcomers on the labour market' (2012, p. 21, italics in the original).

By highlighting the assumptions underpinning the policy discourses, this book moves beyond the focus of European policymaking on 'youth unemployment' and on the 'five million unemployed youth' and provides a more holistic understanding of the various challenges faced by young people. In some respects, while the three policy paradigms identified by Knijn (2012) represent three distinctive policy frameworks, they all share a focus on labour market transitions, without addressing the whole set of challenges faced by young people in other policy areas. This book points out how solving the issues faced by young people in Europe requires a set of interventions that do not always involve employment policies. The transitions during this life-course stage produce needs that are associated with education, skills acquisition and entry into the labour market, the transition out of the family home and into alternative housing arrangements and the process of family formation. The needs arising from these life-course transitions therefore cross-cut a number of social policy areas, including education, training, housing, social security, family policies and also labour market policies.

In many respects the analysis of this new policy environment and the effects of risk on young people's lives has been confined to the sociology of youth (or youth studies), while social policy theory has not contributed to this debate. This book has been constructed with the belief that an integrated approach unifying youth studies and social policy has the potential to clarify the nature of inequality affecting young people and the relevance of welfare structures in mitigating contemporary risks. This is likely to provide a much more holistic understanding of the different resources that young people have access to, and draw on (through the state, the family and the (labour) market), in managing new risks and the role for policy in meeting their needs.

1.3 The structure of the book

Stimulated by the stream organised at the European Network for Social Policy Analysis Conference 2012 'Young People and Social Policy in Europe: New Risks and Emerging Challenges' and by the panel on 'Young People and Social Policy in Europe' at the 2013 inaugural Youth Studies Conference, this book draws together new studies by European scholars in the field of youth policy to identify new and shared risks confronting European youth during the global economic crisis. In order to explore differences and similarities in young people's experiences of risk across Europe, and different types of policy responses, the book combines cross-national analyses with country-specific case studies from different welfare states. The cross-national studies explore differences in youth policies and welfare outcomes across different European welfare states. The case studies consider the nature of, or change within, specific social policy areas or whole welfare states in individual countries, including the 'social, political, economic, cultural and ideological contexts which impinge on the shape and impact of particular social policies' (Clasen, 2004, pp. 94–5). This allows us to explore both the qualitative and quantitative differences in youth policies and welfare outcomes across countries.

The book includes studies from a number of contrasting welfare regimes to explore the different effects that welfare regime structures can have on European young people's exposure to risk and on patterns of youth transitions (Laaksonen, 2000; Walther, 2006). The use of 'welfare regimes' analysis, or attempts to develop typologies or systems of classification to summarise similarities and differences in the design of different welfare states, has been a common feature of comparative social policy research (Kennett, 2004). Most influential in this approach has been the work of Gosta Esping-Andersen (1990), who developed a typology of European welfare states built on two principles. First is decommodification, or the extent to which the state enables its citizens to 'maintain a livelihood' without relying on participation in the labour market. It does this through the provision of social rights that ensure an adequate standard of living. The second is 'stratification', or the extent to which a welfare state promotes a certain system of social relations, and the character of those relations (Esping-Andersen, 1990). Drawing on these principles, Esping-Andersen identified three ideal-type 'welfare regimes': the liberal regime type, in Anglo-Saxon countries such as the United Kingdom, in which social provision is residualist in character – targeted to the needy and often modest in value; the corporatist (or conservative) regime type, found in countries such as France, Germany and Italy, where welfare benefits are strongly linked to occupational status, so that those in secure work are well protected and those in precarious work receive inadequate protection, underpinned by the strong reliance on the role of the family in supporting its members; and the social democratic regime type, typified by Scandinavian countries such as Denmark, Norway and Sweden, characterised by universal services and welfare benefits and a commitment to full employment (Esping-Andersen, 1990).

Since the publication of Esping-Andersen's typology, a number of scholars have identified welfare states that do not fit neatly into the proposed three regime types, and which can be considered another distinctive regime type. For example, some have identified a 'Southern model' typified by Spain, Italy and Greece (Ferrera, 1996), and a post-communist welfare regime, comprising two 'sub-worlds', a Baltic Cluster and an Eastern European Cluster (Castles and Obinger, 2008). Some scholars have challenged Esping-Andersen's work (and indeed the wider welfare regime typology approach), arguing that in order to be 'decommodified', a person must first be a labour market participant, and the focus on decommodification is therefore built on the ideal of the 'citizen worker' to the exclusion of groups for whom commodification (or labour market entry) is a problem (such as women and young people) (O'Connor, 2004). These scholars argue that an emphasis on decommodification fails to recognise the important role of policy in facilitating labour market entry (O'Connor, 2004). In addition to this, as we argue in Chapter 2, there are a number of limitations in applying the welfare regime typology in a context where young people are 'semi dependent'.

In developing a typology of welfare regimes to compare the contexts in which young people undergo transitions to adulthood, Walther (2006) includes in his analysis the role of welfare state policies relevant for young people, including education, training and support for labour market entry. He identifies four 'transition regimes': the universalistic transition regime, found in the Nordic countries such as Sweden and characterised by comprehensive schooling and 'collective social responsibility' for youth transitions, such as rights to state-funded social assistance to support periods in education; the liberal transition regime, found in the United Kingdom, characterised by an individualised approach to youth transitions, including activation policies focused on labour market entry rather than education and training, and a 'deficit' model of youth unemployment that treats it as an issue of individual pathology; the employment-centred transition regime found in continental countries such as Germany and France, characterised by stratified systems of schooling that place children in streams from an early age, and by the polarisation of the labour market between the secure 'core' with generous social security provisions and the periphery with access to low, residual benefits; and the sub-protective transition regime, found in the southern European countries such as Spain and Italy, characterised by informal or insecure work and limited social protection, which rely heavily on family support (Walther, 2006).

Since Walther's (2006) welfare regime analysis of youth transitions, social policy theory has moved on, supplanting this more static welfare regime approach that emphasises government institutions with an approach that focuses on 'welfare mixes' (Powell and Barrientos, 2004), or the role that public and private providers of welfare play in supporting a country's citizens. The analysis in this book builds on the important welfare regime analyses of youth transitions, by proposing an understanding of 'welfare mixes' to clarify the comparatively different contributions made by the state, the family and the labour market to young people's welfare across countries.

In order to do so draws on studies from welfare states that are classified as belonging to different welfare state clusters, in order to draw out the broad assumptions that underpin welfare systems concerning young people. It begins, in Chapter 2, by drawing on an analysis of welfare mixes to understand the way that young people experience and manage contemporary risk during transitions to adulthood. While some youth scholars argue that uncertainty and flexibility create greater choices for young people (Arnett, 2006), and others suggest that the effects of risk are shaped by pervasive structural factors (Bynner, 2005), this chapter uses the notion of the welfare mix to provide a 'middle-range' tool; that is, a method of understanding the complex relationship between individual agency and social and institutional structures as young people navigate life-course transitions in contemporary Europe.

The book is then divided into two parts: Part I – 'Precariousness, Social Exclusion and Youth Policy in Europe' – is concerned with young people's experiences of precariousness, social exclusion and disadvantage in Europe, situated in the context of the global economic crisis. It contains two comparative studies and three case studies of the United Kingdom, Greece and Spain. The five contributions in this part challenge normative understandings of youth precariousness and disadvantage and reflect on the implications for policy. Eldin Fahmy (Chapter 3) provides the first comparative chapter, a study of youth poverty and deprivation in European Union countries. He identifies challenges in the measurement of youth poverty and deprivation in Europe and draws attention to the multi-dimensional and dynamic nature of youth disadvantage. In a comparative analysis of Italy, Spain and the United Kingdom, Annalisa Murgia and Barbara Poggio (Chapter 4) reveal the way in which highly skilled young people are exposed to labour market precariousness, suggesting that high education and skill levels do not always inoculate young people from disadvantage.

The three case studies in Part I provide detailed analyses of young people's experiences of social exclusion and precariousness at the country level, focusing on their labour market opportunities. Clive Sealey (Chapter 5) provides a qualitative analysis of young people's experiences of social exclusion, arguing that, while the emphasis of policy is on individual responsibility for managing labour market risk, for young people, labour market precariousness can be closely linked to structural factors such as local labour market conditions. Lefteris Kretsos (Chapter 6) explores precarious employment and unemployment among young people in Greece, arguing that while these phenomena have been exacerbated by the global economic crisis, they are part of a longer and more pervasive trend that has been building since the 1980s. Alessandro Gentile (Chapter 7) provides a qualitative analysis of young people's experiences of precariousness in Spain. Like the authors of Chapter 4, Gentile explores the experiences of labour market precariousness among young highly skilled or educated people. In this detailed case study of young people in Spain, Gentile also reveals the importance of structural factors in shaping young people's transitions, and points to the central role of familial responsibility in supporting young people to manage labour market risk.

Part II – 'Changing Transitions, Welfare Sources and Social Policies' – focuses on contemporary changes to young people's transitions to adulthood, and the extent to which young people draw on different sources of welfare – the state, market and family – as they navigate these transitions. The authors in this part reveal how normative assumptions underpinning social policies can structure the way in which young people support themselves during these transitions. Lara Maestripieri and Stefania Sabatinelli (Chapter 8) provide the first comparative study, presenting a qualitative analysis of transitions from education to the labour market among young people in ten European countries (Spain, Italy, Switzerland, France, Germany, the Netherlands, the United Kingdom, Poland, Croatia and Sweden). It sets out the ways in which young people's experiences of precarious employment and unemployment are structured by the different 'resource packages' they have access to that can support them through this transition. In Chapter 9 Anna Angelin, Timo Kauppinen, Thomas Lorentzen, Olof Bäckman, Pasi Moisio, Espen Dahl and Tapio Salonen then address the important issue of social protection for young people during periods of unemployment. In a quantitative comparative study of Norway, Finland and Sweden, Angelin and colleagues reveal the way in which the changing nature of youth labour market transitions have challenged the social protection systems in the Nordic countries and have made young people vulnerable to poverty.

The three case studies in Part II provide detailed analyses of the way in which social policies shape youth transitions in three welfare states: France, the United Kingdom and Germany. Tom Chevalier and Bruno Palier (Chapter 10) draw out the tension in support for youth transitions in France between familialism or 'state-sponsored' family support for young people in higher education, and residualist activation schemes for vulnerable young people outside education. They draw attention to the consequent inequalities. Ann Berrington and Juliet Stone (Chapter 11) focus on transitions to residential independence in the United Kingdom. Drawing on an analysis of the British Household Panel Survey, they reveal inequalities in housing transitions among different groups of young adults and the way in which housing policies are reinforcing some of these inequalities, including gender inequalities. Walther R. Heinz (Chapter 12) describes the distinctive features of Germany's school to work transitions, including a highly stratified education system and a strong system of vocational education and training. He argues that, while the impact of the global economic crisis on youth unemployment has been to some extent cushioned in Germany, inequalities persist that are reinforced by the shift towards activation policies that focus on individualised responsibility rather than the creation of labour market opportunities.

The final chapter (Chapter 13) draws out trends in the effects of the global economic crisis on the lives of European young people, and their experiences of disadvantage, precariousness and transitions into adulthood. It sets out the ways in which different social policies, such as education, housing and active labour market policies, both mediate and intensify the effects of the crisis on young people.

References

Arnett, J. (2006). *Emerging Adulthood, the Winding Road from the Late Teens through the Twenties* (New York: Oxford University Press).

Beck, U. (1992). *Risk Society: Towards a New Modernity* (New Delhi: Sage).

Bell, D. and Blanchflower, D. (2011). *Young People and the Great Recession.* IZA Discussion Paper 5674 (Bonn: Institute for the Study of Labour).

Bovenberg, L., Van Soest, A. and Zaidi, A. (eds.) (2010). *Ageing, Health and Pensions in Europe: An Economic and Social Policy Perspective* (Houndmills: Palgrave Macmillan).

Bradshaw, J. (2012). 'The Case for Family Benefits'. *Children and Youth Services Review* 34 (3), 590–6.

Busch, K., Hermann, C., Hinrichs, K. and Schulten, T. (2013). *Euro Crisis, Austerity Policy and the European Social Model: How Crisis Policies in Southern Europe Threaten the EU's Social Dimension* (Berlin: Friedrich-Ebert-Stittung).

Bynner, J. (2005). 'Rethinking the Youth Phase of the Life Course: The Case of Emerging Adulthood'. *Journal of Youth Studies* 8 (4), 367–84.

Callender, C. (2012). 'The 2012/13 Reforms of Higher Education in England: Changing Student Finances and Funding', in Kilkey, M., Ramia, G. and Farnsworth, K. (eds.) *Social Policy Review 24: Analysis and Debate in Social Policy* (Bristol: Policy Press), pp. 75–93.

Castles, F. and Obinger, H. (2008). 'Worlds, Families, Regimes: Country Clusters in European and OECD Area Public Policy'. *West European Politics* 31 (1/2), 321–44.

Clasen, J. (2004). 'Defining Comparative Social Policy', in Kennett, P. (ed.) *A Handbook of Comparative Social Policy* (Cheltenham: Edward Elgar), pp. 91–102.

Coles, B. (1995). *Youth and Social Policy: Youth Citizenship and Young Careers* (London: UCL Press).

Dietrich, H. (2013). 'Youth Unemployment in the Period 2001–2010 and the European Crisis – Looking at the Empirical Evidence'. *European Review of Labour and Research* 19, 305–24.

Esping-Andersen, G. (1990). *The Three Worlds of Welfare Capitalism* (Cambridge: Polity Press).

Evans, K. (2002). 'Taking Control of Their Lives? Agency in Young Adult Transitions in England and the New Germany'. *Journal of Youth Studies* 5 (3), 245–71.

Ferrera, M. (1996). 'The "Southern Model" of Welfare in Social Europe'. *Journal of European Social Policy* 1 (6), 17–37.

Furlong, A. and Cartmel, F. (2007). *Young People and Social Change: New Perspectives* (Maidenhead: Open University Press).

Furlong, A., Woodman, D. and Wyn, J. (2011). 'Changing Times, Changing Perspectives: Reconciling "Transition" and "Cultural" Perspectives on Youth and Young Adulthood'. *Journal of Sociology* 47 (4), 355–70.

Heinz, W. (2009). 'Youth Transitions in an Age of Uncertainty', in Furlong, A. (ed.) *Handbook of Youth and Young Adulthood: New Perspectives and Agendas* (London: Routledge).

Jessoula, M., Graziano, P. and Madama, I. (2010). ' "Selective Flexicurity" in Segmented Labour Markets: The Case of Italian Mid-Siders'. *Journal of Social Policy* 39 (4), 561–83.

Kennett, P. (2004). 'Introduction: The Changing Nature of Comparative Social Policy', in Kennett, P. (ed.) *A Handbook of Comparative Social Policy* (Cheltenham: Edward Eldgar).

Kjorholt, A. and Qvortrup, J. (2012). *The Modern Child and the Flexible Labour Market: Early Childhood Education and Care* (Basingstoke: Palgrave Macmillan).

Knijn, T. (ed.) (2012). *Work, Family Policy and the Transition to Adulthood in Europe* (Basingstoke: Palgrave Macmillan).

Laaksonen, A. (2000). 'Young Adults in Changing Welfare States: Prolonged Transitions and Delayed Entries for under-30s in Finland, Sweden and Germany in the '90s'. *Mannheimer Zentrum fur Europaische Sozialforschung* 12, 1–32.

MacDonald, R. (2011). 'Youth Transitions, Unemployment and Underemployment: Plus ça change, plus c'est la même chose?' *Journal of Sociology* 47 (4), 427–44.

McKee, K. (2012). 'Young People, Homeownership and Future Welfare' (Policy Review). *Housing Studies* 27 (6), 853–62.

Madsen, P.K., Molina, O., Lozano, M. and Møller, J. (2013). 'Labour Market Transitions of Young Workers in Nordic and Southern European Countries: The Role of Flexicurity'. *Transfer* 19 (3), 325–43.

O'Connor, J. (2004). 'Gender, Citizenship and Welfare State Regimes', in Kennett, P. (ed.) *A Handbook of Comparative Social Policy* (Cheltenham: Edward Elgar).

Patterson, L., Forbes, K. and Peace, R. (2009). 'Happy, Stable and Contented: Accomplished Ageing in the Imagined Futures of Young New Zealanders'. *Ageing and Society* 29 (3), 431–54.

Powell, M. and Barrientos, A. (2004). 'Welfare Regimes and the Welfare Mix', *European Journal of Political Research* 43 (1), 83–105.

Roberts, S. (2011). 'Beyond 'NEET' and 'Tidy' Pathways: Considering the 'Missing Middle' of Youth Transition Studies', *Journal of Youth Studies* 14 (1), 21–39.

Saunders, P. (2009). 'Income Support for Families and the Living Standards of Children', in Kamerman, S., Phipps, S. and Ben-Arieh, A. (eds.) *From Child Welfare to Child Well-Being: Children's Well-Being: Indicators and Research* Vol. 1 (Netherlands: Springer), pp. 275–92.

Schoon, I. and Bynner, J. (2003). 'Risk and Resilience in the Life Course: Implications for Interventions and Social Policies'. *Journal of Youth Studies* 6 (1), 1–31.

Standing, G. (2011). *The Precariat: The New Dangerous Class* (London: Bloomsbury Academic).

Taylor-Gooby, P. (2004). *New Risks, New Welfare: The Transformation of the European Welfare State* (Oxford: Oxford University Press).

Theodoropoulou, T. and Watt, A. (2011). 'Withdrawal Symptoms: An Assessment of the Austerity Packages in Europe', ETUI Working Paper 2/2011.

Vickerstaff, S. (2006). 'Life Course, Youth, and Old Age', in Taylor-Gooby, P. and Zinn, J. (eds.) *Risk in Social Science* (Oxford: Oxford University Press), pp. 180–201.

Walker, A. and Naegele, G. (2009). *Social Policy in Ageing Societies: Britain and Germany Compared* (Basingstoke: Palgrave Macmillan).

Walther, A. (2006). 'Regimes of Youth Transitions: Choice, Flexibility and Security in Young People's Experiences across Different European Contexts'. *Young* 14 (2), 119–39.

Yates, S.J. and Payne, M. (2006). 'Not So NEET? A Critique of the Use of "NEET" in Setting Targets for Interventions with Young People'. *Journal of Youth Studies* 9 (3), 329–44.

2
Constructing a Theory of Youth and Social Policy

Lorenza Antonucci, Myra Hamilton and Steven Roberts

2.1 Introduction

This chapter develops a framework for understanding the experiences and policy needs of young people. At present, in spite of a greater focus on young people in social and public policy, there is no coherent conceptual approach to understanding youth and social policy. Contemporary analysis of the risks facing young people has been dominated by the sociology of youth, but the tools and concepts of welfare theory – central to how we can understand and address young people's needs – have not been employed in any systematic way in this field. This chapter aims to fill this gap by discussing the interaction between the sociology of youth and social policy theory.

A framework that draws on both social policy theory and the sociology of youth enables us to provide an integrated understanding of contemporary young people and their needs. Youth is a phase of the life-course that presents several challenges to the wider traditional paradigm of welfare policy, and this chapter sets out how the conceptual framework can help us to conduct social policy research that addresses challenges arising from the semi-dependence, or fluctuating nature of dependence and independence, that characterises the youth phase. The first section clarifies the specific needs arising from life-course transitions during this phase and the differentiated needs arising from the increasingly fragmented nature of youth transitions. The second section stresses the associated inequalities and sets the basis for a fruitful collaboration between the sociology of youth and social policy theory, focusing on how welfare structures mediate inequalities in transitions and periods of dependence and independence. The last section offers a framework based on welfare theory and sets out the relevance of welfare mixes for understanding young people's semi-dependence on the various sources of welfare (family, labour market and state) and the character and distribution of youth inequalities.

2.2   Youth as a specific phase of the life-course

There has been a movement within the discipline of sociology over recent decades towards the conceptualisation of contemporary society in terms of 'risk'. This refers to the way in which discourses of risk are playing an unprecedented formative role in the actions of individuals, groups, businesses and governments. The perceived ubiquitous presence of risks in contemporary society forms the sociopolitical milieu in which individuals, including young people, now conduct themselves (Beck, 2000; Beck and Beck-Gernsheim, 2002). The intensification of risk has been accompanied by the breakdown of the certainties associated with industrialisation, resulting in the increasingly unstable or precarious nature of the traditional structures of work and the family. As a result, the fairly rigid social roles that shaped possibilities for human action (Beck, 2000) have broken down, and individuals are forced to play a much more active role in the construction of their own biographies (Bauman, 2002; Beck and Beck-Gernsheim, 2002). This is part of a broader and widely theorised process of individualisation said to be associated with late modernity, in which individuals are compelled to actively negotiate risk and insecurity on an ongoing basis (Bauman, 2002; Beck, 2000; Beck and Beck-Gernsheim, 2002), a thesis developed most notably by German sociologist Ulrich Beck. This has been accompanied by a shift in emphasis by governments, consistent with a neo-liberal approach to policy, towards greater responsibility placed on individuals to manage these risks, often through self-insurance rather than collective insurance mechanisms (Bowman et al., 2013; Hamilton, 2010, 2014). Individuals are not just required to manage risks as they arise but are increasingly encouraged or required to 'accumulate resources to manage risk across the lifecourse' (Bowman et al., 2013, p. 1). The result has been significant changes to the traditional life-course and its associated biographical management.

Young people have felt the effects of these changes to the life-course most strongly. Young people undergo transitions that are specific to their life-course stage, such as developing skills and transitioning out of education, entering the labour market for the first time, moving out of the family home and starting a family (Vickerstaff, 2006), that make them particularly vulnerable to the risks associated with post-industrial society. These transitions result in heightened exposure to social and structural changes such as labour market restructuring and the increasing demand for educated workers and specialised skills, forcing them to negotiate risks that 'were largely unknown to their parents' (Furlong and Cartmel, 1997).

Contemporary youth transitions are now characterised as being uncertain, fragmented (France, 2007; Furlong and Cartmel, 2007; Heinz, 2009) and 'de-standardised'. In contrast to their counterparts from previous generations who experienced apparently unproblematic transitions between the end of the Second World War and the mid-1970s, the lives of contemporary young Europeans are often characterised as consisting of stuttering steps forward, steps back and pauses, rather than a process of stages of mechanical predictability on a universal path to the fixed end point of 'normal' maturity (Walther et al., 2002). Communal reference points, formerly presented as certainties in respect of the routes taken, the timing of doing so and the previously associated outcomes, are taken to have become relatively meaningless.

'Standardised' transitions from education to work have been replaced by more complex combinations of education, training, periods of work and periods of unemployment. The number of young people participating in higher education has increased (France, 2007) and the new, more flexible, labour market has meant that the types of jobs that young people take up have changed, now more likely to be 'marginal' jobs with little job security (Furlong and Cartmel, 1997). The increasing demand for educated workers and specialised skills in post-industrial society has meant that young people are compelled to engage with the education system or face long-term unemployment (Furlong and Cartmel, 1997). At the same time, education systems are becoming increasingly commodified, with the proliferation of (sometimes substandard) qualifications (Standing, 2011). Young people with a tertiary education are finding it increasingly difficult to build coherent occupational identities. As they graduate from education, they are often compelled by the need for income to take jobs that are temporary or not consistent with their skills and qualifications, making it more difficult to build the career trajectory they desire, and leading to 'status frustration' (Standing, 2011). This is often compounded by large debts that they incurred throughout their study. There are also forms of precarious work designed specifically for young people who are studying or who have recently graduated, such as internships. While apprenticeships were traditionally a form of cheap labour for those in training, apprenticeships often led to secure work. However, internships do not, and are an increasingly pervasive method of employing young people in low or no wage, insecure, positions (Standing, 2011).

Young people therefore make up the 'core' of what Guy Standing (2011) calls 'the precariat'. While young people were facing increasingly precarious work prior to the economic downturn, mass unemployment created by the recession has hit young people hard. Unemployment among young people rose significantly as they dropped out of the labour force at three times the rate of adults. Many entered further education, exacerbating the spiral of 'qualifications' exceeding requirements for the jobs available (Standing, 2011). While young people have traditionally entered the labour market in precarious positions, they are now in precarious work for considerably longer and find it more difficult to gain permanent employment (Standing, 2011). The effects of workforce 'flexibility' have been felt particularly strongly by young people, who are most likely to be affected by longer probationary periods, short-term contracts and low wages (Standing, 2011). Young people are less likely to have access to enterprise benefits, which increases their vulnerability to poverty (Standing, 2011), and as a result of their life-course stage, they also lack contributory welfare state benefits because they have not had the time to develop adequate contribution records.

These risks, or 'new risks', do not concern only the labour market but also the distribution of caring responsibilities and the challenges associated with balancing work and care that result from changing gender roles (Taylor-Gooby, 2004, p. 8). As a result, these risks are also felt acutely by young people at the stage of family formation. The result has been a range of 'new behaviours' such as cohabitation before marriage and living alone (Billari and Liefbroer, 2010) that have altered the traditional pathways from family of origin to family formation. These changes have also meant that youth transitions have become more complex and less linear than in the past (Billari and Liefbroer, 2010; Evans, 2002; Vickerstaff, 2006; Walther, 2005). As youth transitions have become less predictable, young people are faced with greater uncertainty and insecurity during this life-course phase (Vickerstaff, 2006; Walther, 2005). The increasing insecurity has meant that transitions such as entry into the labour market and moving out of the family home have become increasingly 'reversible', creating what have been described as 'yo-yo transitions' (Walther, 2006). For example, young people are increasingly likely to return to the parental home after a period of living independently (see Berrington and Stone in this volume). The reversibility of these transitions, alongside changes to the traditional life trajectory such as delays in marriage and family formation and later labour market entry owing to higher levels of youth unemployment and participation in higher education (Laaksonen, 2000; Vickerstaff, 2006; Walther, 2006) have seen youth become a more discrete and protracted phase of the life-course.

Young people can also be considered to be the 'prime' subjects of the processes of individualisation in late modernity. Young people are at a time in the life-course when the creation of a 'biographical project' takes place – this is the time in the life-course when individuals most intensively 'plan and navigate their own career and lifestyle directions' (France, 2007, p. 61). The 'opening up' of youth transitions has led many to argue that young people are faced with wide-ranging choice in the 'construction of their biography' (France, 2007), leading to a greater emphasis on young people's 'decisions' in the transition to adulthood (Vickerstaff, 2006). Arnett, for example, argues that youth (or what he calls 'emerging adulthood') in late modernity is characterised by optimism, freedom and multiple future possibilities (Arnett, 2006). This 'individualisation' of youth transitions has been reinforced by a process of responsibilisation in which young people become responsible for 'making it', and liable when things become difficult (Furlong and Cartmel, 1997; Walther, 2005). Hence, as a result of their life-course stage, not only are young people exposed to the risks of post-industrial society on a grand scale, but they are expected to play a greater role in the management of those risks. As a consequence, young people have a series of specific experiences and needs that are relevant for social policy.

Youth policy is underpinned by a series of normative assumptions and expectations about young people's social and economic activity and their engagement with the welfare state. What young people are entitled to (or not entitled to), whether these entitlements have conditions attached to them, and how they are encouraged or incentivised to behave have been structured by a normative understanding of what kinds of social and economic activity are acceptable during this phase of the life-course. Youth transitions are to some extent institutionalised in different social policy structures so that differences in welfare regimes can shape the way that transitions are negotiated by young people in different countries (Bynner, 2005; Walther, 2006). A country's social policies may, for example, structure the way in which young people make the transition from school to work, encouraging or compelling them to behave in certain ways (Billari and Liefbroer, 2010). These policies can 'increase subjective risk' or provide 'cushioning mechanisms [which] can serve to increase space for subjectively meaningful transitions' (Walther, 2006, p. 136). These institutional structures com-bine with cultural norms and expectations to create 'climates of nor-mality' in which young people's biographies are embedded (Walther, 2006, pp. 135–6). Responsibilisation has become the 'climate of normal-ity' in which many young people in Europe must now operate. In this climate, policies are focused on the need for young people to make themselves 'employable'. Activation policies, for example, are under-pinned by the principle that young people should take responsibility for their employment participation, advancement and social integra-tion (Walther, 2005). This policy climate increases subjective risk and offers fewer or more limited 'cushioning' mechanisms for young people as they negotiate life-course transitions. It also fails to take account of factors operating beyond the individual level that shape the contexts in which young people operate.

2.3   Inequalities and structural differences in youth transitions

While the degree of agency compelled by the 'opening up' of youth biographies is seen by some as having positive implications, creat-ing greater choice and opportunity for young people (Arnett, 2006; Patterson et al., 2009), others focus on the ways that these changes are coupled with growing risks that young people from all backgrounds are required to face as they make their transition to adulthood. In particu-lar, of great concern to policymakers is the notion that a generation of young people, 'irrespective of class and gender', are at risk of labour mar-ket insecurity and exclusion, and stunted career trajectories (Wyn and Woodman, forthcoming). The effects of these changes on a whole gener-ation of young people present very real challenges for policymakers, but we contend that the challenge is more complex than this. While there are important commonly experienced social and economic conditions, many researchers have drawn attention towards the ways that youth is far from a homogenised experience (Bynner et al., 2002; Fenton and Dermott, 2006; MacDonald and Marsh, 2005; Moreno, 2012; Roberts and Evans, 2013; Roberts and Pollock, 2009). Instead, the youth period is characterised by inequality of opportunity and of outcome as 'old' social divisions – such as class, gender, 'race' and place – continue to create differences in the experience of the transition to adulthood, both across and between nation states, but also, importantly, within them. This is especially the case when considering how these different socio-demographic characteristics intersect.

Young people are endowed with access to different levels and types of social, cultural and economic resources, or what sociologists might sometimes call 'capitals'. It is the possession and convertibility of such capitals that equips (young) people with differentiated capacities to act to mitigate what are deemed to be common, classless, contemporary risks; as such, differentiated compositions of capitals create advantages and disadvantages that underpin inequality, whilst at the same time the process of individualisation actually masks these structural inequalities and imbues all social actors with a sense of responsibility for their own social location.

These class-based and structural differences have been exacerbated by policymakers' decisions in the 'age of austerity'. In Britain, for example, austerity measures have resulted in the removal and/or reduction of programmes which, however meagre, were aimed at reducing economic and educational inequalities. In the UK, the abandonment of the Educational Maintenance Allowance (the payment to pupils entering post-compulsory schooling as a means of lessening the demands of economic necessity) and the Future Jobs Fund (the programme of subsidised youth employment) alongside measures aimed at raising revenue, such as increases in VAT rather than income tax (which is known to disproportionately affect those earning less), and the encouragement for universities to triple tuition fees have all combined into an unequal impact upon working-class young people and their families and communities (Atkinson et al., 2013). Policy changes of this type are typical of a broader trend in which many industrialised nations have deviated from social policies aimed explicitly at moderating wage inequality and poverty, towards welfare state retrenchment, more social assistance premised on means testing and more activation policies. Such developments are argued to have potentially reduced the redistributive capacity of social policies (Emmenegger et al., 2012; for a wider ranging review of how social policymaking contributes to or mitigates inequalities in various European countries see Korpi, 2010).

Even at its most basic level, social class continues to structure young people's transitions to adulthood. Young people from working-class and/or low income backgrounds tend to be disproportionately less likely to participate in higher education (Furlong and Cartmel, 2007) and more likely to make efforts to permanently engage with the labour market at a younger age. The UK's higher education system, for example, is considered to be very hierarchical, with 'old' elite universities and their predominantly middle-class student intakes faring much better in entering the labour market than students from the 'new' higher education institutions. This is compounded by the fact that institutions that exhibit the highest rates of non-completion are the newer universities: those that have a comparatively large proportion of working-class, non-traditional students.

Sarah Evans (2009) documents the intersection of class and gender as a significant influence upon young people's choice of university. Evans illustrates how family ties and gender-specific family obligations (often caring for siblings, parents, grandparents or even having domestic responsibilities in the family home) problematise the idea that even suitably qualified young women are free choice-making, individual agents, responsible for navigating a supposedly democratic higher education system and obtaining attendant future employment success. Evans argues instead that class and gender combine, with particular consequences for the location of the institution of choice, but also result in specific (elite) institutions being viewed as 'foreign fields' – middle-class (often masculine) spaces which symbolically exclude working-class women. Diane Reay's findings serve to summarise these education-based analyses particularly well. She argues that 'regardless of what individual working-class males and females are able to negotiate and achieve for themselves within education, the collective patterns of working-class trajectories remain sharply different from those of the middle classes' (Reay, 2006, p. 294). Issues related to the pervasiveness of class-based inequality are also paralleled in research about young people's 'chosen' employment outcomes. Quinn et al. (2008, p. 34), for instance, looked at the journey young people make from education into low-level jobs without training (JWT) and conclude that 'the impact of class on channelling these young people into JWT is indisputable'.

Given that we know that class correlates highly with educational achievement and participation, we can also note the ways in which the risk of unemployment is unevenly distributed, with tertiary levels of education linked to a lower risk of unemployment (OECD, 2013). This is made clear if one considers the unemployment situation in the UK, where, despite a sharp increase, recent graduates have been about a third less likely to be unemployed than non-graduates aged 21–30 (ONS, 2013). Similarly, when comparing the rates of unemployment between those who graduated five or more years ago (3 per cent) to the rest of the non-graduate adult population over 30 years old (just over 6 per cent), higher education experience again stands this group in good stead.

It is incontestable that precariousness, certainly in respect of flexible (involuntary) part-time and temporary work, has been on the rise for several decades, and that this shift represents a transition in employment relations (Kalleberg, 2009). These increases, which have been driven by the transformation from manufacturing to service-based economies (a process sometimes called deindustrialisation), have led to concerns that perhaps 'we are all precarious now'; indeed, this is part of Standing's (2011) argument about the ever-expanding precariat. Young people as a collective are particularly affected by atypical employment forms. There is evidence of growing precariousness among those with higher education qualifications, with graduates increasingly finding themselves embroiled in longer and more drawn out 'entry tournaments' (Marsden, 2007) to land graduate-level jobs, experiencing a perceived underemployment of their skill level as they compete for roles that were once the preserve of their lower-qualified contemporaries, and even facing spells of unemployment. However, the distribution and experience of labour market precariousness among young people is heavily structured by social inequalities.

Hence, while these contemporary conditions may affect an entire generation of young people, they do not affect them equally. Evidence points towards growing numbers of jobs at both the bottom and top of the waged economy (Goos and Manning, 2007), resulting in hourglass-shaped labour markets, characterised by a polarisation between 'lovely and lousy jobs'. Lousy jobs are those which are lacking in security, requiring high levels of flexibility and generally low paid, with many being 'zero hours' contracts. This type of working arrangement, which is more often found in industries where young people are concentrated, allows employers to respond flexibly to demand and therefore guarantees employees no minimum number of weekly hours. However, while a 'lovely' job tends to be those that are well paid, secure and granting autonomy, even at this level many jobs are flexible and involve short-term contracts. Yet the experience of apparently precarious work is far from uniform. Will Atkinson (2010) documents the ways in which redundancy and flexible work can be used advantageously by some middle-class people, such as presenting opportunities to take a break and/or take time to retrain, but it is seemingly an issue of huge concern for those further down the social hierarchy.

While inequality has often been associated with or described in reference to differences in material standards of living, we need to understand it as much more than this. Increasingly, research has also considered what is sometimes termed as agency inequalities, which reflect the differences in people's range of real choices of alternative activities (Korpi, 2010). Sociologist Beverly Skeggs (2012) recently contended that the experience of working-class young people and middle-class graduates in becoming part of the precariat was likely to be comparatively very different in the longer term. Pointing towards the significant issue of intergenerational inheritance, she notes there are distinct class divisions in prospective wealth and property transference which reinforce patterns of wealth inequality and present precarious middle-class young people with a psychological safety net. This knowledge, especially when combined with the capacity to mobilise other social, cultural and economic resources (Roberts, 2013), is likely to produce qualitatively very different experiences of precariousness. Here, we get a sense of how young people come to experience their own situation as a product of their own choices, while at the same time ignoring the ways their agency might be 'bounded' (Evans, 2002).

What this suggests is that 'old' inequalities, in combination with new risks, create challenges for social policy. These challenges become enhanced because we know that 'it is in the course of making transitions [to adulthood] that social class, gender and ethnic divisions among young people widen, deepen and are consolidated' (Roberts, 2000, p. 6). Recognising this fact points to the need for a framework that better sets out the relevance of welfare structures for the character and distribution of youth inequalities. We need a theory that enables us to capture the dynamic interplay of both structure and agency if social policy is to fully and appropriately respond to the welfare needs of young people.

2.4   Understanding inequality and risk through the analysis of the 'welfare mixes'

There are two coexisting tendencies involved in understanding young people's social condition. Section 2.2 of this chapter remarked on the challenges faced in youth transitions, the ongoing process of individualisation and diffusion of social risk that challenges young people's lives, and the capacity of social policy to respond to young people's evolving social needs. Section 2.3 stressed how social structures continue to be dominant in the distribution of social risks, and the need for constructing theories on youth transitions that explain processes of inequality. Youth studies have grappled with the extent to which this process of individualisation has increased agency, providing young people with greater choice in the 'construction of their biography', and the way that structural inequalities continue to exert an influence, particularly in the distribution of risks (Furlong and Cartmel, 2007).

Most recently, a middling tendency (Threadgold, 2011) has emerged, which combines an understanding of structures with the need to explore processes of individualisation and of the role of the agency. The tendency towards middle-ground theoretical positions that situate themselves between structural and agential explanations of inequality has been criticised by some commentators. Woodman (2009), who believes that social class is no longer up to the task of explaining contemporary inequality, argues that proponents of this middle-ground approach incorrectly use the individualisation thesis (proposed by Ulrich Beck) as a straw man to argue that class still matters. However, middle-ground theories also provide a degree of vitality and relevance (Threadgold, 2011). Middle-ground positions allow us to explain how the 'reflexive self', rather than replacing class, becomes the medium by which it is produced and reproduced (Skeggs, 2004, p. 60; Furlong and Cartmel, 2007). Only then can social policy begin to mitigate its effects.

According to the concept of 'structured individualism', one such middle-ground approach, individualised pathways are determined by structural boundaries, such as the labour market, government policies and family, that provide or limit choices and opportunities (France, 2007, p. 71). However, as structural boundaries and opportunities vary greatly across Europe, the balance between structure and agency in different countries remains unclear, as does the function of the different sources of welfare in shaping youth transitions. The application of welfare theory offers a framework for understanding how young people negotiate risk by drawing on sources of welfare (from the state, the market and the family), including how young people's experiences of the process of individualisation are shaped by different institutional structures. It helps us to understand the constraints and opportunity structures in which young people navigate these risks, suggesting that the balance between structure and agency varies depending on different welfare structures.

2.4.1   Welfare regimes as structures

For many years, the starting point for the analysis of sources of welfare in European social policy has been the influential regime analysis by Esping-Andersen (1990). While subject to subsequent evolutions and critiques (Arts and Gelissen, 2002; Ferrera, 1996; Lewis, 1997), welfare regime analysis goes beyond a simple analysis of the social policy resources available to young people (such as social security, housing support, educational support and so on) and facilitates a consideration of the way in which they interact, allowing us to identify the assumptions underpinning whole welfare systems.

As stated by Heinz, welfare systems are one of the different 'transitional arrangements' that vary greatly across societies as young people approach adulthood (2009, p. 5). Within each welfare system, young people are granted the peculiar status of 'both semi-dependency and semi-independency... [with] some rights and responsibilities in decision-making about their future, and some support and guidance in doing so' (Coles, 1995, p. 7). Different configurations of rights and responsibilities across welfare states shape the way that transitions are negotiated by young people (Bynner, 2005; Walther, 2006), creating different models of semi-dependence across countries. For example, researchers focusing on youth transitions regimes have found that transitions in southern European countries are characterised by a certain form of semi-dependence (Micheli and Rosina, 2010) and that this can be ascribed to southern familism and to a lower value placed on independence from family both by young people and their families (Van de Velde, 2008). These differences also reflect norms about intergenerational support embedded in southern transitional regimes (Leccardi and Ruspini, 2006; Moreno, 2012; Walther, 2006). In the case of welfare state arrangements in liberal countries, scholars have identified the strong trend towards individualisation, or the responsibility of the individual young person to manage risks such as unemployment and poverty (Furlong and Cartmel, 2007; Lemke, 2001).

In liberal regimes, where we have seen the development of a strong notion of personal responsibility in youth (Stenner and Marshall, 1999), the notion of 'full adulthood' has become closely associated with 'self-sovereignty' (Sennett, 2003, p. 113) and the 'shame of dependency' on state-based welfare provision (Dean, 2004, p. 33). Even in countries that rely on more familial models of welfare provision, the individualisation of risk is an increasing trend (Rosina et al., 2007). As Swartz and O'Brien interestingly note, 'in those countries with limited welfare states, the private and hidden nature of interfamily support may not only reproduce existing inequalities, but may also legitimate and reinforce ideologies of independence and individualism' (Swartz and O'Brien, 2009, p. 223).

As pointed out by Walther, welfare regime analysis has been used in the comparative analysis of youth transitions in order to 'identify variations in the interplay between structure and agency in different transition contexts' (Walther, 2006, p. 120). Welfare regime analysis therefore represents a 'middle-range' theory that combines the analysis of individualisation with that of institutional structures. While welfare theory has effectively established the importance of considering welfare regimes as structures around young people, this analysis can be deepened by looking beyond the apparatus of the welfare state to examine the relationship between different sources of welfare – formal and informal – or 'welfare mixes' across countries that young people draw on to manage risk.

2.4.2 From welfare regimes to welfare mixes

What is neglected by the simple focus on youth welfare regimes is a discussion of the theoretical assumptions behind the formation of the above-mentioned clusters (Liberal, Continental, Southern-European and Scandinavian). While welfare regime analysis focuses on the outcomes of Esping-Andersen's regime division, the analysis of 'welfare mixes' clarifies how the different combination of welfare sources in each country leads to different levels to decommodification and defamilisation in young people's lives. As stated by Powell and Barrientos:

> A specific articulation of the market, state and family, production of welfare produces specific welfare outcomes, measured in terms of de-commodification or de-familialism, as well as specific stratification effects that reinforce the welfare mix, ensuring path dependence. Nevertheless, conceptually, the welfare mix is the basis upon which the welfare regime is built.
>
> (Powell and Barrientos, 2004, p. 85)

Considering 'welfare mixes' means analysing the comparative relevance of the three main sources of welfare in different contexts. An approach that draws on the concept of the welfare mix implies that the typology of regimes identified by Esping-Andersen (1990) is not necessarily valid for youth transitions, and there is a need instead to identify 'youth regimes' by exploring the comparative relevance of formal and informal sources of support across the state, the market and informal networks.

The analysis of the 'welfare mix' takes into account that welfare regime divisions are now less clear-cut as a consequence of common pressures from globalisation (Mishra, 1999). It also allows us to better understand how welfare states have changed, and continue to change. A welfare mix analysis overcomes the main limitation of the original analysis of welfare regimes by Esping-Andersen (1990), which 'is anchored in the old, passive politics of the welfare state' (Powell and Barrientos, 2004, p. 87). Welfare states have undergone significant change since the development of welfare regime analysis. Not only was the original welfare regime division constructed with data from the 'golden age of the welfare state', but it focuses on income maintenance programmes, rather than the 'active' policies that have emerged to deal with new social risks (Powell and Barrientos, 2004). As we have stressed above, activation policies have a particularly strong impact on young people as newcomers to the labour market. In addition to this, the effects of austerity described in the previous section have affected the 'welfare mixes' available to young people in Europe. Therefore, focusing on the welfare mix, rather than on regimes, means also capturing the 'new structure of welfare in an era of privatization' (Ascoli and Ranci, 2002), understanding how young people manage risk when welfare state provisions are limited.

In fact, the way that young people draw on sources of welfare to manage risk is connected to their specific position vis-à-vis social policy. The period of youth transitions implies a sort of 'semi-dependence': a passage between childhood dependence and adult independence (Coles, 1995, p. 7). In this condition of semi-dependence, young people across Europe use a different combination of the three main sources of welfare (state, family and the labour market) to cope with social risks. As Powell and Barrientos observe, 'the welfare state, the family and the market are seen as three sources of managing social risks' (Powell and Barrientos, 2004, p. 98). Young people commonly undertake the dual processes of becoming economically independent (understood as earning an income on the market) while remaining to some extent dependent on their families (particularly for financial support and accommodation). Because of this, when understanding youth social policy, we need to understand the way in which the welfare state interacts with other sources of welfare in young people's lives, such as the market and family, and the role of the state in setting normative standards in young people's engagement with all three sources of welfare. For Walther, increasingly, 'situations of youth-like dependency and adult autonomy may co-exist simultaneously within the same biography' (2006, p. 121). By capturing both social risks and welfare structures, the analysis of 'welfare mixes' is better equipped than 'welfare regimes' to offer 'middle-range welfare theories'.

Furthermore, an analysis of welfare mixes clarifies the dynamics of youth inequality both across countries and within countries. The comparison across European countries enables the welfare mixes available to young people to be compared: given the existing diversity in the mixes of welfare available, Europe represents a social laboratory for understanding how the different structures influence processes of individualisation (as in Evans, 2002). Appreciating the cross-national diversity allows scholars to overcome what appears to be a 'generalisation fallacy' in youth studies, where conclusions are drawn by focusing on Anglo-Saxon countries (Bynner and Chisholm, 1998), all examples of the liberal model of welfare regime. On the contrary, a comparative analysis of welfare mixes across Europe clarifies, for example, the specific function of state sources and the roles these play in sustaining the transitions of young people in northern Europe, and the role of family sources, which is central in southern Europe but is becoming increasingly important across the rest of the continent. The analysis of the welfare mixes indeed implies a holistic understanding of the sources of support available to young people, namely the specific function of family, state and labour market sources and how the balance between them changes over time.

Moreover, the analysis of welfare sources available during young people's semi-dependence can further our understanding of stratification and inequality within each country. Compared with the analysis of totally dependent individuals (children), in which it is possible to assume a direct transmission of inequality from parents, such an assumption is not possible in the protracted status of semi-dependency of young people (Furlong and Cartmel, 2007, p. 140). Young people are in fact between a certain level of dependency (on family and on the welfare state) and a status of independence coming from their own participation in the labour market. As a result, the reproduction of social inequalities is more complex in this group. An analysis of welfare sources can help us to understand this complex process, such as how different combinations of labour market conditions, family circumstances and welfare state arrangements may mitigate or entrench social inequalities. For example, the declining role of labour market and state sources in sustaining young people's independence and the increasing reliance on family sources are both processes that can potentially reinforce the transmission of social disadvantage across generations and the reproduction of inequalities.

A welfare mix analysis allows us to deepen our understanding of not just the function of each source of welfare in helping young people to manage risk, but their comparative relevance in contemporary welfare states. A welfare mix analysis of the way in which young people manage risk reveals major changes in the role of different sources of welfare in supporting them through transitions to adulthood. In late modernity, young people face major challenges in their transitions to the labour market, intensified by the global economic crisis. The diffusion of precarious jobs and the increasing impact of underemployment on youth transitions (MacDonald, 2011; Standing, 2011) challenge the extent to which young people can depend on labour market sources to sustain their independence, creating a further protraction of semi-dependency in their transitions. Family is becoming a more central source of welfare for young people, and intergenerational transfers are becoming more important as they undergo transitions such as higher education and training, labour market entry and, in some cases, family formation. We know much less about the role of state sources in supporting youth transitions with direct welfare provisions, such as systems of student support, housing and social security (as in Antonucci, 2011; Laaksonen, 2000) – while a number of contributions in this book aim to fill this gap by discussing welfare state interventions in housing, social security and education. Recent studies in the field have also pointed out the emerging tensions in work and family life faced by young people – 'newcomers' to work and family life across Europe (Knijn, 2012). At the same time, states are winding back public provision as a source of welfare. Austerity measures across Europe are limiting the availability of state sources for young people: processes of welfare state retrenchment and austerity across Europe have a particularly strong impact on young people (compared with other age groups) as a category affected most acutely by 'new social risks' (Taylor-Gooby, 2004, 2013).

These changes have important implications for youth inequalities that this book sets out to explore. While a welfare source analysis allows us to identify changes to the comparative relevance of welfare sources that are common to all European welfare states, it also allows us to explore trends within different European welfare states. This book will shed light on some of these trends in the welfare sources that are made available to young people during their transitions to adulthood, and the implications that they have for the character of youth transitions and youth inequalities across different nations.

2.5 Youth studies and welfare theory: A framework for supporting youth transitions?

In conclusion, youth studies provides a comprehensive analysis of the contemporary conditions facing young people. It provides extensive discussion of the risks that young people face in late modernity and the effects of those risks on the contemporary youth biography. Most particularly, youth studies emphasises the replacement of traditional, linear pathways from adolescence to adulthood by uncertain and fragmented pathways, or 'choice biographies'. This process has been described in youth studies as 'individualisation'. For some youth sociologists, young people now construct their biographies from a range of options and opportunities in a manner that is less constrained by social institutions and structures than those of their forebears. But while some scholars (such as Arnett) have argued that the process of individualisation presents young people with greater agency in their life choices, others studying the sociology of youth (such as Bynner) have argued that young people's transitions continue to be shaped by structural constraints such as class and gender, and by institutional constraints such as education and labour market structures. Some of these scholars have argued that the process of individualisation has actually deepened structural inequalities rather than freeing young people from their shackles. There has been significant debate in the sociology of youth about whether individual agency or structural constraints forms the dominant feature of contemporary youth transitions. A recent tendency in this debate has been to provide middle-ground explanations of youth transitions, such as 'structured individualism', that attempt to account for both the process of individualisation and the continued relevance of structures, without placing priority on one or the other.

However, what has been missing in this debate is due recognition of the importance of welfare structures (and the social policies in which they are embedded) in shaping the way that contemporary risks are experienced and negotiated by young people. Including an analysis of welfare structures is essential to identifying young people's needs arising from these contemporary conditions, and how best to meet them. But an analysis of this kind is also central to understanding how those needs are generated. Moreover, an analysis of welfare structures helps us to understand the process by which contemporary risks generate different forms of need among European young people. Welfare structures shape the extent to which young people can exercise agency, and the extent to which they are constrained by structures. An analysis of welfare structures therefore has the potential to operate as a 'middle-ground' approach to the contemporary conditions facing young people.

Welfare regime analysis goes some way to providing a middle-range theory of youth transitions, but has some downfalls when applied to young people. Welfare regime analysis emerged in the 1980s and 1990s from more predictable labour market and income maintenance structures, and is focused on the role of the state in decommodifying individuals from reliance on the market. However, the labour market has changed considerably so that it is now characterised by insecurity, and welfare states have also changed in orientation to place greater responsibility on the individual for managing risk. Young people have been particularly affected by precarious work and the individualisation agenda (through activation programmes, for example) and 'commodification', rather than decommodification, has become a key policy issue. But perhaps most significantly, welfare regime analysis focuses on the welfare state apparatus. However, young people, as a result of their life-course stage, draw on a unique mix of formal and informal sources (including support from the welfare state) as they move between different forms of dependence on the state, the market and their families.

As a result, a 'welfare mix' approach provides a more appropriate framework for understanding the relationship (much debated in youth studies) between individual agency and structural constraints in contemporary youth transitions. It explores not just the relative importance of each individual source of welfare but the ways in which these interact to produce welfare outcomes. This approach, unlike a welfare regime approach, is also able to make sense of the 'semi-dependence' identified in youth studies as characteristic of the youth phase. The approach asks: in each country, to what extent must young people rely on the state, the labour market and the family – and different combinations of all three – to support themselves during transitions to adulthood? To what extent does a country's 'welfare mix' allow individual young people to pursue subjectively meaningful transitions and make plans for the future (or 'construct their own biography')? And to what extent does a country's welfare mix mitigate or perpetuate social inequalities? This framework allows us to respond to some of the major questions raised in youth studies about how young people experience and manage risk, while simultaneously pointing to the ways in which policy can address their needs. In the first application of a welfare mix approach to the study of young people, drawing on new research from social policy scholars, this book will shed light on some of these trends in the welfare sources that European young people have access to, and the implications that they have for the character of youth transitions and youth inequalities across different nations.

References

Antonucci, L. (2011). 'University Students in Transition to Adult Age. Comparing Italy and England'. *Italian Journal of Social Policy* 15 (3), 271–89.

Arnett, J. (2006). *Emerging Adulthood, the Winding Road from the Late Teens through the Twenties* (New York: Oxford University Press).

Arts, W.A. and Gelissen, J.P.T. (2002). 'Three Worlds of Welfare Capitalism or More? A State-of-the-Art Report'. *Journal of European Social Policy* 12 (2), 137–58.

Ascoli, U. and Ranci, C. (eds.) (2002). *Dilemmas of the Welfare Mix. The New Structure of Welfare in an Era of Privatization* (New York: Springer).

Atkinson, W. (2010). *Class, Individualization and Late Modernity* (Basingstoke: Palgrave Macmillan).

Atkinson, W., Roberts, S. and Savage, M. (eds.) (2013). *Class Inequality in Austerity Britain: Power, Difference and Suffering* (Basingstoke: Palgrave Macmillan).

Bauman, Z. (2002). 'Individually, Together', in Beck, U. and Beck-Gernsheim, E. (eds.) *Individualisation* (London: Sage), pp. x–xix.

Beck, U. (2000). 'Living Your Own Life in a Runaway World: Individualisation, Globalisation and Politics', in Hutton, W. and Giddens, A. (eds.) *Global Capitalism* (New York: The New Press), pp. 164–74.

Beck, U. and Beck-Gernsheim, E. (2002). *Individualisation* (London: Sage).

Billari, F.C. and Liefbroer, A.C. (2010). 'Towards a New Pattern of Transition to Adulthood?'. *Advances in Life Course Research* 15, 59–75.

Bowman, D., Bodsworth, E. and Zinn, J. (2013). 'Gender Inequalities and Risk During the "Rush Hour" of Life'. *Social Policy and Society* 12 (2), 277–86.

Bynner, J. (2005). 'Rethinking the Youth Phase of the Life Course: The Case of Emerging Adulthood'. *Journal of Youth Studies* 8 (4), 367–84.

Bynner, J. and Chisholm, L. (1998). 'Comparative Youth Transition Research: Methods, Meanings and Research Relations'. *European Sociological Review* 14 (2), 131–50.

Bynner, J., Elias, P., McKnight, A., Pan, H. and Pierre, G. (2002). *Young People's Changing Routes to Independence* (York: Joseph Rowntree Foundation).

Coles, B. (1995). *Youth and Social Policy: Youth Citizenship and Young Careers* (London: UCL Press).

Dean, H. (2004). *The Ethics of Welfare* (Bristol: Policy Press).

Emmenegger, P., Häusermann, S., Palier, B. and Seeleib-Kaiser, M. (2013). *The Age of Dualization: The Changing Face of Inequality in Deindustrializing Societies* (Oxford: Oxford University Press).

Esping-Andersen, G. (1990). *The Three Worlds of Welfare Capitalism* (Cambridge: Polity Press).

Evans, K. (2002). 'Taking Control of Their Lives? Agency in Young Adult Transitions in England and the New Germany'. *Journal of Youth Studies* 5 (3), 245–69.

Evans, S. (2009). 'In a Different Place: Working-class Girls and Higher Education'. *Sociology* 43 (2), 340–55.

Fenton, S. and Dermott, E. (2006). 'Fragmented Careers? Winners and Losers in Young Adult Labour Markets'. *Work, Employment & Society* 20 (2), 205–21.

Ferrera M. (1996). 'The "Southern Model" of Welfare in Social Europe'. *Journal of European Social Policy* 1 (6), 17–37.

France, A. (2007). *Understanding Youth in Late Modernity* (London: Open University Press).

Furlong, A. and Cartmel, F. (1997). *Young People and Social Change: Individualization and Risk in Late Modernity* (Buckingham: Open University Press).

Furlong, A. and Cartmel, F. (2007). *Young People and Social Change: New Perspectives* (Buckingham: Open University Press).

Goos, M. and Manning, A. (2007). 'Lousy and Lovely Jobs: The Rising Polarization of Work in Britain'. *The Review of Economics and Statistics* 89 (1), 118–33.

Hamilton, M. (2010). 'Welfare Reform and Provision for Old Age in Australia and Britain', in Marston, G., Moss, J. and Quiggin, J. (eds.) *Risk, Welfare and Work* (Melbourne: Melbourne University Press).

Hamilton, M. (2014). 'The "New Social Contract" and the Individualisation of Risk in Policy'. *Journal of Risk Research*, 1–15.

Heinz, W. (2009). 'Youth Transitions in an Age of Uncertainty', in Furlong, A. (ed.) *Handbook of Youth and Young Adulthood: New Perspectives and Agendas* (London: Routledge).

Kalleberg, A.L. (2009). 'Precarious Work, Insecure Workers: Employment Relations in Transition'. *American Sociological Review* 74 (1), 1–22.

Knijn, T. (2012). *Work, Family Policies and Transitions to Adulthood in Europe* (Basingstoke: Palgrave Macmillan).

Korpi, W. (2010). 'Class and Gender Inequalities in Different Types of Welfare States: The Social Citizenship Indicator Program'. *International Journal of Social Welfare* 19 (1), 14–24.

Laaksonen, A. (2000). 'Young Adults in Changing Welfare States: Prolonged Transitions and Delayed Entries for under-30s in Finland, Sweden and Germany in the '90s'. *Mannheimer Zentrum fur Europaische Sozialforschung* 12, 1–32.

Leccardi, C. and Ruspini, E. (2006). *A New Youth? Young People Generations and Family Life* (London: Ashgate).

Lemke, T. (2001). ' "The Birth of Bio-politics": Michel Foucault's Lecture at the College de France on Neo-liberal Governmentality'. *Economy and Society* 30 (2), 190–207.

Lewis, J. (1997). 'Gender and Welfare Regimes: Further Thoughts'. *Social Politics* 4 (2), 178–81.

MacDonald, R. (2011). 'Youth Transitions, Unemployment and Underemployment'. *Journal of Sociology* 47 (4), 427–44.

MacDonald, R. and Marsh, J. (2005). *Disconnected Youth? Growing Up in Britain's Poor Neighbourhoods* (Basingstoke: Palgrave Macmillan).

Marsden, D. (2007). 'Labour Market Segmentation in Britain: The Decline of Occupational Labour Markets and the Spread of "Entry Tournaments" '. *Sociétés* 28, 965–98.

Micheli, G. and Rosina, A. (2010). 'The Vulnerability of Young Adults on Leaving the Parental Home', in Ranci, C. (ed.) *Social Vulnerability in Europe. The New Configuration of Social Risks* (Basingstoke: Palgrave Macmillan), pp. 189–218.

Mishra, R. (1999). *Globalization and the Welfare State* (Cheltenham: Edward Elgar).

Moreno, A. (2012). 'The Transition to Adulthood in Spain in a Comparative Perspective: The Incidence of Structural Factors'. *Young* 20 (1), 19–48.

OECD (2013). *Education at a Glance 2013: OECD Indicators* (Paris: OECD Publishing).

ONS (2013). 'Graduates in the UK Labour Market 2013, Office for National Statistics', 19 November 2013, available at http://www.ons.gov.uk/ons/dcp171776_337841.pdf

Patterson, L.G., Forbes, K.E. and Peace, R.M. (2009). 'Happy, Stable and Contented: Accomplished Ageing in the Imagined Futures of Young New Zealanders'. *Ageing and society* 29 (3), 431–54.

Powell, M. and Barrientos, A. (2004). 'Welfare Regimes and the Welfare Mix'. *European Journal of Political Research* 43 (1), 83–105.

Quinn, J., Lawy, R. and Diment, K. (2008). *Young People in Jobs without Training in South West England* (Exeter: South West Observatory Skills and Learning, University of Exeter).

Reay, D. (2006). 'The Zombie Stalking English Schools: Social Class and Educational Inequality'. *British Journal of Educational Studies* 54 (3), 288–307.

Roberts, K. (2000). 'Problems and Priorities for the Sociology of Youth', in Bennett, A., Cieslik, M. and Miles, S. (eds.) *Researching Youth* (Basingstoke: Palgrave).

Roberts, K. and Pollock, G. (2009). 'New Class Divisions in the New Market Economies: Evidence from the Careers of Young Adults in Post-Soviet Armenia, Azerbaijan and Georgia'. *Journal of Youth Studies* 12 (5), 579–96.

Roberts, S. (2013). 'Youth Studies, Housing Transitions and the "Missing Middle": Time for a Rethink?'. *Sociological Research Online* 18 (3), 11.

Roberts, S. and Evans, S. (2013). ' "Aspirations" and Imagined Futures: The Im/possibilities', in Atkinson, W., Roberts, S. and Savage, M. (eds.) *Class Inequality in Austerity Britain: Power, Difference and Suffering* (Basingstoke: Palgrave Macmillan).

Rosina, A., Micheli, G.A. and Mazzucco, S. (2007). 'An Analysis of Young People's Risk of Difficulties on Leaving the Parental Home'. *Italian Journal of Social Policy*, 4 (3), 95–111.

Sennett, R. (2003). *Respect: The Formation of Character in an Age of Inequality* (London: Penguin Books).

Skeggs, B. (2004). *Class, Self, Culture (Transformations: Thinking Through Feminism)* (London: Taylor and Francis).

Skeggs, B. (2012). 'Cruel Optimism', Thinking Allowed (Radio broadcast). *BBC Radio* 4, 13 February 2012.

Standing, G. (2011). *The Precariat: The New Dangerous Class* (London: Bloomsbury).

Stenner, P. and Marshall, H. (1999). 'On Developmentality: Searching the Varied Meanings of "Independence" and "Maturity" Extant amongst a Sample of Young People in East London'. *Journal of Youth Studies* 2 (3), 297–316.

Swartz, T.T. and O'Brien, K.B. (2009). 'Intergenerational Support during the Transition to Adulthood', in Furlong, A. (ed.) *Handbook of Youth and Young Adulthood: New Perspectives and Agendas* (London: Routledge).

Taylor-Gooby, P. (2004). *New Risks, New Welfare* (Oxford: Oxford University Press).

Taylor-Gooby, P. (2013). *The Double Crisis of the Welfare State and What We Can Do About It* (Basingstoke: Palgrave Macmillan).

Threadgold, S. (2011). 'Should I Pitch My Tent in the Middle Ground? On "Middling Tendency", Beck and Inequality in Youth Sociology'. *Journal of Youth Studies* 14 (4), 381–93.

Van de Velde, C. (2008). *Devenir Adulte. Sociologie Comparée de la Jeunesse en Europe (Become Adult. Comparative Sociology of Youth in Europe)* (Paris: Presses Universitaires de France, collection Le Lien Social).

Vickerstaff, S. (2006). 'Life Course, Youth, and Old Age', in Taylor-Gooby P. and Zinn, J. (eds.) *Risk in Social Science* (Oxford: Oxford University Press), pp. 180–201.

Walther, A. (2005). 'Risks and Responsibilities: The Individualisation of Youth Transitions and the Ambivalence between Participation and Activation in Europe'. *Social Work & Society* 3 (1), 116–27.

Walther, A. (2006). 'Regimes of Youth Transitions: Choice, Flexibility and Security in Young People's Experiences across Different European Contexts'. *Young* 14 (2), 119–39.

Walther, A., Stauber, B., Biggart, A., du Bois-Reymond, M., Furlong, A., López Blasco, A., Mørch, S. and P. J. Machado (eds.) (2002). *Misleading Trajectories - Integration Policies for Young Adults in Europe?* (Opladen: Leske+Budrich).

Woodman, D. (2009). 'The Mysterious Case of the Pervasive Choice Biography: Ulrich Beck, Structure/Agency and the Middling State of Theory in the Sociology of Youth'. *Journal of Youth Studies* 12 (3), 243–56.

Wyn, J. and Woodman, D. (forthcoming, 2014). *Youth Studies Matters* (London: Sage).

Part I

Precarity, Social Exclusion and Youth Policy in Europe

3
The Complex Nature of Youth Poverty and Deprivation in Europe

Eldin Fahmy

3.1 Introduction

The global economic crisis, with its dire impacts for European youth, draws attention to the importance of research into inequalities in youth transitions in order to better understand the drivers of disadvantage and to improve policy responses. Drawing upon *2009 EU Survey of Income and Living Conditions* data for 28 countries, this chapter examines the nature, extent and distribution of disadvantage among 16–29-year-olds living in Europe. Since the groundbreaking work of Peter Townsend (for example, 1979, 1987), it has been well established that indirect, income-based estimates of poverty provide unreliable estimates of command over resources and need to be supplemented with direct measures of social and material deprivation. This lack of correspondence reflects both technical limitations in income measurement, and the more basic conceptual limitations of income measures in estimating individuals' and households' capacity to realise social needs. In this chapter it is argued that this is especially important in relation to youth, where household income estimates are highly imprecise measures of young people's command of resources and financial well-being.

Drawing on data from the *2009 EU-SILC Deprivation Module*, this chapter therefore examines the nature and structure of youth disadvantage based upon three operational measures: relative low income; material and social deprivation; and subjective poverty. In doing so the varying profile of vulnerability to youth disadvantage both within and between member states is examined, together with the extent to which such variations may be 'explained' by the effects of different youth welfare regimes. The chapter concludes with some observations on how further analysis could inform the development of policies to tackle youth disadvantage.[1]

3.2   What do we already know about youth poverty in Europe?

Existing research shows that young people in Europe are often more vulnerable to income poverty than older working age adults. Panel datasets such as the *Luxembourg Income Study* (LIS) and especially the *European Communities Household Panel Survey* (ECHP) have been key resources in the empirical investigation of youth poverty. Kangas and Palme's (2000) analysis of LIS data for eight OECD countries (including six European countries) reveals that rates of income poverty amongst young people under 25 are substantially higher than for most other age groups, and that this is a consistent cross-national pattern in the life-course of poverty. These authors conclude that:

> In most countries, the young have replaced the old as the lowest income group. The persistent poverty of the later years has gone; a passing poverty of early adulthood has arrived.
>
> (2000, p. 350)

Based upon an analysis of ECHP data for young Europeans aged 17–35, Iacovou and Berthoud (2001) also found that young men and women are more vulnerable to income poverty than older respondents, and that this effect is especially pronounced for young people who have left the parental home. Subsequent analysis of ECHP data by Iacovou and Aassve (2007) reveals substantial cross-national variations in income poverty rates amongst European youth, with especially high rates in the 'social democratic' countries such as Finland and Denmark (attributed to early domestic transitions), and in 'southern' countries such as Italy and Spain (associated with high overall rates of income poverty).

However, also using ECHP data, Mendola et al. (2008) find the relationship between income poverty rates and poverty *persistence* to be far from uniform across European societies as a result of national differences in welfare provision and labour market performance. In particular, it is argued that high rates of youth income poverty in Scandinavian countries (associated with early domestic transitions) do not in general result in long-term poverty persistence. This finding appears to be consistent with Halleröd and Westberg's (2006) analysis of panel data for Swedish youth aged 19–25. These authors find that the personal incomes of Swedish youth tell us little about their current living standards or future prospects. They argue that economic deprivation during youth is not a good guide to subsequent social and material deprivation. Poverty persistence in the Nordic countries is better explained in terms of the reproduction of existing class and gender inequalities (Halleröd and Westberg, 2006; Julkunen, 2002). Family support plays a strong role in preventing deprivation amongst youth in all European countries, alongside the timing of domestic transitions, cohabitation/marriage and labour market participation, which appear to be protective factors both in avoiding poverty entry and in facilitating poverty exit (see also Aassve et al., 2006; Fahmy, 2007).

Given the above evidence, understanding heterogeneity of institutional forms and opportunity structures across European societies is clearly central in explaining and responding to vulnerability to youth poverty. Variations in public welfare provision, housing markets, family structure and population demography are all known to influence vulnerability to youth poverty (for example, Iacovou, 2002; Vogel, 2002). Collectively, these factors highlight the importance of understanding the role of cross-national differences in welfare regimes in shaping youth transitions, and in determining vulnerability to poverty and wider forms of disadvantage. Walther and Pohl (2005) propose a typology of youth transition regimes based upon cross-national variations in education, training, labour market entry, welfare policy provision, gender norms and models of youth inclusion. However, whilst this represents a significant conceptual advance in understanding cross-national variations in youth welfare in Europe, it does not currently provide a robust empirical basis for a comprehensive classification of all European social systems. As a result, the following analyses are based upon a descriptive, geographically based classification of welfare systems which distinguishes between northern Europe (Denmark, Finland, Iceland, Sweden, Norway), north-west Europe (Ireland, the United Kingdom), western Europe (Belgium, France, the Netherlands, Austria, Luxembourg), eastern Europe (the Czech Republic, Estonia, Latvia, Lithuania, Poland, Slovakia, Hungary), southeast Europe (Bulgaria, Romania) and southern Europe (Cyprus, Greece, Italy, Malta, Portugal, Spain). As such the following analyses make no specific causal assumptions about the effects of different youth transition regimes on poverty vulnerability, though the overlaps are clear with regard to existing welfare regime classifications (for example, Esping-Andersen, 1990; Ferrera and Rhodes, 2000; Gallie and Paugam, 2000; Titmuss, 1974).

3.3 Youth inclusion and the impacts of the economic crisis in Europe

The evidence reviewed above consistently shows that young Europeans are more likely to live in low income households than older Europeans. However, the potential effects of the global economic crisis have focused attention on young people's circumstances and prospects and the extent, nature and dynamics of youth poverty. European economies have been amongst those most severely affected by the economic downturn, and young Europeans in particular have suffered disproportionately as a result of rising unemployment, employment insecurity and in-work poverty (for example, Bell and Blanchflower, 2011; Gush and Taylor, 2012; ILO, 2010). For example, since the economic crisis, the unemployment rate amongst 15–24-year-olds has risen dramatically across the EU member states from 15 per cent (February 2008) to 23 per cent (June 2012) – levels which are unprecedented in the post-1945 era (EC, 2012a).

It is well established that unemployment is strongly associated with increased vulnerability to poverty, and amongst Europe's young people these effects are therefore likely to be pronounced, especially in southern Europe, the Baltic states and Ireland, where unemployment is highest (Özdemir et al., 2010). Recent OECD research shows that not only have market incomes become more unequal across OECD member states since the economic crisis but that income poverty rates have risen substantially amongst young people in many EU member states, especially Estonia, Ireland, Greece, the Netherlands, Italy, Spain and the UK (OECD, 2013).

More widely, the effects of recession also need to be understood in the context of increased global economic competition and changing patterns of economic exchange associated with globalisation. For example, Buchholz et al. (2009) argue that young adults are the main 'losers' from globalisation processes in Europe. Despite some significant variations across European societies as a result of institutional and social differences, globalisation appears to have intensified the effects of educational and class inequalities in shaping labour market risks and outcomes for young people, resulting in increased employment uncertainty and postponed family formation. More generally, it is widely argued that changes in the social and economic terrain of youth transitions in recent decades have resulted in new risks and/or the deepening of existing inequalities associated with class and ethnicity, and that this may have intensified with the economic recession (for example, Buchmann and Kriesi, 2011;

Catan, 2004; Edward and Weller, 2010; Schizzerotto and Lucchini, 2002; Smith, 2009).

These observations highlight the importance of investigating the social and material circumstances of European youth. However, it is also likely that the direct effects of the recession upon young people's circumstances and their long-term prospects will not be known fully for some time, as a result of the 'lags' between economic shocks and their impacts on households' income situation and subsequent living standards (and also as a result of delays in the release of relevant survey data). The long-term effects of increased youth unemployment and fiscal austerity are especially difficult to estimate, though existing evidence points to the permanent material and psychological 'scarring' effects of recession (Bell and Blanchflower, 2011; Burgess et al., 2003; Gregg and Tominey, 2004).

The EU Youth Strategy for 2010–18 states that the economic crisis has 'hit young Europeans with unprecedented levels of unemployment and the risk of social exclusion and poverty' (2012b, p. 2), and the development of more effective policy responses to remedy this situation is therefore a pressing priority. To date, EU youth policy has focused primarily upon the quality of school to work transitions through, for example, initiatives to improve tertiary education and training, the promotion of labour market activation and job creation programmes, and efforts to improve youth mobility between EU member states. It has focused on promoting employability through investments in 'human capital', intended to promote wider economic competitiveness and growth (for example, EC, 2012b). The EU's ambitious long-term vision for promoting 'sustainable' and 'inclusive' growth, the *Europe 2020* strategy, also adopts a 'human capital' approach, with headline targets focusing on reducing early school leaving and increasing tertiary educational attainment, and additional targets for increasing employment participation and promoting (employment-related) skills acquisition and (labour) mobility (EC, 2010). More recently, the European Commission (2013) has acknowledged the urgency of addressing the youth unemployment crisis through concerted action including the Youth Guarantee activation programme, investment in youth through the European Social Fund and Youth Employment Initiative, and increased support for intra-EU labour mobility.

However, this agenda reflects 'social integrationist' assumptions about the nature and causes of social disadvantage, which have rightly been questioned as a framework for understanding poverty and social exclusion in contemporary societies (see, for example, Levitas, 1996, 1998).

As applied to the situation of youth, this discourse privileges inclusion through paid work as the preferred route to social inclusion for youth – indeed, inclusion is largely conceptualised *as* participation in paid work. Aside from the implicit economic reductionism associated with this approach, it also tends to deflect attention away from a focus on young people's capacity to realise *social* entitlements to an adequate standard of living, as well as to meet normative standards concerning social well-being and participation. Addressing this latter agenda requires us to investigate young people's access to material resources (principally income), and associated material and social living standards.

Moreover, given the scale of the problem facing European youth it is unlikely that labour market interventions on their own will be sufficient to insulate young Europeans from the risk of poverty and social exclusion. As part of the *Europe 2020* agenda, the EU is committed to achieving a 25 per cent reduction in the share of the EU population at risk of poverty and social exclusion by 2020. Given the evidence reviewed here, considerably more emphasis upon tackling youth poverty and exclusion will be needed if comparable reductions in the risk of poverty and social exclusion are to be achievable for Europe's youth. To achieve this, better evidence is needed on the incomes and living conditions of young Europeans, including how different measures of disadvantage compare with respect to Europe's youth population. This chapter seeks to improve the evidence base by examining the social profile of vulnerability to poverty defined in relation to three measures of disadvantage: income, deprivation and subjective measures.

3.4   Aims and methods

What, then, does this chapter seek to contribute to this existing knowledge base? First, it updates our understanding of cross-national variations in youth poverty in Europe on the basis of the most up-to-date and comprehensive data derived from the *EU Survey of Income and Living Conditions* (EU-SILC). Second, the chapter seeks to advance understanding of youth poverty by examining the relationship between three different operational measures of poverty: measures based upon relative low income, material and social deprivation, and subjective poverty. Existing work in this area has focused on indirect, income-based measures of poverty. However, it is well established that the empirical overlaps between indirect, income-based measures and other operational measures are not substantial (for example, Bradshaw and Finch, 2003; Haggenaars and de Vos, 1988; Whelan et al., 2001). The relationship between indirect income measures and both objective measures of social and material deprivation and subjective perceptions of income adequacy and economic strain amongst young people is not currently well understood (see, however, Iacovou and Berthoud, 2001; Fahmy, 2007; Hallerod and Westberg, 2006). This raises some fundamental questions about the 'best' way to measure cross-national variations in youth poverty. This chapter therefore addresses the following questions:

- How many young people are experiencing poverty across Europe and how do rates vary between European countries?
- To what extent do different measures of poverty identify the same populations as poor?
- How does the social profile of vulnerability to poverty vary, based upon different measures and in different European countries?

3.4.1   Data and indicators

The results reported here are based on analysis of the 2009 EU-SILC UBD cross-sectional file and comprises data on over 500,000 individuals and 200,000 private households in 28 European countries. The sample includes approximately 62,000 respondents aged 16–24 with national sample sizes in the approximate range 1,000–5,000 (see Appendix Table A.1 for further details). The dependent variables investigated here are defined as follows:

Income poverty. In this chapter, and for consistency with the Eurostat definition, young people are defined as 'income poor' where their total equivalised household incomes (in purchasing parity units) are less than 60 per cent of national median incomes in their country of residence. Three points are worthy of note here. First, as is common practice in income measurement and analysis, incomes are measured at the household level and subsequent analysis is applied at the individual level. This approach assumes that incomes are pooled within households and that all household members have equal access to the resources derived from this income. Whilst incomes are usually shared to some degree within households, researchers are often unable to ascertain whether the intrahousehold distribution of resources is equal or reflects social differences associated with age, gender, economic status and so on. Second, there is no compelling scientific case for setting an income poverty threshold at the 60 per cent median income threshold (as opposed to, say, 40 per cent, 50 per cent or 70 per cent), and the extent and social distribution of youth poverty will to some extent depend upon the specific threshold chosen. In this chapter convention is followed in order to facilitate comparison with official EU estimates that use the 60 per cent median measure. Third, median income thresholds are calculated relative to national income distributions, not relative to Europe-wide income data. This means that the same income (in purchasing parity units) may have very different implications for respondents' poverty status in different countries, depending on the national distribution of income.

Social and material deprivation. Though the multidimensional nature of poverty is now widely accepted, existing work in this area has mostly focused on income. The few studies that have investigated youth deprivation do not provide extensive information on the statistical properties of the deprivation indicators used. As a result, it is not possible to assess whether these items truly measure our underlying construct of interest (validity), whether they give consistent results (reliability) and whether their combination gives an accurate indication of the intensity of deprivation (additivity). Using data from the 2009 EU-SILC Deprivation module, the most extensive and up-to-date source of survey evidence on this topic in Europe, this chapter builds on extensive validation work undertaken by Guio et al. (2012). These authors develop deprivation measures that are reliable, valid and additive in all 27 EU member states. In line with Guio et al.'s recommendations, the deprivation index used here comprises a simple additive scale of 12 items widely viewed by European publics as contemporary 'necessities of life', where households lacking five or more items are classified as 'deprivation poor' (see, for example, EC, 2007; Guio et al., 2009).[2]

Subjective poverty. Subjective poverty is operationalised in terms of economic strain. EU-SILC respondents are asked to rate the degree of financial difficulty their household experiences in 'making ends meet', and households are identified here as subjectively poor if they report 'difficulty' or 'great difficulty' in doing so. Whilst subjective measures are sometimes used simply in order to validate objective income and deprivation measures of poverty, others have argued that subjective measures constitute a valid approach to poverty measurement in their own right (for example, Hagenaars, 1986; Hagenaars and de Vos, 1988). At the same time, it should be noted that 'felt need' (Bradshaw, 1972) does not correspond with existing normative or relative definitions since subjective perceptions of what constitutes minimally adequate living standards may vary. Moreover, the absence of felt need in this sense may not necessarily imply the absence of social and material deprivation, or that income is sufficient to meet these needs.

The analyses below begin by reporting observed frequencies for the proportion of young Europeans experiencing poverty according to low income, deprivation and subjective measures, and compare these rates with those for adults aged over 25. The EU-SILC is a sample survey and inferential statistics are therefore needed in order to make valid inferences beyond this sample to the wider population. In the analyses that follow, relative risk ratios are therefore calculated to estimate the risk of poverty as defined above for young Europeans aged 16–24 and for adults aged 25+. Statistical significance for these values (and therefore their external validity) is estimated using Pearson Chi Square with continuity correction, although it is also possible to derive 95 per cent confidence intervals for these relative risk ratios (which arguably are more informative). In Table 3.4, the social and demographic structure of poverty in Europe is examined according to income, deprivation and subjective measures. Since many of these predictors are intercorrelated (for example, age and educational attainment), a multivariate approach is necessary in order to estimate the independent effect of different respondent characteristics on the odds of poverty. This can be done using binary logistic regression resulting in odds estimates (exp(B)) which for categorical predictors describe the odds of poverty in comparison with a specified reference group, and controlling for the effects of other predictor variables included in the model.

3.5   Findings

3.5.1   Do different measures produce different estimates of youth poverty?

The percentage of young people experiencing poverty in Europe according to low income, deprivation and subjective measures is set out in Table 3.1, which also compares youth poverty rates to those for all adults aged over 25. It is clear that low income, deprivation and subjective measures result in very different estimates of the extent and geographical distribution of youth poverty. Although at the European level low income and deprivation estimates give broadly similar results (15.1 and 20.9 per cent respectively), the relationship between low income and deprivation is highly variable between countries. Amongst eastern and south-east European youth, rates of social and material deprivation are generally higher than levels of income poverty, whilst the reverse is clearly the case in much of the rest of Europe with the exceptions of Portugal and Malta. Broadly speaking, these data suggest that youth deprivation is more of a pressing

Table 3.1 Poverty amongst young Europeans aged 16–24 (% and 16–24/25+ ratios), 2009

Region	Country*	Income		Deprivation		Subjective	
		%	Risk	%	Risk	%	Risk
East	HU	17.8	1.97	41.9	1.06	63.0	1.20
	CZ	11.5	1.82	12.5	[1.11]	32.7	1.25
	SK	13.8	1.53	19.5	1.10	33.8	1.09
	PL	18.6	1.44	22.5	[0.94]	37.8	1.11
	LT	18.1	[0.99]	26.4	0.88	33.8	[0.99]
	EE	14.3	[0.98]	11.1	0.86	25.4	1.34
	LV	19.8	0.89	34.7	0.88	48.7	[1.03]
	SI	9.3	0.74	10.1	0.53	27.8	1.08
North	NO	33.5	3.34	4.0	1.73	9.2	1.50
	SE	26.4	2.03	1.9	[1.07]	9.7	1.46
	DK	32.7	2.01	4.3	1.41	14.5	1.84
	FI	25.1	1.61	3.7	[0.91]	8.8	1.39
	IS	15.2	1.39	2.0	[1.13]	16.0	[1.01]
North-west	IE	16.7	1.30	10.8	[1.15]	27.3	1.17
	UK	18.8	1.21	7.0	[0.85]	21.5	1.47
South	IT	25.2	1.39	10.4	[0.99]	44.7	1.28
	PT	18.8	1.24	24.2	[0.92]	53.6	1.21
	GR	20.6	1.23	15.5	0.87	60.1	1.06
	ES	20.0	1.21	8.3	0.83	37.5	1.25
	MT	10.6	[0.91]	13.1	0.81	54.6	1.21
	CY	9.2	0.60	7.5	0.70	50.5	1.14
South-east	RO	25.9	1.35	57.2	[1.01]	52.8	1.13
	BG	18.4	[0.96]	55.4	0.94	62.9	[1.00]
West	FR	23.0	2.10	13.6	1.17	24.5	1.46
	LU	18.6	1.95	5.2	[1.03]	7.7	[1.10]
	NL	22.5	1.85	1.4	0.35	11.9	1.23
	DE	21.2	1.33	11.1	0.80	11.6	1.19
	BE	16.4	1.17	10.4	[1.08]	24.5	1.26
	AT	11.9	1.00	5.9	0.64	15.7	[1.09]
ALL		20.9	1.40	15.1	[0.98]	29.9	1.22
Coeff. of variation (CV)		.315		.937		.557	

Notes: 'Risk' describes the relative risk of poverty for young respondents compared with older respondents (the ratio of event probabilities). Statistical significance assessed using Pearson Chi Square with continuity correction. [ ] = not significant at p <.05 level. The coefficient of variation (CV) is a measure of the overall variability of estimates, the ratio of standard deviation to the mean (CV = sd/mean).

Source: EU-SILC UDB 2009 Cross-sectional file, revised March 2012 (author's calculations).
* See Appendix Table A.2 for country labels.

problem in eastern and south-east Europe, whilst income poverty is more widespread across Europe as a whole, including in more prosperous regions such as northern and western Europe. As such, there is also less between-country variability in income poverty rates compared with rates of social and material deprivation amongst European youth.

However, both income and deprivation measures provide much lower estimates of youth poverty than subjective measures of economic strain. Across Europe as a whole, one third (33.8 per cent) of young people live in households reporting '(great) difficulty' in making ends meet. In comparison with income and deprivation measures, crossnational variations in subjective poverty are even more pronounced. Rates of subjective poverty are especially high in eastern, south-east and southern Europe and generally lower in northern, north-west and western Europe. In this respect the profile of subjective poverty correlates quite closely with deprivation, though rates of subjective poverty are somewhat higher than might be expected amongst young people in southern Europe, given levels of observed material and social deprivation amongst youth in these countries.

3.5.2 How do rates of youth poverty in Europe compare with those for older adults?

While the analyses reviewed in Section 3.2 point to higher rates of income poverty amongst young Europeans compared with older citizens, deprivation and subjective measures yield a much less consistent pattern between countries. Overall, there is less between-country variability in the relationship between relative low income and age than is the case for subjective poverty, and especially for deprivation approaches as measured by the coefficient of variation. With regard to relative low income, rates of youth poverty are considerably higher for young people than older adults in northern and western Europe, and in some parts of eastern Europe (for example, Slovakia, Hungary, the Czech Republic, Poland). However, in contrast, and with the notable exceptions of Norway, Denmark and (to a lesser extent) France and Slovakia, rates of youth deprivation are broadly comparable with those for older adults, and in many cases are actually much lower (for example, the Netherlands, Austria, Slovenia). Across Europe as a whole, young people are somewhat more likely to live in households reporting '(great) difficulty' in making ends meet than older adults, and this effect is especially marked in northern Europe, France and the UK.

3.5.3   How many young Europeans are experiencing poverty according to these measures?

As Table 3.2 shows, across Europe as a whole 11.5 million young people are income poor, 8.4 million young people experience relative deprivation and 16.5 million young people live in households reporting '(great) difficulty' in making ends meet. In terms of total numbers,

Table 3.2   Young Europeans aged 16–24 experiencing poverty: totals (in thousands) and as a percentage of total youth poverty by country and region, 2009

Region	Country*	Income		Deprivation		Subjective	
		N	%	N	%	N	%
East	PL	910	7.9	1,102	13.2	1,853	11.3
	HU	217	1.9	509	6.1	765	4.6
	CZ	138	1.2	155	1.9	395	2.4
	SK	112	1.0	158	1.9	275	1.7
	LT	85	0.7	124	1.5	159	1.0
	LV	61	0.5	107	1.3	151	0.9
	EE	26	0.2	20	0.2	46	0.3
	SI	22	0.2	13	0.2	66	0.4
North	SE	283	2.5	20	0.2	99	0.6
	DK	186	1.6	24	0.3	82	0.5
	NO	181	1.6	21	0.3	49	0.3
	FI	143	1.2	21	0.2	50	0.3
	IS	6	0.1	1	0.0	6	< 0.1
North-west	UK	1,380	12.0	514	6.1	1,570	9.5
	IE	109	0.9	70	0.8	177	1.1
South	IT	1,378	12.0	567	6.8	2,446	14.9
	ES	895	7.8	372	4.5	1,679	10.2
	GR	216	1.9	162	1.9	631	3.8
	PT	203	1.8	262	3.1	579	3.5
	CY	10	0.1	8	0.1	55	0.3
	MT	6	< 0.1	7	0.1	29	0.2
South-west	RO	705	6.1	1,564	18.7	1,441	8.8
	BG	160	1.4	486	5.8	552	3.4
West	DE	1,798	15.6	939	11.2	982	6.0
	FR	1,552	13.5	916	11.0	1,659	10.1
	NL	399	3.5	24	0.3	209	1.3
	BE	197	1.7	124	1.5	293	1.8
	AT	123	1.1	60	0.7	161	1.0
	LU	9	0.1	2	0.0	4	< 0.1
ALL		11,508	100	8,354	100	16,464	100

Source: EU-SILC UDB 2009 Cross-sectional file, revised March 2012 (author's calculations).
* See Appendix Table A.2 for country labels.

approximately half of all 'poor' young Europeans live in just three or four countries, though these countries differ for income poverty (France, the UK, Italy, Germany), deprivation (Romania, Poland, France) and subjective poverty (Italy, Poland, Spain, France).

3.5.4 What is the multidimensional profile of youth disadvantage amongst young Europeans?

Table 3.3 shows the frequency of different combinations of disadvantage for young people aged 16–24, and for older adults. Across Europe as a whole, a smaller proportion of young people (55.3 per cent) experience no disadvantage according to these measures than is the case for older adults (62.5 per cent). Similarly, greater proportions of young people experience a singular instance of disadvantage (25.9 per cent) and combinations of two indicators (13.2 per cent) than is the case for older adults (21.0 and 11.9 per cent respectively). Young people are also more likely to experience multidimensional disadvantage across all three measures than is the case for older adults, with 5.6 per cent of young Europeans (or more than 2.5 million people) reporting low income, relative deprivation and subjective poverty compared with 4.6 per cent of older adults. Unfortunately, even with the very large samples available in the EU-SILC it is not possible to reliably estimate the distribution of

Table 3.3 Poverty amongst young Europeans aged 16–24: multidimensional classification by region (column %), 2009

| | Aged 16–24 by region | | | | | | All aged 16–24 | All aged 25+ |
	North	North-west	West	South	East	South-east		
Not poor	67	65	69	46	51	29	55.3	62.5
Deprivation only	<1	1	1	1	3	9	2.1	2.9
Income only	21	8	12	6	5	2	8.7	5.9
Subjective only	5	14	7	28	16	11	15.1	12.2
Income & deprivation	1	2	2	<1	1	3	1.1	1.0
Income & subjective	4	5	3	8	3	1	4.5	2.8
Deprivation & subjective	1	3	2	5	13	28	7.6	8.1
Income, deprivation & subjective	1	3	3	5	7	17	5.6	4.6
N	8,976	4,164	12,838	13,956	18,889	4,122	62,945	391,396

Source: EU-SILC UDB 2009 Cross-sectional file, rev. March 2012 (author's calculations).

different combinations of youth poverty between European countries, though it is possible to do so at a regional level. As Table 3.3 shows, in most regions of Europe, combinations of disadvantage are relatively uncommon amongst young people. Nevertheless, approximately one in eight (13 per cent) young people in eastern and over one quarter (28 per cent) of young people in south-east Europe live in households reporting both social and material deprivation and difficulty in making ends meet. Whilst multidimensional poverty is generally not widespread amongst European youth, nearly one in twelve (7 per cent) young people in eastern Europe, and one in six (17 per cent) young people in south-east Europe are classified as experiencing poverty according to all three measures.

How, then, does the social profile of vulnerability to poverty vary based upon different measures across Europe? Table 3.4 shows the multivariate odds of experiencing low income, deprivation and subjective poverty for selected respondent characteristics based upon binary logistic regression. Overall, sex, age group, household type and nationality explain approximately half of the variability in objective measures of poverty (such as low income, deprivation), but results in a rather less well-fitting model with regard to subjective poverty. In other words, subjective poverty appears to be more weakly associated with socioeconomic and demographic differences than is the case for low income and deprivation. Controlling for variations in sex, household type and nationality, young people are more likely to experience income poverty and less likely to experience deprivation in comparison with older adults. Thus, young people aged 16–19 are 12 per cent more likely (1:1.12), and those aged 20–24 are 71 per cent more likely (1:1.71) to experience relative low income in comparison with older respondents. In contrast, older adults aged 35+ are about 45 per cent (1:1/.69) more likely to experience deprivation than 16–19-year-olds, and about 22 per cent (1/.82) more likely to experience deprivation than 20–24-year-olds.

3.6   Discussion

How, then, should we interpret these findings, and what are their implications for research practice and policy in this area? First, these data should be interpreted in the light of theoretical models of youth transition 'regimes' and how these vary between and within countries. It is clear that youth-specific processes of impoverishment at least partly explain between-country variability in levels of youth poverty. In particular, variations in the timing and quality of youth transitions associated

Table 3.4 Low income, deprivation and subjective poverty in Europe by selected respondent characteristics: frequencies and multivariate odds ratios, 2009

	Deprivation			Income			Subjective		
	%	exp(B)	se	%	exp(B)	se	%	exp(B)	se
Sex									
Male	12.9	ref		15.4	ref		25.0	ref	
Female	15.3	.48	.01	17.1	.51	.01	26.5	.53	.00
Age group									
16–19	15.2	.69	.02	21.7	1.12	.02	31.3	.81	.02
20–24	15.1	.82	.02	20.2	1.71	.02	28.7	1.04	.01
25–29	14.2	.82	.02	15.1	1.14	.02	26.4	1.06	.01
35+	15.5	ref	14.8	24.3	ref			ref	
Household type									
Single	19.7	ref	26.0	24.9	ref			ref	
Couple, no children	11.4	.26	.01	11.9	.23	.01	17.4	.33	.01
Couple with children	10.2	.34	.01	15.6	.30	.01	24.8	.57	.01
Single parent	23.6	1.25	.02	34.7	[.97]	.02	40.9	1.34	.02
Other	18.3	.48	.01	12.9	.20	.01	33.6	.76	.01
Educ. attainment									
Lower secondary or less	22.2	1.96	.01	23.2	2.24	.01	35.3	2.35	.01
Upper secondary	16.0	1.28	.01	13.8	1.08	.01	24.2	1.28	.01
Post-secondary	6.3	ref	7.8	12.3	ref			ref	
Nationality									
Other EU state	13.5	.79	.04	18.7	1.21	.03	28.0	1.17	.03
Country of residence	15.3	ref	15.1	24.5	ref			ref	
Any other country	27.9	2.06	.02	31.6	2.49	.02	42.8	2.08	.02
Nagelkerke R sq.		.55			.58			.34	
N		431,046			430,943			430,167	

Source: EU-SILC UDB 2009 Cross-sectional file, rev. March 2012 (author's calculations). Binary logistic regression models (method = enter). Values greater than 1 indicate increased odds of poverty in comparison with the specified reference group. [ ] = Not significant at .05 level.

with leaving the parental home, setting up home with a partner, finishing education and finding work, and starting a family can have a decisive impact upon poverty vulnerability amongst young people (for example, Iacovou and Aassve, 2007; Vogel, 2002). These are interrelated processes, and variations in the 'transition mix' will often therefore be critical. These processes are subject to substantial regional differences associated with specific transition regimes that reflect the wider context of the governance and delivery of social policy for youth, for example in relation to education, activation, housing and social support policies in European countries (for example, Helve and Evans, 2013; Walther, 2006; Walther and Pole, 2005).

Second, it is evident that the extent and geography of youth poverty is highly sensitive to the measure used, and these findings therefore should be interpreted in light of a clear conceptualisation of poverty itself. Given the evidence reviewed above, it has with some justification been argued that income-based measures alone provide an unreliable basis for inference regarding material hardship during youth (for example, Hallerod and Westberg, 2006) and especially for between-country comparisons concerning youth disadvantage. In particular, whilst incomes are measured at the household level (and assume pooling of resources within households), we are often dealing with quite different household units depending on the timing of housing transitions, since the age at which young people leave the parental home varies widely across European countries (for example, Iacovou and Berthoud, 2001; Vogel, 2002). However, whilst leaving home often has a decisive impact on total household income for young people, its effects on social and material deprivation amongst young people is not currently well understood. It is largely for this reason that the 2012 EU youth report argues that it is 'difficult' to make meaningful cross-national comparisons in rates of youth income poverty (2012a, p. 50). The relationship of youth income poverty to other dimensions of youth disadvantage in Europe is therefore especially worthy of note here.

High levels of youth income poverty in northern European countries appear to run counter to expectations, with social democratic welfare regimes generally being characterised by relatively low levels of income inequality (for example, Lelkes and Gasior, 2012). To a large extent these findings reflect between-country variations in the timing of domestic transitions, with young people typically living independently at a much younger age in northern Europe than elsewhere. Nevertheless, these data do not identify similarly high levels of social and material deprivation amongst northern European youth, nor do they point to widespread perceptions of economic hardship. A broadly similar pattern is evident elsewhere in north-west Europe and western Europe.

How, then, should we explain this apparent contradiction? First, evidence of high levels of income poverty amongst northern and western European youth partly reflects existing practice in the measurement of income poverty within the EU. The EU's official measure of low income is a measure of the relative distribution of incomes *within* European countries not *between* them. Thus, whilst young people in northern Europe are income poor relative to the situation in northern European states (mostly as a result of leaving the parental home), they are not income poor relative to the distribution of incomes across Europe as a whole. Were we to adopt a relative income standard based upon the distribution of incomes across Europe as a whole a very different picture emerges, with income poverty overwhelmingly concentrated in eastern and south-east Europe (and to a lesser extent southern Europe) (see Appendix Table A.2).

More importantly, the apparent mismatch between income and deprivation measures in many northern, north-west and western European countries reflects the dynamics of poverty over time. Whilst poverty is often measured on a cross-sectional basis, the relationship between incomes and living standards is dynamic: as Townsend (1979) argues, social and material deprivation arises as a result of insufficient command of resources (principally income) *over time*. Thus when a household's income falls people generally seek to mitigate the effects of declining incomes on living standards at least in the short term, resulting in a (temporary) mismatch between income and deprivation. Cross-sectional data can shed only limited light on this relationship not least as a result of the limitations of the EU-SILC survey design in researching young adults' circumstances (see e.g. Iacovou et al., 2012). However, further panel analysis of the EU-SILC data is clearly needed to further explore the issue. However, on the basis of this theory of poverty dynamics, and in light of recent evidence on this question in Sweden (Hallerod and Westberg, 2006), youth income poverty in northern Europe appears to be mostly transitory.

Whilst vulnerability to poverty is quite widespread amongst northern European youth (that is, they have low incomes), it is not matched by high levels of deprivation, and for older cohorts household incomes are generally sufficient to avoid income poverty. In other words, after the initial income 'shock' associated with leaving the parental home, young people's incomes appear to recover over time with no observable effects in terms of increased vulnerability to social and material deprivation. Indeed, the relative transience of low income amongst northern European youth might be attributable to the *effectiveness* of northern European welfare systems in mitigating the effects of early domestic transitions on living standards. Certainly, there is compelling international comparative evidence of the positive role of welfare generosity (and especially social transfers) in reducing overall poverty rates, and the 'Nordic model' has generally been held to be highly effective in poverty reduction (for example, Brady, 2005; Kenworthy, 1999; Scruggs and Allen, 2006; Smeeding, 2006). Nevertheless, the relatively short-lived nature of low income amongst northern European youth is not a rationale for inaction, not least since we lack reliable evidence on the long-term effects of low income during youth for the quality of youth transitions and subsequent outcomes (though see Bell and Blanchflower, 2011; Burgess et al., 2003; Gregg and Tominey, 2004, for a discussion of the effects of youth unemployment).

However, a very different picture emerges when we consider the situation of youth in eastern, south-east and southern Europe. Here, social and material deprivation and subjective poverty are much more widespread both amongst young people and amongst older adults, results which consistently point to the endemic nature of deprivation amongst youth and its persistence across the life-course. These findings might also suggest that the delivery of social welfare in 'post-Communist' and 'Mediterranean' policy regimes may be less effective in mitigating the risk of social and material deprivation both amongst young people and for older adults. As a result, the current context of economic crisis and social welfare retrenchment may further diminish young people's resilience to periods of unemployment and labour market precariousness in southern, eastern and south-east Europe, with long-term consequences for their capacity to achieve minimally adequate living standards and levels of well-being and societal participation.

Finally, the profile of subjective poverty amongst youth is quite similar to that of social and material deprivation in European countries, suggesting that respondents' subjective evaluations are broadly consistent with objective measures of deprivation. Nevertheless, in nearly every country included in this analysis, rates of subjective youth poverty are higher than those pertaining to older adults, despite substantial variability in the relationship between age and objective measures of deprivation. This may simply reflect age-related differences in respondents' subjective responses to their circumstances (that is, that young people are perhaps less accepting of inadequate income). However, it is also possible that existing deprivation measures do not adequately reflect the experience of deprivation during youth. Whilst the EU-SILC deprivation indicators are certainly valid measures of deprivation across European populations as a whole, their adequacy across the life-course is currently not well understood and they are not designed with the specific intention of understanding deprivation during the youth phase, where different indicators may be needed to reflect differences in lifestyles and consumption patterns across the life-course.

At a theoretical level, this also raises some difficult questions about the identification of relevant comparator groups and, in particular, whether these should describe contemporary living standards within nation states or at a European level. If, following Townsend (1979), we are to understand poverty as relative to prevailing norms, patterns of consumption and lifestyles, then from a cross-national perspective the question of relevant comparator groups is crucial. As discussed above, the EU's preferred measure of income poverty is relative *within* countries not *between* them, whereas the opposite is the case in the measurement of relative deprivation since the same indicators are adopted across European countries. The consequence is quite a different pattern of results at the cross-national level. Since the proposed deprivation indicators included in these analyses are widely viewed as 'necessities of life' in European countries, there is certainly a case for a common approach to the measurement of deprivation across Europe. However, it is much less clear that adopting a similar approach is warranted in the measurement of low income within Europe (for a discussion see Fahey, 2007). Nevertheless, this makes meaningful cross-national comparisons in the extent of income poverty and material and social deprivation much more challenging.

3.7 Conclusion

What, then, is the 'best' way to measure youth poverty and what are the implications for policy? This chapter finds relatively little overlap between income, deprivation and subjective measures of poverty amongst European youth. The three measures identify quite different groups of young people as living in poverty. Since this leads to very different national estimates of youth poverty rates and vulnerability, it has potentially serious implications for policies to tackle youth poverty. The lack of overlap between measures is partly explicable in terms of definitional differences in the specification of comparator groups where relative income measures are estimated at the country level and deprivation-based measures seek to establish a Europe-wide standard. The lack of overlap also reflects the limitations of cross-sectional data in representing poverty dynamics, and concerns over the validity of existing measures. A youth-specific deprivation index is likely to provide for more sensitive measurement of social variations in vulnerability to poverty amongst young people, though with obvious limitations in terms of the comparability of poverty estimates across the life-course. However, in the absence of a consistent and reliable measurement framework for understanding the relationship between income and deprivation across European youth, it may be safest to conclude with Bradshaw and Finch (2003) that we should consider a range of different measures of poverty in order to effectively triangulate results based upon different methods.

When we consider youth poverty using a range of different objective and subjective measures the following pattern emerges. In terms of the overall extent of youth poverty, rates of youth poverty appear to be consistently high across income, deprivation and subjective measures in Poland, Latvia, Romania, Bulgaria and Portugal. In general terms poverty rates appear to be higher in 'post-communist' and 'Mediterranean' welfare systems, though relative low income is endemic amongst youth across much of Europe. To a large extent this general finding corroborates existing evidence on the spatial distribution of poverty in Europe (for example, Atkinson and Marlier, 2010; Lelkes and Gaisor, 2012). However, when we compare national rates of youth poverty across all measures with that experienced by older adults in European countries, it is clear that there is a specific problem of youth poverty in some European countries, but this does not appear to map closely onto any existing welfare regime typology. In Norway, Denmark, Ireland and France rates of youth poverty are consistently higher than those for older adults according to income-based, deprivation and subjective measures. This highlights the limitations of general typologies of welfare regime in informing our understanding of the nature and dynamics of youth welfare in Europe, and therefore also of the general drivers and specific trigger events associated with youth poverty vulnerability (see, for example, Mendola et al., 2008; Vogel, 2002). A more specific focus on understanding regimes of youth transition and welfare is needed if we are to better identify effective policies in very different national contexts for supporting young people's transitions and insulating them from the risk of poverty and social exclusion in these difficult times.

Appendices

Table A.1 Sample sizes: persons in households (unweighted)

Code	Country	ALL	16–24
AT	Austria	13,610	1,452
BE	Belgium	14,721	1,643
BG	Bulgaria	15,047	1,673
CY	Cyprus	9,283	1,357
CZ	Czech Republic	23,302	2,549
DK	Denmark	15,025	1,757
EE	Estonia	13,542	2,394
FI	Finland	25,157	3,161
FR	France	25,611	2,977
DE	Germany	28,368	2,507
GR	Greece	18,035	1,710
HU	Hungary	25,053	3,085
IS	Iceland	8,545	1,335
IE	Ireland	12,641	1,280
IT	Italy	51,196	4,735
LV	Latvia	14,403	1,828
LT	Lithuania	12,852	1,636
LU	Luxembourg	11,406	1,090
MT	Malta	10,213	1,294
NL	Netherlands	23,687	2,149
NO	Norway	13,855	1,772
PL	Poland	38,541	5,161
PT	Portugal	13,013	1,371
RO	Romania	18,703	1,975
SK	Slovakia	16,137	2,790
SI	Slovenia	29,576	4,350
ES	Spain	36,865	3,850
SE	Sweden	18,441	2,654
UK	United Kingdom	19,380	1,824
ALL		576,208	67,359

Source: EU-SILC UDB 2009 Cross-sectional file, rev. March 2012.

Table A.2 Youth income poverty based on 60 per cent national median threshold and 60 per cent Europe-wide median threshold, 2009 (percentage poor)

Region	Code		EU median	Country
East	HU	Hungary	95.7	11.8
	LT	Lithuania	89.7	18.7
	PL	Poland	89.7	14.7
	SK	Slovakia	88.1	10.8
	LV	Latvia	81.0	21.7
	EE	Estonia	75.5	14.7
	CZ	Czech Republic	71.4	7.7
	SI	Slovenia	19.2	12.1

Table A.2   (Continued)

Region	Code		EU median	Country
North	SE	Sweden	13.2	14.8
	FI	Finland	9.1	16.3
	DK	Denmark	8.2	17.5
	NO	Norway	7.8	13.3
	IS	Iceland	4.4	11.9
North-west	UK	United Kingdom	15.2	16.8
	IE	Ireland	3.0	14.4
South	PT	Portugal	62.4	16.3
	GR	Greece	36.8	17.8
	MT	Malta	30.0	12.4
	ES	Spain	26.5	17.6
	IT	Italy	20.9	19.9
	CY	Cyprus	6.4	13.3
South-west	RO	Romania	99.5	22.2
	BG	Bulgaria	98.3	19.4
West	DE	Germany	11.2	16.5
	FR	France	10.4	13.4
	NL	Nederland	9.2	14.8
	BE	Belgium	8.7	14.8
	AU	Austria	5.0	12.2
	LU	Luxembourg	2.1	11.8
ALL			40.7	15.5

Notes

1. The analyses reported here were conducted as part of the Second Network for the analysis of EU-SILC ('Net-SILC2') project on income and living conditions in Europe led by Ann-Catherine Guio, Dave Gordon and Eric Marlier (Grant 10602.2010.004-2011.146). I am grateful to Eurostat for access to the data for these purposes. The work upon which this chapter draws was first presented at European Social Policy Analysis Network Annual Conference, Edinburgh, 6–8 September 2012, and I am grateful for the many helpful contributions and suggestions of participants.
2. The items comprising the deprivation index describe individual respondents lacking the following items: some new clothes*; two pairs of shoes*; some money for oneself*; leisure activities*; drink/meal monthly*; replace worn-out furniture*; meat, chicken, fish or equiv.; unexpected expenses; holiday; arrears; computer and Internet*; home adequately warm. Asterisk indicates 'enforced lack' (where respondents are asked and subsequently respond that they lack these items because they cannot afford them). See Guio et al. (2012) for further details.

References

Aassve, A., Iacovou, M. and Mencarini, L. (2006). 'Youth Poverty and Transition to Adulthood in Europe'. *Demographic Research* 15, 21–50.

Atkinson, A. and Marlier, E. (eds.) (2010). *Income and Living Conditions in Europe* (Brussels: Eurostat).

Bell, D. and Blanchflower, D. (2011). 'Young People and the Great Recession'. *IZA Discussion Paper 5674* (Bonn: Institute for the Study of Labour).

Bradshaw, J. (1972). 'The Taxonomy of Social Need', in McLachlan, G. (ed.) *Problems and Progress in Medical Care* (Oxford: Oxford University Press).

Bradshaw, J. and Finch, N. (2003). 'Overlaps in Dimensions of Poverty'. *Journal of Social Policy* 32 (4), 513–25.

Brady, D. (2005). 'The Welfare State and Relative Poverty in Rich Western Democracies, 1967–1997'. *Social Forces* 83 (4), 1329–64.

Buchholz, S., Hofäcker, D., Mills, M., Blossfeld, H-P., Kurz, K. and Hofmeister, H. (2009). 'Life Courses in the Globalization Process: The Development of Social Inequalities in Modern Societies'. *European Sociological Review* 25 (1), 53–71.

Buchmann, M. and Kriesi, I. (2011). 'Transition to Adulthood in Europe'. *Annual Review of Sociology* 37, 481–503.

Burgess, S., Propper, C., Rees, H. and Shearer, A. (2003). 'The Class of '81: The Effects of Early-Career Unemployment on Subsequent Unemployment Experiences'. *Labour Economics* 10 (3), 291–311.

Catan, L. (2004). *Becoming Adult: Changing Youth Transitions in the 21st Century* (Brighton: Trust for the Study of Adolescence).

EC (European Commission) (2007). *Poverty and Social Exclusion.* Special Eurobarometer 279.

EC (European Commission) (2010). *Europe 2020: A Strategy for Smart, Sustainable and Inclusive Growth.* COM(2010) 2020 final. EC: Brussels.

EC (European Commission) (2012a). *EU Youth Report: Status of the Situation of Young People in the European Union.* SWD(2012)257 final. EC: Brussels.

EC (European Commission) (2012b). *EU Youth Strategy, 2010–1: Implementation of the Renewed Framework for European Cooperation in the Youth Field.* COM(2012) 49 final. EC: Brussels.

EC (European Commission) (2013). *Working Together for Europe's Young People: A Call to Action on Youth Unemployment.* COM(2013) 447 final. EC: Brussels.

Edward, R. and Weller, S. (2010). 'Trajectories from Youth to Adulthood: Choice and Structure for Young People before and during Recession'. *Twenty-First Century Society* 5 (2), 125–36.

Esping-Andersen, G. (1990). *The Three Worlds of Welfare Capitalism* (Cambridge: Polity Press).

Fahey, T. (2007). 'The Case for an EU-wide Measure of Poverty'. *European Sociological Review* 23 (1), 35–47.

Fahmy, E. (2007). 'Poverty and Youth Transitions in Europe', in Colley, H., Hoskins, B., Parveva, T. and Boetzelen, P. (eds.) *Social Inclusion for Young People: Breaking Down the Barriers* (Strasbourg: Council of Europe).

Ferrera, M. and Rhodes, M. (2000). *Recasting European Welfare States* (Ilford: Cass).

Gallie, D. and Paugam, S. (eds.) (2000). *Welfare Regimes and the Experience of Unemployment in Europe* (Oxford: Oxford University Press).

Gregg, P. and Tominey, E. (2004). 'The Wage Scar from Youth Unemployment'. *Centre for Market and Public Organisation Working Paper 04/097* (CMPO: University of Bristol).

Guio, A.-C., Fusco, A. and Marlier, E. (2009). 'A European Union Approach to Material Deprivation Using EU-SILC and Eurobarometer Data'. *IRISS Working Paper 2009–19* (Luxembourg: CEPS/INSTEAD).

Guio, A.-C., Gordon, D. and Marlier, E. (2012). *Measuring Material Deprivation in the EU: Indicators for the Whole Population and Child Specific Measures* (Brussels: Eurostat).

Gush, K. and Taylor, M. (2012). 'Employment Transitions and the Recession', in McFall, S. (ed.) *Understanding Society: Findings, 2012* (Colchester: ISER).

Hagenaars, A. (1986). *The Perception of Poverty* (Amsterdam: North Holland).

Hagenaars, A. and de Vos, K. (1988). 'The Definition and Measurement of Poverty'. *Journal of Human Resources* 23 (2), 211–21.

Halleröd, B. and Westberg, A. (2006). 'Youth Problem: What's the problem? A Longitudinal Study of Incomes and Economic Hardship among Swedish Youth'. *Acta Sociologica* 49 (1), 83–102.

Helve, H. and Evans, K. (2013). *Youth and Work Transitions in Changing Social Landscapes* (London: Tufnell Press).

Iacovou, M. (2002). 'Regional Differences in the Transition to Adulthood'. *Annals of the American Academy*, 40, 580.

Iacovou, M. and Aassve, A. (2007). *Youth Poverty in Europe* (York: JRF).

Iacovou, M. and Berthoud, R. (2001). *Young People's Lives: A Map of Europe* (Colchester: ISER, University of Essex).

Iacovou, M., Kaminska, O. and Levy, H. (2012). 'Using EU-SILC Data for Cross-Sectional Analysis: Strengths, Problems and Recommendations'. *ISER Working Paper2012–03* (ISER: University of Essex).

ILO (International Labour Organisation) (2010). *Global Employment Trends for Youth* (Geneva: ILO).

Julkunen, I. (2002). 'Social and Material Deprivation among Unemployed Youth in Northern Europe'. *Social Policy and Administration* 36 (3), 235–53.

Kangas, O. and Palme, J. (2000). 'Does Social Policy Matter? Poverty Cycles in the OECD Countries'. *International Journal of Health Services* 30, 335–52.

Kenworthy, L. (1999). 'Do Social-Welfare Policies Reduce Poverty? A Cross-National Assessment'. *Social Forces* 77 (3), 1119–39.

Lelkes, O. and Gaisor, K. (2012). *Income Poverty and Social Exclusion in the EU.* Policy Brief January 2012 (Vienna: European Centre for Social Welfare Policy and Research).

Levitas, R. (1996). 'The Concept of Social Exclusion and the New "Durkheimian" Hegemony'. *Critical Social Policy* 46, 5–20.

Levitas, R. (1998). *The Inclusive Society? New Labour and Social Exclusion* (London: Macmillan).

Mendola, D., Busetta, A. and Aassve, A. (2008). 'Poverty Permanence among European Youth'. *ISER Working Paper 2008–04* (Colchester: ISER).

OECD (Organization for Economic Cooperation and Development) (2013). *Crisis Squeezes Income and puts Pressure on Inequality and Poverty.* OECD.

Özdemir, E., Sanoussi, F. and Ward, T. (2010). *The Potential Effects of the Recession on the Risk of Poverty.* Social Europe Research Note 6/2010. European Commission.

Schizzerotto, A. and Lucchini, M. (2002). 'Transitions to Adulthood during the Twentieth Century. A Comparison of Great Britain, Italy and Sweden'. *EPAG Working Paper* 2002–36 (Colchester: University of Essex).

Scruggs, L. and Allen, J. (2006). 'The Material Consequences of Welfare States: Benefit Generosity and Absolute Poverty in 16 OECD Countries'. *Comparative Political Studies* 39 (7), 880–904.

Smeeding, T. (2006). 'Poor People in Rich Nations: The United States in Comparative Perspective'. *Journal of Economic Perspectives* 20 (1), 69–90.

Smith, D. (2009). 'Changes in Transitions: The Role of Mobility, Class and Gender'. *Journal of Education and Work* 22 (5), 369–90.

Titmuss, R. (1974). *Social Policy* (London: Allen & Unwin).

Townsend, P. (1979). *Poverty in the UK: A Survey of Household Resources and Standards of Living* (London: Harmondsworth).

Townsend, P. (1987). 'Deprivation'. *Journal of Social Policy* 16 (2), 125–46.

Vogel, J. (2002). 'European Welfare Regimes and the Transition to Adulthood: A Comparative and Longitudinal Perspective'. *Social Indicators Research* 59 (3), 275–99.

Walther, A. (2006). 'Regimes of Youth Transitions: Choice, Flexibility and Security in Young People's Experiences across Different European Contexts'. *Young* 14 (2), 119–39.

Walther, A. and Pohl, A. (2005). *Thematic Study on Policy Measures Concerning Disadvantaged Youth*. Final Report to European Commission DG Employment and Social Affairs.

Whelan, C., Layte, R., Maître, B. and Nolan, B. (2001). 'Income, Deprivation and Economic Strain: An Analysis of the European Community Household Panel'. *European Sociological Review* 17 (4), 357–72.

4
At Risk of Deskilling and Trapped by Passion: A Picture of Precarious Highly Educated Young Workers in Italy, Spain and the United Kingdom

Annalisa Murgia and Barbara Poggio[1]

4.1 Introduction

Recent decades have seen growing academic debate on the relationship between tertiary education and secure career pathways. In Europe in the 1990s, globalisation, the tertiarisation of the economy, the deregulation of labour markets, the onset of structural unemployment and the 'democratisation' of university (Blasutig, 2011) broke down the existing relationship between higher education and secure career pathways. The assumption that expanding higher education will automatically increase economic growth and reduce social inequalities has been challenged (Ballarino, 2007; Schomburg and Teichler, 2006), forcing researchers to revise their theoretical tools and interpretative models.

In addition to changes in the relationship between higher education and work, research suggests that in many European countries there is a widening gap between full-time ongoing contracts providing job security and social protection on the one hand, and short-term contracts which provide only limited access to the welfare system on the other (Bentolila et al., 2008; Boeri, 2010; Boeri and Garibaldi, 2007; Dolado et al., 2002). While these changes concern the whole labour market, specific and alarming effects are felt by highly educated young workers.

The 'endemic and persisting' mismatch between the demand for and supply of qualified labour (Schomburg and Teichler, 2006) has meant that, increasingly, young people entering the labour market are unable to capitalise on their educational investment (Wolbers, 2003). Whilst high educational levels have traditionally played an important role in protecting individuals against unemployment and underemployment, the recent data show that the protection effect of higher education has been eroded by the economic crisis. Samek Lodovici and Semenza sum it up in a passage worth quoting at length:

> Possibly for the first time, during the current economic recession we are witnessing a waste of young highly-educated human resources in most European countries. Although inactivity and unemployment are more widespread among young people with low educational attainment, a growing share of young graduates are also ending up there, while those having jobs are increasingly employed in temporary and low-qualified positions.
>
> (Samek Lodovici and Semenza, 2012, p. 8)

In this complex context, this chapter builds on the debate by exploring the relationship between tertiary-educated young people and the spread of temporary work in Europe. It sets out the risks faced by young graduates – especially since the onset of the economic crisis – such as work and income discontinuity and access to social protection, and the implications of insecure and short-term work for their career prospects and private and family lives.

The chapter is based on the findings of the project 'Trapped or Flexible? Risk Transitions and Missing Policies for Young Highly Skilled Workers in Europe', financed by the European Commission and conducted during 2011.[2] The project was a comparative study which combined quantitative analysis of the employment patterns of highly educated young people in the 27 member countries of the European Union with three qualitative case studies conducted in Italy, Spain and the United Kingdom. This chapter is based on the qualitative component of the project, interviews with young highly qualified young people aged 25–34 years who had been in work for five years (or slightly more). All participants were at the time of the interview either working in jobs that matched their skill sets but were only temporary, or in jobs that were significantly below their skill levels.

The chapter will first provide a general overview of the European labour market and policy context, and then set out the results from interviews conducted with highly qualified young people in Italy, Spain and the United Kingdom. Finally, the results of focus groups with key informants concerned with labour market policies in the three case study countries will be presented. Drawing on these results, the concluding section will set out proposals for action to support highly qualified young workers.

4.2   Theoretical framework

The changing nature of work has for some time prompted those working in the field to redefine the traditional interpretative categories constructed around work, such as the secure, on-going job (Sennett, 1998; Standing, 2011). In increasingly globalised and interconnected contemporary societies, the nature of both work and wider social relationships is increasingly heterogeneous and fluid (Bauman, 2005; Beck and Beck-Gernsheim, 2002). In this context, the images and meanings attributed to work are redefined as people move more frequently between jobs, between employment and unemployment, and between training and work, thus giving rise to new professional pathways and, in general, to new life-stories (Gherardi and Murgia, 2012).

In the highly tertiarised countries of Europe, the traditional categories of typical/atypical, paid/unpaid, regulated by a contract/irregular, work therefore lose their heuristic capacity (Brophy and de Peuter, 2007; Glucksmann, 2005; Strangleman, 2007); and so does the dualism which classifies working activities as skilled or unskilled (Brine, 2006). The work of Pierre Bourdieu has been pioneering in this regard. For Bourdieu, the problems of the new economy are not concentrated in specific sectors of the labour market, for instance illegal, temporary or low-skilled work. Rather, he describes an entire '*génération précaire*' (Bourdieu, 1998), which he defines as a new era marked by the 'institution of insecurity and domination through precariousness' (Bourdieu, 2003, p. 29). Highly educated young people, who were once protected by their educational qualifications, are today emblematic of the above-mentioned social phenomena that are changing people into entrepreneurs of their own 'human capital' (Armano and Murgia, 2014; Chicchi and Leonardi, 2011; Neilson and Rossiter, 2008; Ross, 2009). They are a particularly interesting group of subjects because they are the protagonists of the 'new spirit of capitalism' (Sennett, 2006). Their endeavour to free themselves from the oppressive uniformity of mass society and to express their creativity and individual autonomy through work has in fact been incorporated by the contemporary capitalist model itself (Boltanski and Chiapello, 1999).

This chapter will explore the narratives of highly qualified young people as they navigate these changes. These narratives concern both work and other areas of life (housing independence, starting a family, free time and access to social protection). In so doing, it will explore: how the biographies of those who aspire to become so-called 'knowledge workers' are articulated; what kinds of professional trajectories they are able to construct when employment takes the form of fixed-term contracts; and how highly qualified young people have been affected by the current financial crisis.

4.3   Overview of the quantitative data on highly qualified workers in Europe

A brief outline of European labour market trends reveals that the current economic crisis has generated further insecurity for this particular category of highly educated and skilled workers, especially the youngest ones (Bradley and Devadason, 2008; Samek Lodovici and Semenza, 2012). According to a recent report of the International Labour Organisation (2012), temporary work has grown significantly over the last few decades for both adults and young people. However, the increase among young people has been much greater: in advanced economies more than one young person in every three is unable to obtain a permanent job, and this figure has increased since the onset of the economic crisis (from 36.3 per cent in 2008 to 37.1 per cent in 2010). In the EU27 in 2010, more than 50 per cent of young people aged between 15 and 24 were working on fixed-term contracts (see Figure 4.1). In many countries, temporary work was also widespread among workers in the 25–39 age group (Eurostat, 2011).

If one specifically considers the frequency of temporary employment among *qualified* workers, very different patterns emerge among member countries. While in the majority of member states (11 out of 19), workers with a primary education level are less likely to transit rapidly to permanent work, the relation between transition rates and education level is not linear. Figure 4.2 shows that, in the majority of member states, workers with a secondary education are *more* likely to transition to permanent contracts than new graduates. This means that in the majority of cases temporary workers with high education levels are not more likely than their counterparts with lower education levels to obtain permanent jobs (Torchio, 2012).

In Portugal, Finland, Italy, Cyprus and the Czech Republic, among graduates aged 15–24, the incidence of temporary work is on average six percentage points higher than that observed for all the other levels of education. For the highest-educated workers aged 25–39, the incidence

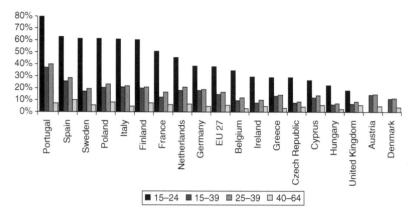

Figure 4.1   Incidence of temporary work in Europe on total dependent employment by age in 2010
Source: Samek Lodovici and Semenza (2012), p. 32.

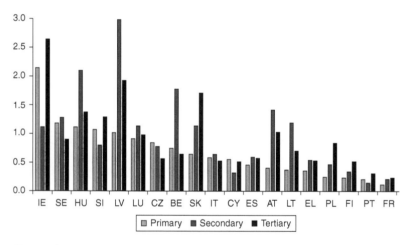

Figure 4.2   Transition rates from temporary to permanent contracts, by education level (2005–07)
Source: European Commission (2010a), p. 142.

of temporary work is on average seven percentage points higher in Austria and Italy (European Commission, 2010a). These countries are characterised by segmented labour markets and have undertaken 'two-tier reforms' – alternatively called 'reforms at the margin' (Bentolila et al., 2008; Boeri, 2010) – by substantially deregulating the use of temporary contracts while maintaining stringent redundancy rules on permanent contracts (Samek Lodovici and Semenza, 2012). In many European countries, therefore, a university education does not offer a guarantee of stable employment.

Secondary analysis of the Eurostat (2011) data in the three case study countries reveals that young highly educated workers experience labour market insecurity differently in the three countries. In the case of young graduates in Italy, working on a fixed-term contract often does not represent a stepping stone towards a more stable job, particularly among women. While training contracts (apprenticeships and traineeships) can provide a stepping stone, freelance contracts – particularly common among the highly qualified – do not. In addition, the wage penalty for temporary workers is relatively high and growing (Samek Lodovici and Semenza, 2012). In Italy, family background also plays a central role in the construction of work trajectories congruent with one's training and experience (Murgia et al., 2012).

In Spain, the situation is more concerning than in Italy because the incidence and persistence of precarious work is even higher and characterised by 'random transitions', or trajectories that seem to lead 'anywhere', since employment experiences do not necessarily help to build a coherent profile (Samek Lodovici and Semenza, 2012). Low wages are also becoming more common: in 2009 the annual average earnings of a temporary worker were only 69.6 per cent of those of a permanent worker (Arestis and Sawyer, 2012). In this situation, precarious work leads to precarious living conditions, including an inability to develop long-term plans such as achieving housing independence and starting a family (González Gago et al., 2012).

In the United Kingdom, unlike the two Mediterranean countries, the main issue for highly educated young workers is skill mismatch and over-qualification, rather than temporary work. English graduates do not typically enter forms of precarious work, but their first jobs are likely to be lower-skilled and in fields unrelated to their degrees. However, the current crisis has increased unemployment and involuntary temporary work among the young highly qualified in the UK as well, and lengthened the transition period for graduates into work (Hadjivassiliou et al., 2012).

The next few sections describe the policy context in Italy, Spain and the United Kingdom, before presenting the results of the qualitative analysis of interviews with highly qualified young people. The analysis highlights differences in the way that these labour market challenges are perceived by young people themselves. Distinctive national pictures emerge, reflecting different cultural approaches and differences

in institutional regulation models. It is nevertheless possible to identify a common trajectory followed by the European countries in their
intensive use of non-standard contracts (Herrmann, 2008). Similarities
emerge in the treatment of young graduates across the Mediterranean
and conservative welfare regimes, hitherto characterised by work-based
social rights; in the traditional 'coordinated market economies' typical
of most continental European countries (Bosch et al., 2009; Gautié and
Schmitt, 2011); and in liberal economies such as the United Kingdom
(Madsen, 2010).

4.4   Policy context

In this section the policy context in the three case study countries is
described, to provide a sense of the environments in which the young
interviewees sought work. In recent years, while a small number of
European countries have introduced initiatives targeted at highly qualified young people, such as Germany (Misko, 2006), Sweden (Thorsen
and Brunk, 2009) and Greece (European Commission, 2010a), none
of the three case study countries has policies or programmes targeted
specifically at this group. In all three countries, there have been some
attempts to facilitate workforce entry and improve social protection
among *all* young people, but broader deregulation of the labour market has undermined these attempts and many young people remain in
precarious work.

In the United Kingdom in the 1980s, a process of radical and
widespread deregulation of the labour market reduced the level of legal
protection for all workers. In subsequent decades, Spain and Italy exhibited a similar process of work flexibilisation through the introduction of
temporary contractual forms (Samek Lodovici and Semenza, 2012).

In Spain, whilst temporary employment dates back to the 1980s with
the introduction of fixed-term employment promotion contracts, it pro-
liferated towards the end of the following decade. This was despite an
attempt in the second half of the 1990s to encourage permanent contracts for some groups, such as young people aged 16–30. In response
to the large increase in youth unemployment, new flexicurity-oriented
measures were introduced between 2010 and 2012, which increased severance pay for fixed-term contracts and provided deductions for firms
that recruited young people under 30 on permanent contracts, in order
to reduce temporary employment among young people (González Gago
et al., 2012).

In Italy, the labour market has been reformed largely through
the deregulation of workforce-entry contracts. From 1997, with the

ostensible aim of increasing labour market flexibility to favour youth employment, a series of policies were introduced to increase flexibility in work contracts. In reality, however, the consequences of the reforms were problematic precisely for young people. The increased flexibility 'translated into a significant share of young people holding atypical labour contracts, facing lower job security, lower contributions and lower expected pension benefits' (European Commission, 2011, p. 26). The few attempts to curb precarisation and to support young people (including the Agreement on Welfare, Labour Market and Pensions for Equity and Sustainable Growth promoted by the centre-left government in 2007 and the ambitious Action Plan – Italy 2020 proposed in 2009 by the centre-right government) have been short-sighted and have not produced significant improvements (Murgia et al., 2012). Nor has the recent labour market reform law (2012) brought substantial changes – although it introduces some correctives in regard to the indiscriminate use of freelance contracts and better regulation of apprenticeships.[3] It has not addressed the range of insecure contractual forms still in effect, nor has it introduced universal protection in the case of job loss or a guaranteed minimum wage (Treu, 2013).

In both Italy and Spain, certain contractual forms, such as training contracts, apprenticeships and study grants targeted specifically at young people, have been introduced in order to improve their chances of workforce entry. But insufficient attention has been paid to their implementation, so that in many cases they have turned into disguised forms of underpaid and temporary work, exacerbating precarisation and producing labour market segregation. In the Italian case, the effectiveness of these types of training contracts is unclear (Rhodes, 2012), partly owing to inadequate monitoring (Brunello, 2010).

In Spain, temporary contracts tailor-made for young workers were introduced in 1980 by the Worker Status, initially targeted at highly skilled workers, with the aim of supporting newly qualified young people to acquire professional skills in their field.These were followed by apprenticeship contracts for young workers, internship contracts and training contracts. There are also two kinds of workforce entry that do not entail the establishment of employment relationships between workers and companies: scholarships and contracts for services (González Gago et al., 2012). All these contractual forms have become increasingly widespread owing to their significant benefits for companies, given that they do not require payment of social security contributions and the regulation of wages through collective agreements; nor do they offer benefit or severance pay in the event of contract termination. However, they have increased the precariousness of young workers (Working Lives Research Institute, 2012). Spain's labour market is particularly polarised between 'insiders', protected employees (mostly men aged over 30) with secure work and adequate social protection, and 'outsiders', temporary employees (mostly young people and women) with little access to social protection or to training and job creation (Dubin and Hopkin, 2013).

In the UK there are no special contracts for young workers as such. But the transition from school to work is eased by the widespread use of apprenticeships and other dedicated measures such as the Graduate Talent Pool programme (2009) which provides internships for young graduates, and a package of measures called the Young Person's Guarantee (2009), among them the Future Jobs Fund, which offers those still unemployed six months after graduation access to internships, training courses or support for self-entrepreneurship (European Commission, 2010b). However, although internships have proved to be important instruments for workforce entry, they have substantial shortcomings, particularly the fact that many of them are unpaid (Hadjivassiliou et al., 2012).

In the three case study countries, there are significant differences in the extent to which social protection exists to mitigate the risks associated with the deregulation of the labour market. In Italy, subordinate employment contracts generally provide some insurance protection for sickness and maternity, even though these conditions are less favourable than those attached to standard contracts. 'Quasi-subordinate' workers, who are like freelancers but with only one employer, are largely excluded from social protection measures (Working Lives Research Institute, 2012). In Spain the level of social security has always been low, and since the recent financial crisis, the social protection system has been further retrenched (Perkiö, 2013). Since 2006, Spain has had an Active Income for Insertion Programme which, organised at the regional level, provides a minimum workforce-entry income, although it is subject to stringent conditions and is limited in its effectiveness (Rodriguez Cabrero, 2009).

In the United Kingdom, legal provisions offering employment protection for younger people have existed for some time. In 1999 a national minimum wage was introduced, which covers various categories of young people (Low Pay Commission, 2011).[4] If they have paid sufficient national insurance contributions, young people are entitled to (contribution-based) Job Seekers Allowance (JSA) when they are unemployed. If they have not paid contributions they are entitled to the means-tested (or 'income-based') JSA, paid at a similar rate. Apprentices, interns and some part-time workers do not pay enough national insurance contributions to be entitled to contribution-based JSA should they become unemployed (Eurofund, 2013). In most cases, self-employed people are also only entitled to income-based JSA.

Given the mixed nature of policies that support young people's transitions from education to work, and the relative dearth of policies targeted specifically at highly qualified young people, the 'Trapped or Flexible' research project explored the implications of temporary employment for highly qualified young workers in different policy contexts and labour market regimes. Drawing on qualitative interviews with young people in the three case study countries, the following sections will describe their experience of temporary work and its associated difficulties.

4.5   The study: methodology

The project set out to explore precarity among highly qualified and skilled young people. It adopted a mixed method approach and included several phases. During the first phase of the project, a map was compiled of policies to support young workers with temporary jobs in the 27 European Union member countries. The purpose was to audit policies aimed at extending the rights of workers with permanent jobs to temporary workers. The second phase drew on quantitative and qualitative research techniques to undertake three case studies conducted in Italy, Spain and the United Kingdom.

Each case study involved a statistical analysis of labour market data to evaluate the incidence of non-standard employment and how this has changed during the global economic crisis, with a specific focus on highly qualified young people. This was followed by 75 qualitative semi-structured interviews, conducted in 2011 in the three countries (between 20 and 30 interviews in each country). The interviews were carried out in Milan, Trento and Bologna in Italy, Madrid in Spain, and Brighton in the United Kingdom. All of the interviewees had high educational qualifications (degrees, masters and in some cases doctorates). At the time of the interview, they were all aged between 25 and 34 years old with at least five years of work experience, and were employed on temporary contracts. In around half of the cases the interviewees had jobs which matched their skills; the rest had been forced to accept low-skilled jobs.

Subsequently, the principal findings of the interviews with highly qualified young people were discussed in focus groups with key informants concerned with national labour market policies: policymakers, training and vocational organisations, social security institutes, trade unions and employers' associations. One focus group (each with six to ten participants) was conducted in each country, in Rome, Madrid and London. Analysis of both the interviews and the focus groups highlighted the marked lack of policies intended to remedy the work precarity of young people in general, particularly among highly qualified young people.

4.6   Findings from the study

In what follows we shall present some of the main findings from the analysis of the interviews conducted with highly qualified and highly skilled young people in Italy, Spain and the United Kingdom. The discussion of the findings is divided into three sections: in the first, the focus is on dimensions that more directly concern the sphere of work, such as the unstable and temporary nature of the contractual arrangement, economic precarity and skill-downgrading. The second section will consider the impact of the employment conditions on personal experience, paying specific attention to (i) the difficulties of reconciling private life and work, and (ii) the consequences that temporary work may have for the life-course, particularly during career interruptions for maternity or illness, and in regard to planning for the future. The third section concentrates on the effects of a lack of social protection, which – despite profound changes in labour markets and the normative systems that regulate them – is still difficult to access for persons employed on fixed-term contracts, particularly if freelance or semi-freelance, widely used among highly qualified young people.

4.6.1   Experiences of work precarity by highly skilled workers

The first finding from the analysis of the interviews is that entry into employment was never recounted as a linear transition from the status of student to that of worker, but instead as a somewhat uneven process subject to constant interruptions and changes in direction. For the interviewees in the United Kingdom, the discontinuity most often consisted of a sequence of work experience placements, mostly unpaid, while for those in Italy and Spain it consisted largely of brief episodes of work, often on unrenewed contracts. In this latter case, a crucial juncture for many of the interviewees was when the contract was close to expiry, which was described as a situation characterised by ambivalence on the part of the employers, and by a consequent sense of uncertainty on the part of the young workers.

In March they gave me a six-month contract, so it lasted until August. In September I went back, knowing that the contract would last from September 2010 to September 2011. But the days passed and this contract didn't arrive. So I waited for a day, I waited for two, I waited for a week, I waited for three... soon it was the end of October... Then I went to knock on the door of the personnel manager and I got the answer 'Don't think that if you break my balls every day I'll give you a contract'. As a consequence I still haven't got a contract.

[Italy]

The perception of the precarious nature of work produced increasing demotivation in the young interviewees, together with a fear of skills loss. For these interviewees, the manner in which temporary work was performed meant that they did not perceive it as 'real' work; rather, it consisted of brief experiences that did not offer opportunities for growth and learning; nor did it foster a sense of belonging to a work group. Consequently, these young people felt extraneous to the environments in which they worked and where they would remain for only a few months.

Temporary employment is what really wears you down. I work as a substitute in bank branches during periods when there is a great amount of work. For example, I had to go to a branch near a beach during the summer. There is no time to go beyond your specific tasks and you cannot learn anything. I only could stay in the same job for three months maximum. Stability would make me happier and stimulate me to learn.

[Spain]

From this perspective, unemployment – traditionally defined as the lack of a job – assumed a more nuanced meaning, in that there were more tenuous boundaries between those who were in employment and those who were not. It also changed the semantic referent of the concept of 'stability', which seemed to concern the ability to rely not only on a permanent job but also on a steady income and work, and especially on the absence of the need to search for a job.

As regards the English interviewees in particular, their distress derived mainly from the fact that their first work experiences took the form of internships, usually unpaid. Several of their stories pointed to the willingness of people with high qualifications to accept precarious employment if they perceived it as an opportunity to obtain a job matching their qualifications in the future. This consolidated the tendency among employers to resort to internships so that they could use qualified young personnel at low cost.

> Most of my internships were unpaid and this changed my outlook. After doing my third or fourth internship, and obtaining my degree and Masters, I was starting to think what else do I need to get employment?! My outlook changed from wanting to get work experience in my first internship to that's enough now, I would rather go to Tesco and get a paid job that is unrelated to what I am seeking than do another unpaid job. I felt silly for offering up services for free when I am a well-qualified graduate.
>
> [United Kingdom]

In all three countries, the economic dimension of precarious work formed another distinctive feature of the working conditions of the interviewees. For many of the interviewees, their work was poorly paid and this was a source of great frustration. Nor was work discontinuity compensated for by a higher wage, as envisaged by the paradigm of flexibility.

> When I was studying for my degree I had been working 20 hours a week in a hamburger restaurant. Five years later, I worked as an economics researcher. However, my salary (per hour) was lower. Thus, I have realised that educational level and salary do not correspond at all.
>
> [Spain]

The situation in the United Kingdom seemed less problematic in this regard, because the difficulties were encountered primarily during the workforce-entry phase, after which the situation seemed to improve progressively. For example, one of the graduates interviewed recounted that his employer's pay structure rewarded organisational loyalty and length of service, which meant that pay was low at entry level: when he was offered employment, his salary was £13,000 and when he was made permanent he received a £500 rise, after which he would be getting a £500 rise every year. In fact, the main difficulty for the graduates interviewed in the United Kingdom seemed not to concern pay levels, but instead the bank debts incurred in order to pay university fees, and the difficulty of renegotiating them in view of the low incomes received from first employment.

The way banks treat graduates considerably exacerbates their misery.

[United Kingdom]

Most English graduates accumulate large debts (fees, living expenses and so on) and they cannot afford to pay them off with their low wages from temporary work. Banks offer reasonable overdrafts with no interest payable to students. However, upon graduation, banks begin treating all account holders as if they have obtained a secure job with a reasonable income, and subsequently reduce the overdraft facility and charge interest (Hadjivassiliou et al., 2012). Several graduate interviewees commented that banks should continue to offer loans to young graduates on better terms.

A feature shared by interviewees in all three countries was the perception that their professional trajectories were leading nowhere, and that educational credentials acquired with years of study could not guarantee satisfactory working conditions and the construction of a professional profile that will be attractive to the market. For many of the young people interviewed, the impossibility of constructing a coherent career, the risk of skill loss and being forced to accept jobs that are considered greatly below their education levels and skills were major sources of anxiety and frustration.

> You feel frustrated. When I was studying I did not expect to be in my thirties having such difficulties. I thought that in a couple of years I could get a decent one thousand-euro job. But even that has become almost impossible.

[Spain]

The perception of being over qualified for one's job was therefore among the main issues reported by the interviewees. The most qualified of them had come to believe that their educational credentials were formal obstacles against workforce entry; an aspect which increased their sense of inadequacy and their demotivation owing to an increasing discrepancy between expectations and the reality.

> An electrical technician would be much better at my job than I am, and I also believe that he'd be much more interested, more motivated, and find it much more enjoyable. I did materials physics ... honestly, there's nothing about machines that interests

me ... yes, I'm interested in knowing how they work ... but when after six months I've understood how things work, once I've understood everything, it doesn't interest me anymore. Yes, it's a job and I should do it as best I can ... but intellectually it really doesn't interest me.

[Italy]

The problem of de-skilling was reported by interviewees in all three countries. In the United Kingdom, in fact, even though the chances of obtaining a job after the initial internship seemed to be higher than in the other two countries, opportunities to find a job consistent with qualifications were described as limited. Albeit to a lesser extent than in Spain and Italy, in the United Kingdom we also collected stories related to disheartening experiences of applying for jobs well below one's professional skills. This situation increased the concern among participants about the ability to secure a job, and in particular one that would be at an appropriate skill level.

This is one of the main reasons why this particular category of young people is often caught in what can be called a 'passion trap'. On the one hand, they are in search of jobs that allow them to express their passion; that is, build on the skills that they have acquired and use them in the job profile in which they have invested. On the other hand, employment instability, a lack of protection and in many cases the impossibility of doing the job for which they have been trained, produce stress, suffering, dissatisfaction and anxiety about the future.

4.6.2   Impacts on private and social life

A second aspect explored by the interviews was the relationship between work trajectories and other spheres of life, and in particular the impact of precarious employment on the biographical experiences of individuals. A difficulty raised by interviewees in all three countries was the tendency for work to invade all other life spheres. However, once again, differences were apparent between the United Kingdom and the two Mediterranean countries. The interviewees in Italy and Spain emphasised the difficulties of living independently, of achieving work/life balance and of the construction of a family project, particularly for women. While most of the young interviewees in Spain and Italy strived not to be 'burdens' on their families, the discontinuous nature of their labour market attachment meant that they were forced to rely on the support and resources of their families. Consequently, several interviewees expressed concern about achieving or maintaining independent housing. At the same time, some interviewees described their families' anxiety over a situation perceived to be at odds with the investment that they and their families had made in their education.

> Coming back home is a personal defeat and the family perception contributes, to a certain extent, to this negative sensation. I know they are not going to condemn me, but they experience this as a collective failure, though they try to be optimistic so as not to increase my frustration.
>
> [Spain]

Discontinuous employment, economic precarity and the lack of housing independence also tended to discourage longer-term projects for the future, inducing the young people interviewed – and especially the women – to live from day to day without being able to plan for couple formation or to make choices concerning parenthood.

> I have never thought of having children because I cannot even imagine it in my current situation. I do not even know where I am going to be in the next three months.
>
> [Spain]

> I don't have children … and I mean … I think that without a steady job having a child in my present situation wouldn't be easy … I live alone, so if I'm late one evening, and get home at ten o'clock, thank heavens I only have myself to think about, so that's fine. I don't know what having a family would entail. That I don't know. I certainly see a difficult situation, not an easy one.
>
> [Italy]

Family formation was therefore a matter of great concern, above all for young women working on fixed-term contracts characterised by scant protection and the difficulty of exercising rights, even when legally stipulated, because of the brevity of contracts and the uncertainty of their renewal or stabilisation. This concern is supported by the Eurostat data (2011) which suggest that, although important gender differences in the workplace persist throughout Europe, female temporary workers face significantly greater challenges than permanent ones, especially as regards life choices such as exit from the family of origin, cohabitation and family formation.

The precarious situation of many placed enormous pressure on them to be available for demanding work schedules, which meant that they were forced to postpone – sometimes even to abandon –

specific life projects, particularly those tied to housing independence and parenthood. The interviewees described work situations in which they had to be constantly available to respond to the needs of their organisations. In all three countries, the fear of possible dismissal or non-renewal of the contract exacerbated this condition, generating the phenomenon of 'super' or 'extreme' work (Holmes and Ryan, 2008).

In the United Kingdom, several graduate interviewees with fixed-term jobs regularly stayed late in the office because of 'unrealistic deadlines'. Graduates often found themselves working 'too much', and pressured to be constantly available for work. When the employer expects one to be available to work seven days a week and 'requests to work could come as late as 11pm the night before a shift', it is difficult to make plans and to apply for different jobs or further education (for example, PhD applications). The accounts of long working hours in the UK were very similar to those made by young people in Italy and Spain, who described jobs where 'the week basically doesn't exist, on Saturday and Sunday you have to get something ready for Monday...' Very few of the young people interviewed had clearly defined work schedules. In addition to the 'de-structuration' of working hours, there was an evident 'intensification' and 'densification' of working hours (Gallino, 2001), to the point that the job 'killed off all the rest of the time'.

4.6.3   Difficulty in access to employment rights and social security

The interweaving between the experience of a *precarious job* and a *precarious life*, together with the relations that occur in every country between the regulation of labour rights and the welfare system, also translated for the interviewees into a perception of precarity in regard to social protection. This was more marked in the stories recounted by the young highly skilled workers in Italy and Spain. The interviewees repeatedly reported scant or sometimes non-existent opportunities to exercise social rights granted to other workers: pension rights, sickness benefits, paid maternity or parental leave, training, and unemployment benefits. The following excerpts from the interviews conducted with a Spanish lawyer and an Italian archaeologist highlight both the lack of institutional concern about these issues and the differential treatment accorded to permanent and temporary personnel in the same work context:

> In my opinion, it seems that the government does not care about the informal economy. I spent more than two years in a lawyer's office

without any contract. And I have never seen a labour inspection. It is an extremely widespread situation among young lawyers.

[Spain]

In the long run, after ten years on a project contract, you can't take it anymore! ... You can't work on an archaeological site without at least sickness or injury coverage ... I'll give you an example. The construction industry agreement provides for lay-off benefit in the case of bad weather. So if the weather is bad and you don't have alternative work in the office, you get lay-off benefit, so you go home, but the day's work is paid. With my 'project contract', the pay was already less than one thousand euros, for forty hours a week on the building site. If it started to rain ... I always give the example of my first pay packet with this firm, which was six hundred and twenty euros ... [laughs] which was just about what I spent on petrol driving to and from work.

[Italy]

Through their stories, the interviewees denounced both frequent abuses by employers, who sometimes did not propose an ongoing contract, and the scant rights associated with the contractual forms on which they were hired, especially if they were for freelance or semi-freelance work. Nevertheless, the aspiration of many of these young people was not so much to obtain a lifelong permanent job but rather to have access to forms of protection that would assure income continuity during life phases of unemployment, especially when there was no family support available.

The three things that I can cite are certainly social security, because at the moment I'm not paying supplementary contributions, so I'm not really building a pension, although it's not that I have ... I've started thinking about it. Maternity, because even if I don't have a partner, if I had one, I know that wanting to have children would be a problem ... for me certainly, but for her as well, knowing how the world is going. And then, a problem that I've already had several times, income ... in the sense that what I need is income support. For example, these months I've been earning only intermittently ... it's not fair that I'm not eligible for unemployment benefits like a worker who's laid off and gets redundancy payment for six months.

[Italy]

Concerning the young people in the UK, a number of graduates felt they needed more protection and security in their employment (for example, the lack of sickness or maternity benefits was mentioned during the interviews). Despite the graduates having mixed feelings about their current situation, this was considered by the majority to be an outcome of their own choice. The work experience they were gaining from their temporary roles was seen as a step in order to pursue a chosen career.

Having revealed the difficulties described by the young interviewees – difficulties owing mainly to professional downgrading and the lack of rights stipulated in temporary contracts and, more generally, in the local or national welfare state – the next and concluding section discusses the policy proposals put forward by the key informants in focus groups conducted in Italy, Spain and the United Kingdom. The purpose of these proposals is to promote the quality of work and the rights of this specific target group of workers by improving working conditions and strengthening the social protection available to mitigate social risks such as unemployment, mismatch and underemployment.

4.7   Conclusions and implications for policy

The effects of the precarisation of work in Europe, exacerbated by the economic crisis, have been felt particularly strongly by the younger generation, and they have not spared highly qualified young people. The research presented in this chapter shows that, despite possession of greater skills and higher educational credentials – both of which are crucial resources in the knowledge economy – workers with high qualifications and skills are today exposed to the constant risk of unemployment, lack of income and social marginality. Furthermore, the interviews provided information not only on work precarity but also on its implications for the other spheres of life – from residential independence to family formation – and the complicated interweaving between access to work and different forms of social protection.

In addition to the individual consequences for both careers *strictu sensu* and the interweaving between work and personal life, this phenomenon entails a social cost. The waste of high-skilled human capital hampers growth, increases the risk of poverty, exacerbates inequalities between the generations, reduces tax revenues and generates greater social expenditure (Barbier, 2011; Standing, 2011). It is therefore a matter of urgency to develop policies targeted at this hitherto neglected category of young people. For such policies to be effective, they should take account of the complex relationship between labour market precarity, its impact on personal and family life and the capacity to plan for the future, and the lack of social protection afforded to young people.

Key informants with expertise in national labour market policies provided some recommendations for policies to address the risk of precarity among highly qualified young people. In general, they stressed the need to shift from an approach to young people's workforce participation that was still geared towards increased labour market flexibility, towards a closer integration of the existing education, training, employment and social protection systems. The key informants placed an emphasis on the introduction – where not already present – of social shock absorbers, such as a basic or minimum income, that could offset the flexibilisation of the labour market. This would create greater employment security and reduce the current asymmetry in access to social protection across the different contractual forms.

Overall, there was significant overlap in the recommendations provided by the Spanish and Italian informants compared with those offered by English informants. This can be interpreted in the light of different welfare and institutional regimes in the three countries (Esping-Andersen, 1990; Marsden, 1999) and of a consequent greater affinity in the experiences of young Italian and Spanish interviewees compared with young English interviewees. According to the quantitative data, in Spain and Italy there has been a general erosion of the quality of work, and the central issues for young people with tertiary education are over-qualification, short-term work and low wages. In contrast, in the UK the main issues for this group are over-qualification and skills mismatch, rather than the temporary nature of contracts. These differences also emerged in the qualitative interviews, where we observed that work continuity, lack of social protection and low pay were raised as critical issues by highly qualified young Spanish and Italian people. In the UK, however, the main issue to emerge was, more specifically, the link between the education system and the labour market and in particular the internship system, to the extent that this could become a tool to normalise unpaid or low-paid work.

Consistent with these findings, the policy recommendations collected in Italy and Spain were primarily focused on work discontinuity, low pay and lack of social protection. Key informants suggested tools both to protect young people from the negative effects of short-term contracts and to discourage employers from using them. In contrast, in the

UK the focus of the recommendations was on workforce *entry* (rather than workforce continuity or progression). Key informants focused on the need to better support transitions from education to work, and to ensure that internships are properly regulated to avoid exploitation by employers.

For example, the Italian key informants suggested that firms should continue to pay an allowance to workers on temporary contracts after their contracts have ceased so that they have an interval of time, albeit a short one, to look for another job. They also identified the need to recognise length of service in the temporary contract system, so that people are not once again treated as entry-level (in terms of both skills and pay) each time they commence a new contract. The Spanish key informants suggested that labour market flexibility needed to be compensated by a better social safety-net mechanism (for example, through reform of the severance pay system). Informants in both Italy and in Spain emphasised the need to decouple access to welfare and type of contract. However, in the UK key informants focused on the links between the educational system and the labour market, suggesting that existing policies that provide young graduates with counselling and guidance were insufficient and that a more active policy intervention is required. Incentives for employers to hire a percentage of new recruits on the basis of their potential rather than their experience and more incentives to support youth entrepreneurship were two suggestions provided here. UK key informants also identified the need for a clear policy on internships, improving the terms and conditions associated with them (for example, by obliging employers to pay at least the intern's accommodation and travel expenses).

In conclusion, the precarisation of work and its implications for other spheres of life should prompt European countries to reconsider the relationship between their employment systems and welfare regimes, so that the younger generation, which is particularly affected by the proliferation of temporary jobs, is not excluded from the exercise of employment rights and from full access to social protection. The growing cleavage between 'insiders' (those in permanent work) and 'outsiders' (those in precarious work on the periphery) has dramatically increased social and economic inequalities – and all the more so in the present economic crisis. Whether temporary contracts create precarisation or become the source of opportunities for workers depends not only on personal resources, qualifications and skills – as well evidenced by the stories of highly educated young people – but also, and especially, on the political choices of countries.

Notes

1. This chapter is the result of joint work by the authors. However, if for academic reasons individual responsibility must be attributed, Annalisa Murgia wrote Sections 1, 2, 3 and 6 and Barbara Poggio Sections 4, 5 and 7.
2. The project partners were: IRS – Istituto per la Ricerca Sociale of Milan, the Department of Sociology and Social Research of the University of Trento, the Centro di Ricerche e Servizi Avanzati per la Formazione 'Amitié' of Bologna, the Institute for Employment Studies of Brighton and the Centro de Estudios Economicos Tomillo S.L. Di Madrid. The project was financed by the European Commission, Directorate-General for Employment, Social Affairs and Equal Opportunities through the Pilot project to 'encourage conversion of precarious work into work with rights' (VP/2010/016). The project's results were published in the volume *Precarious Work and Young Highly Skilled Workers in Europe. Risk Transitions and Missing Policies*, edited by Manuela Samek Lodovici and Renata Semenza, Milano, Angeli, 2012.
3. Introduced by the Monti government, the Fornero Reform, which takes its name from the Minister of Labour, led to an extensive reform of the labour market, especially in regard to flexible and temporary work, apprenticeships, unfair dismissal and independent contractors. It regulated the duration and renewal of fixed-term contracts. In regard to apprenticeships, their minimum duration was fixed, a limit was set on the number of apprentices an employer could have and the continuation of the employment relationship was made obligatory for a certain proportion of an employer's apprenticeship contracts.
4. The National Minimum Wage is the hourly rate below which adult workers must not be paid. Full entitlement applies to workers aged 21 and over, while a lower minimum rate applies to 18–20 year olds.

References

Arestis, P. and Sawyer, M. (2012). *The Euro Crisis* (London: Palgrave MacMillan).

Armano, E. and Murgia, A. (2014). 'The *Precariousnesses* of Young Knowledge Workers. A Subject-Oriented Approach'. *Global Discourse: An Interdisciplinary Journal of Current Affairs and Applied Contemporary Thought* 3 (3/4), 486–501.

Ballarino, G. (2007). 'Sistemi formativi e mercato del lavoro', in Regini, M. (ed.) *La sociologia economica contemporanea* (Laterza: Roma-Bari).

Barbier, J-C. (2011). 'Employment Precariousness in a European Cross-National Perspective – A Sociological View over 30 Years of Research', presented at the seminar *De-standardisation of Employment*, Koln University.

Bauman, Z. (2005). *Liquide Life* (Cambridge: Polity Press).

Beck, U. and Beck-Gernsheim, E. (eds.) (2002). *Individualization. Institutionalized Individualism and Its Social and Political Consequences* (London: Sage).

Bentolila, S., Dolado, J. and Jimeno, J. (2008). 'Two-tier Employment Protection Reforms: The Spanish Experience'. *CESifo DICE Report*, 6, 4.

Blasutig, G. (2011). 'Le condizioni occupazionali dei giovani laureati e le nuove sfide per le politiche del lavoro', presented at the ESPANET conference.

Boeri, T. (2010). 'Institutional Reforms and Dualism in European Labor Markets', in Ashenfelter, O. and Card, D. (eds.) *Handbook of Labor Economics* (Amsterdam: Elsevier).

Boeri, T. and Garibaldi, P. (2007). 'Two-tier Reforms of Employment Protection Legislation: A Honeymoon Effect'. *Economic Journal* 117 (521), 357–85.

Boltanski, L. and Chiapello, E. (1999). *Le nouvel esprit du capitalisme* (Paris: Gallimard).

Bosch, G., Lehndorff, S. and Rubery, J. (eds.) (2009). *European Employment Models in Flux: A Comparison of Institutional Change in Nine European Countries* (Basingstoke: Palgrave).

Bourdieu, P. (1998). 'La précarité est aujourd'hui partout', in Bourdieu, P. (ed.) *Contre-feux* (Paris: Liber-Raison d'agir).

Bourdieu, P. (2003). *Firing Back: Against the Tyranny of the Market 2* (London: Verso).

Bradley, H. and Devadason, R. (2008). 'Fractured Transitions: Young Adults' Pathways into Contemporary Labour Markets'. *Sociology* 42 (1), 119–36.

Brine, J. (2006). 'Lifelong Learning and the Knowledge Economy: Those That Know and Those That Do Not: The Discourse of the European Union'. *British Educational Research Journal* 32 (5), 649–65.

Brophy, E. and de Peuter, G. (2007). 'Immaterial Labour, Precarity, and Recomposition', in McKercher, C. and Mosco, V. (eds.) *Knowledge Workers in the Information Society* (Lanham: Lexington Books).

Brunello, G. (2010). 'The Situation of Youth in the European Labour Market', in European Parliament - DG for Internal Policies (ed.) *The Situation of Youth in the European Union*, IP/A/EMPL/NT/2009-14, May 2010.

Chicchi, F. and Leonardi, E. (eds.) (2011). *Lavoro in frantumi. Condizione precaria, nuovi conflitti e regime neoliberista* (Verona: Ombre Corte).

Dolado, J., Garcia-Serrano, C. and Jimeno, J. (2002). 'Drawing Lessons from the Boom of Temporary Jobs in Spain'. *Economic Journal* 112, 270–95.

Dubin, K. and Hopkin, J. (2013). 'Flexibility for Some, Security for Others: The Politics of Welfare and Employment in Spain', in Clegg, D., Graziano, P. and Jessoula, M. (eds.) *The Politics of Flexicurity in Europe: Labour Market Reform in Hostile Climes and Tough Times* (Basingstoke: Palgrave).

Esping-Andersen, G. (1990). *The Three Worlds of Welfare Capitalism* (Cambridge: Polity Press).

Eurofund (2013). 'United Kingdom: Young People and Temporary Employment in Europe', Available from: http://www.eurofound.europa.eu/emcc/erm/studies/tn1304017s/uk1304019q.htm (accessed on 2 January 2014).

European Commission (2011). *Commission Staff Working Document on EU Indicators in the Field of Youth*, Brussels, 25.03.2011 SEC(2011) 401 final.

European Commission (2010a). *Employment in Europe 2010* (Brussels: European Commission).

European Commission (2010b). *Youth Employment Measures 2010* (Brussels: European Commission).

Eurostat (2011). *Labour Force Survey – Annual Results 2010* (Brussels: European Union).

Gallino, L. (2001). *Il costo umano della flessibilità* (Laterza: Roma-Bari).

Gautié, J. and Schmitt, J. (eds.) (2011). *Low-wage Work in the Wealthy World* (New York: Sage).

Gherardi, S. and Murgia, A. (2012). 'By Hook or By Crook: Temporary Workers between Exploration and Exploitation'. *Research in the Sociology of*

Organizations, Special Issue on 'Managing "Human Resources" by Exploiting and Exploring People's Potentials', 37, 75–103.

Glucksmann, M. (2005). 'Shifting Boundaries and Interconnections: Extending the "Total Social Organization of Labour" '. *Sociology Review* 53 (2), 19–36.

González Gago, E., González Olcoz, S. and Segales Kirzner, M. (2012). 'Spain: Random Transitions in the Labour Market', in Samek Lodovici, M. and Semenza, R. (eds.) *Precarious Work and Young Highly Skilled Workers in Europe. Risk Transitions and Missing Policies* (Angeli: Milano).

Hadjivassiliou, K.P., Higgins, T., Rickard, C. and Speckesser, S. (2012). 'The UK: Longer Labour Market Transitions and Deskilling', in Samek Lodovici, M. and Semenza, R. (eds.) *Precarious Work and Young Highly Skilled Workers in Europe. Risk Transitions and Missing Policies* (Angeli: Milano).

Herrmann, A. (2008). 'Rethinking the Link between Labour Market Flexibility and Corporate Competitiveness: A Critique of the Institutionalist Literature'. *Socio-Economic Review* 6 (4), 637–69.

Holmes, A. and Ryan, J. (2008). 'Where Will Commoditization Take Us?', Working Paper n. 31/WP/2008, http://dx.doi.org/10.2139/ssrn.1287500 (accessed on 12 October 2013).

International Labour Organisation (2012). *Global Employment Trends for Youth 2012* (Geneva: International Labour Office).

Low Pay Commission (2011). *National Minimum Wage* (London: Low Pay Commission).

Madsen, P.K. (2010). 'Flexicurity and Upward Transitions: The Magic Bullet?', presentation at the conference 'Flexicurity to the benefit of workers', Gent.

Marsden, D. (1999). *A Theory of Employment Systems: Micro-foundations of Societal Diversity* (Oxford: Oxford University Press).

Misko, J. (2006). *Vocational Education and Training in Australia, the United Kingdom and Germany* (Adelaide: National Centre for Vocational Education Research).

Murgia, A., Poggio, B. and Torchio, N. (2012). 'Italy: Precariousness and Skill Mismatch', in Samek Lodovici, M. and Semenza, R. (eds.) *Precarious Work and Young Highly Skilled Workers in Europe. Risk Transitions and Missing Policies* (Angeli: Milano).

Neilson, B. and Rossiter, N. (2008). 'Precarity as a Political Concept, or, Fordism as Exception'. *Theory, Culture & Society* 25 (7/8), 51–72.

Perkiö, J. (2013). 'Basic Income Proposals in Finland, Germany and Spain'. *Transform!*, Discussion Paper n. 2, Available from: http://transform-network.net/uploads/tx_news/Paper_no2_perkioe_EN.pdf (accessed on 13 November 2013).

Rhodes, M. (2012). 'Coordination, Cooperation and Conflict in Labor Market Reform: Spain and Italy in the Crisis', paper for presentation at the Collegio Carlo Alberto, Turin, 22 November 2012.

Rodriguez Cabrero, G. (2009). 'Assessment of Minimum Income Schemes in Spain, Peer Review in Social Protection and Social Inclusion and Assessment in Social Inclusion', Available from: http://ec.europa.eu/social/main.jsp?catId=89&langId=en&newsId=1416&moreDocuments=yes&tableName=news (accessed on 13 October 2013).

Ross, A. (2009). *Nice Work If You Can Get It: Life and Labor in Precarious Times* (New York: New York University Press).

Samek Lodovici, M. and Semenza, R. (eds.) (2012). *Precarious Work and Young Highly Skilled Workers in Europe. Risk Transitions and Missing Policies* (Angeli: Milano).

Schomburg, H. and Teichler, U. (2006). *Higher Education and Graduate Employment in Europe: Results from Graduate Surveys from Twelve Countries* (Dordrecht: Springer).

Sennett, R. (1998). *The Corrosion of Character. The Personal Consequences of Work in the New Capitalism* (London: Norton & Company).

Sennett, R. (2006). *The Culture of the New Capitalism* (London: New Heaven).

Standing, G. (2011). *The Precariat. The New Dangerous Class* (London: Bloomsbury).

Strangleman, T. (2007). 'The Nostalgia for Permanence at Work? The End of Work and its Commentators'. *Sociological Review* 55 (1), 81–103.

Thorsen, Y. and Brunk, T. (2009). 'Sweden: Flexicurity and Industrial Relations', Eironline, Available from: http://www.eurofound.europa.eu/eiro/studies/TN0803038s/se0803039q.htm (accessed on 12 October 2013).

Torchio, N. (2012). 'Recent Trends and Features of Precarious Work in Europe', in Samek Lodovici, M. and Semenza, R. (eds.) *Precarious Work and Young Highly Skilled Workers in Europe. Risk Transitions and Missing Policies* (Angeli: Milano).

Treu, T. (2013). 'Flessibilità e tutele nella riforma del lavoro'. *Giornale di diritto del lavoro e di relazioni idustriali* 35, 1–51.

Wolbers, M.H.J. (2003). 'Job Mismatches and Their Labour Market Effects among School Leavers in Europe'. *European Sociological Review* 19 (3), 249–66.

Working Lives Research Institute (2012). *Study on Precarious Work and Social Rights* (London, London Metropolitan University).

5
Social Exclusion, Risk and the UK Youth Labour Market

Clive Sealey

5.1 Introduction

Previous chapters have highlighted how the notion of risk has become a prevailing feature of social policy for young people. At the core of this emphasis in the UK, and in many other countries, has been the rejection of the notion of structure as the predominant feature of social inequality, as evident in a number of youth policies. On the contrary, current policies have focused on providing individual interventions to manage social risk. This is apparent within youth social exclusion policies, which often emphasise the lack of labour market participation by 'troublesome youth' as the primary cause of such social exclusion.

This chapter presents empirical evidence on the labour market experiences of marginalised youth in the UK, and thus the relevance of policies that rely on labour market participation to overcome social exclusion. It is based on research carried out using extensive qualitative data collection and analysis. The findings suggest that social exclusion of young people in local settings is reinforced by their reliance on local labour market structures, attendant incomes, and family sources and welfare agencies. The chapter first discusses the evolution of social exclusion policies in the UK, presenting the principles of current policies oriented towards tackling social exclusion via labour market participation. Secondly, it explicates the experiences of young socially excluded people in fragmented labour markets and trapped in the low-income cycle. In addition, the chapter shows how household income and family structures play a central role in shaping young people's choices in the labour market. Furthermore, this part will discuss the relatively limited role of welfare agencies, contrasting it with the influence of informal networks. Finally, the chapter emphasises the implications of the findings, presenting the limits of individualised youth social policy.

5.2 Social exclusion in contemporary youth social policy

This section briefly charts the fundamental shift in youth policy over the last 30 years, from an emphasis on the 'social integration' of youth, to the contemporary policy discourse of youth social exclusion as defined by the individualised, troublesome labour market experiences of youth.

5.2.1 From 'social integration' to the 'individualist turn'

The contemporary emphasis on risk contrasts somewhat with the immediate post-war period in the UK, when the 'social integration' of young people became a clear aim of the nascent welfare state (France and Wiles, 1997). At this time, the state took greater responsibility for the management of individual risk and security by offering universal social services and education. Consequently, young people born in the years during and immediately after the Second World War 'enjoyed the redistribution of social resources brought by the Welfare State which meant that they were healthier and better educated than ever before' (Spence, 2005, pp. 48–9). This was characterised first by education, followed principally by employment, with further education for a limited minority, wherein the ultimate objective of such transitions was labour market participation. This was as a consequence of 'youth' becoming defined as more a period of semi-dependence between childhood (dependence) and adulthood (independence) (Jones, 2002). For example, the emphasis in policy on full employment as an economic goal created jobs and resources for young people in the form of apprenticeships. This increased the possibilities for social inclusion through the expansion of citizenship rights, not only in terms of employment rights but also social, political and civil rights. Policies such as the statutory establishment of youth work following on from the 1944 (Butler) Education Act and the Abermarle Report in 1960 (France and Wiles, 1997) articulated this, as did codified educational requirements for all young people under 16, also from the 1944 Act. Taken together, these changes meant that the prospects for the social mobility of young people during this immediate post-war period increased appreciably and became fairly stable and uniform in comparison to the pre-war period (Graham and McDermott, 2006).

In this context, the significance of the 'individualist turn', as Crompton (2010, p. 20) argues, in theoretical and political debates over the last 30 years has 'played its part in shifting the analysis of social inequality to the individual level'. Such an individualist turn is especially evident in relation to young people (Spence and Wood, 2011), for whom the transition from modernity to late modernity has been the most profound (Smith, 2010). For example, the end of full employment as a policy goal resulted in unemployment being deemed a price worth paying; this was especially the case with youth employment, with young people disproportionately affected compared with other labour market groups, in particular in structural employment (MacDonald, 2000).

This 'individualist turn' ultimately reflects the shift away from the 'social integration' of youth as identified above, wherein the notion of human interdependence, so important to Titmuss's conception of social welfare in much of the post-war welfare system (Welshman, 2004), has been realigned towards making the links between social interaction opaque and less interdependent (Jordan, 1996). The curtailment of state support means that children born after the 1970s were expected to rely more upon either themselves or their parents. This is in contrast to their counterparts born in the 1940s, who enjoyed state grants, such as those in higher education. This and other changes that eroded young people's social rights in important areas of social welfare, such as employment and housing, have resulted in a shift for young people away from dependence on the state to a prolonged period of dependence on themselves and/or their family (Cobb-Clark and Ribar, 2009). This realignment links to Kim et al.'s (1994, p. 2) generalised notion of 'individualism', which 'pertains to societies in which the ties between individuals are loose: everyone is expected to look after himself or herself and his or her immediate family'.

5.2.2 Youth social exclusion as individualised exclusion from the labour market

The economic restructuring of the late 1970s onwards, which brought with it a virtual collapse of the youth labour market, stimulated a series of policy responses. Most significantly, these included the introduction and then widespread growth of youth training schemes, in tandem with a number of welfare reforms that sharply reduced young people's benefits entitlements. In this context, minimum age school leavers, especially, were often excluded from employment, exempted from social security benefits available to older workers and left with training alternatives that provided limited value. This pattern of withdrawal of support and moves towards more individualist thinking has continued for more than three decades. Current social policies are, indeed, deeply influenced by the turn of New Labour policies, which included in their agenda the goal of tackling youth social exclusion. The 'third way' approach of New Labour exemplified this changed focus, positing 'agency as the primary bearer of contemporary risk' (Fudge and Williams, 2006, p. 585). This notion became appropriated and adopted into policies less concerned with dealing with the causes of disadvantage and more with the potentiality of reflexive individualisation, as expressed through agency, as the primary way to overcome disadvantage (Smith, 2010). Indeed, perhaps the most significant application by New Labour of reflexive individualisation into policy was in relation to youth social exclusion. Here, New Labour put in place a range of social exclusion policies intended to manage young people's transitions in the context of uncertainty and risk and which reflected the 'third way' approach (Cieslik and Pollock, 2002). Examples of such policies include the Connexions Service,[1] the New Deal for Young People,[2] *Youth Matters: Next Steps*,[3] the proposal to raise the compulsory school leaving age to 18, the introduction of diplomas, the consideration of vocational education and training, and the Educational Maintenance Allowance.[4] More specifically, within their flagship policies of the Connexions Service and the New Deal for Young People, while the imperative was 'emphasising opportunity and securing [young people's] labour market participation' (Bradford, 2005, p. 65), this was primarily because the government proclaimed that 'any job is better than no job' (Lindsay et al., 2007, p. 541), with little concern for the quality of jobs which such employment policies produced. This is a point made by Levitas (2005) in her consideration of the discourse of New Labour. She argues that New Labour's approach exemplified 'an inconsistent combination of SID [Social Integrationist Discourse] and MUD [Moral Underclass Discourse]' (p. 28), in which 'paid employment is the central means of social integration and social control, and unemployment the overriding element in social exclusion' (p. 48), but alongside a tone that invokes the idea that a lack of social exclusion originates from individual pathology or a lack of moral responsibility.

More contemporarily, the fog of 'austerity' has ostensibly made it harder to discern an explicit social exclusion focus in relation to the current Coalition government's youth policy, as evidenced by the downgrading and scrapping of most of the previous government's youth policies. Perhaps totemic in this respect was the political discourse articulated in the aftermath of the 2011 riots, wherein a political consensus suggested that 'troublesome youth' lay at the heart of the issue (Cooper, 2012). Prime Minister David Cameron, in particular, was keen to make this point in his speech to the House of Commons a few days after the disturbances:

> The young people stealing flat screen televisions and burning shops; that was not about politics or protest, it was about theft... At the heart of all the violence sits the issue of the street gangs. Territorial, hierarchical and incredibly violent, they are mostly composed of young boys, mainly from dysfunctional homes.
>
> (Hansard, 2011)

This is despite the fact that the majority of those charged were actually 'adults', not 'juveniles' (MOJ, 2012). While acknowledging that the academic notion of troublesome youth is not new (for example, Hedidge, 1979), its contemporary political use increasingly articulates a latent discourse of young people and youth as disconnected from mainstream society, with lack of labour market participation given as the primary marker of such troublesome youth (see also MacDonald et al., 2005). This discourse has been reflected in Coalition youth policy in two significant ways (St Croix, 2012). On the one hand negative portrayals of youth (as exemplified by the quote from David Cameron, above) are perpetuated; on the other hand, successful young people are defined as those with the skills that enable them to get good jobs, with the potential to become economically productive adults and contribute to the economy, rather than being dependent on the state (indicated by the indifference towards increased youth unemployment and levels of young people Not in Education, Employment or Training (NEETs), removal of the Educational Maintenance Allowance and increasing the cost of higher education). Such a dualism not only reflects continuity with the previous approach of New Labour on labour market participation, but also more precisely demarcates Coalition policy as 'underpinned by an idea of individualistic choice-making supported by a "compassionate" market and unaffected by political, social and economic inequalities' (St Croix, 2012).

This makes relevant this chapter's focus on the labour market experiences of marginalised youth. As outlined above, youth policy in the UK has over the last 30 years or so moved away from the emphasis on 'social integration' towards an 'individualist turn', with the changed emphasis towards social exclusion as a prime example of this shift. In particular, social exclusion has been expressed as a process engendered by 'the excluded' themselves, resulting in specific focus on youth excluded from the labour market. The following analysis presents empirical evidence for the lived reality of the labour market experiences for marginalised youth, and thus considers the relevance of this individualist turn within youth social exclusion policy.

5.3 Methods and context

The research was carried out using an extensive qualitative data collection and analysis process. Relevant ethical clearance was received for the research. Participants for this research in two deprived localities in Birmingham, England's second largest city by population, were identified through 'gatekeepers' in the form of a Connexions centre and a youth and community centre.

In both localities there is an emphasis on service sector employment, particularly public sector education and private caring businesses, and a complete lack of manufacturing employers. In contrast, a neighbouring affluent locality in the city is home to a large manufacturing company, and generally there is a greater variety of employers. This difference is significant because while public sector jobs typically pay above private sector jobs (Rogers, 2012), caring occupations pay just around 60 per cent of national average (ONS, 2008b), while manufacturing jobs typically pay higher than service sector jobs, often at or above average earnings (ONS, 2008a). This means that in both absolute and relative terms, the types of jobs typically available to participants were low paid in comparison to more affluent neighbouring localities. These opportunity structures in the local labour market form an important backdrop when developing an analysis of the participants' labour market outcomes. After all, as Green and White (2007) highlight, the 'bounded horizons' of one's immediate locality are important in constraining the labour market behaviour of young people, whereby a reluctance to travel outside their immediate locality plays an important restricting role in labour market entry and advancement.

The first part of the research process was an initial sampling questionnaire to around 30 young people at these centres. This survey instrument was built around the notion of 'at risk', defined as factors which are likely to contribute to social exclusion (Allard, 2005; Bullen et al., 2000). The notion of young people 'at risk' has become a prevailing concept in explaining disadvantage. The questionnaire highlighted individuals particularly 'at risk' of social exclusion, and the four most at risk individuals from each locality were chosen to participate in the next stages of the research, making eight research participants in total, aged 19–21. The 'at risk' social exclusion profile of selected research participants from the Sampling Questionnaire is shown in Table 5.1.

Data was then collected, using intensive qualitative research methods that focused on the direct measurement of social exclusion by use of a modified form of the Diary-Diary Interview Method (DDIM) (Zimmerman and Weider, 1977). The original DDIM is a two-stage data collection process. In stage 1, participants are asked to maintain a two-week diary of their activities, broken up into time spheres. In the second stage, the diary is converted into a question-generating/data-generating device, whereby the diary narrative is used to formulate questions to ask of the diarist in a diary interview, in order to 'clarify the detail of everyday life in the scene [and] in the process, discover the structure of relevancies that inform, render sensible, and give value to such activities' (Zimmerman and Weider, 1977, p. 490). The modification occurs with the addition of a further follow-up interview stage, giving a tripartite framework for data collection and analysis. In total, data collection took approximately ten weeks, encompassing two weeks between diary completion and diary interview, and eight weeks between diary interview and follow-up interview.

Methodologically, the strength of such localized, in-depth, small-case research is that it offers the possibility of developing a 'thick description' of the profile of the structure, relations, attitudes and dynamics within local communities. Ethnographic-based approaches such as the DDIM, then, provide an opportunity to delve below the surface of events and facts to reveal underlying meaning (Maginn, 2007). Moreover, McDowell (2001) suggests that representing the mundane details of everyday lives of marginalised young people rather than focusing on any 'spectacular' behaviour may be a better way of capturing the social context circumstances and restricted opportunities that they face. The main themes to emerge from the research are detailed below.

5.4   Research findings

5.4.1   Fragmented labour market transitions and the low-income cycle

All of the participants indicated that they had had numerous jobs, and recounted similar experiences. David and Mikealae both stated that previous voluntary work was important in attaining their present jobs, and Lance's previous job was also gained through an initial voluntary placement, suggesting such work was an important way for participants to acquire employment. Furthermore, of the three participants who were

Table 5.1 'At Risk' social exclusion profile of research participants (names have been changed to protect anonymity)

	Ashley	Sharon	Larry	Gemma	Rod	Mikealae	Lance	David	Total
	Male	Female	Male	Female	Male	Male	Male	Male	
	21	20	19	19	20	20	20	20	
Member of ethnic minority	✓					✓			3
Living in locality 2+ years		✓	✓	✓	✓		✓	✓	6
No examinations/GCSE/GNVQ as highest level of examinations passed or taken	✓	✓	✓	✓	✓		✓		6
Receipt of free school meals	✓	✓	✓	✓	✓	✓	✓	✓	8
Truanting from school	✓	✓	✓	✓		✓			5
Unemployed	✓	✓	✓	✓			✓		5
Income less than £133 per week for a single person	✓	✓	✓	✓		✓	✓		6
Lived in care	✓								1
Permanent exclusion from school	✓	✓	✓						3

Table 5.2   Changes in participants' labour market circumstances between diary interviews and follow-up interviews (eight weeks)

Mikealae	Taken new second job
David	Taken new second job in factory
Rod	Offered new job but said no
Lance	Secured new work placement in type of job wanted
Sharon	N/A
Ashley	1. Obtained Construction Skills Certifications Scheme (CSCS) card – necessary for working in labouring/manual jobs 2. Offered new nine-month computer course – but not able to take up if working, so looking for work
Larry	N/A
Gemma	Taken part-time temporary work in three different jobs

presently working, none was in a roles he or she had actively planned to do, but rather had stumbled upon it. As Table 5.2 shows, in the relatively short period between the two interviews, there had been some significant changes in the labour market status for most participants.

Notwithstanding the fact that data collection took place during the late summer months of July–September, it is nevertheless possible to argue that these changes highlight the transitory and dynamic nature of participants' existence as young people, and thus the individualised nature of their life in general, in that there are some relatively significant changes in such a short period of time. However, the rather fragmented and disrupted nature of participants' work experiences, and the fact that six out of eight participants had some kind of change in their labour market status suggest that it was the transitory nature of the labour market itself which contributed significantly to their labour market status, and further discussion of these changes reinforced the inherently unstable nature of the labour market – a finding consistent with other youth research that has identified high levels of churn between low and no pay (Shildrick et al., 2012).

In addition to having fragmented transitions, the participants also showed an individualised strategy of coping with unemployment, and this was centred on improving their prospects in the labour market, as evidenced by Gemma's consideration:

> … it's not that I don't wanna work I do wanna work but there's just not like the jobs that are coming up ain't what I want and I've applied

for them anyway and I still don't get them it's like what I've applied for Sainsbury's and everything . . . it does irritate me it's not like I've got nothing to put on a CV my CV is quite good so I just can't understand what it is . . .

However, the study emphasises also the persistence of fragmented transitions to adulthood during labour market participation. For those working, the inadequacy of in-work income was something which was outlined as impacting on their lives, in line with the recent findings of Shildrick et al. (2012) that show the existence of a 'low-pay, no-pay cycle'. For example, Rod worked for 40 hours a week, but was only legally entitled to the national minimum wage, which gave him an income he described as both 'ridiculous' and 'inadequate', and led to frustration and anger, as related below:

> . . . it's not fair you know what I mean . . . I'd just like a bit more money, like I'm working really hard and I'm thinking at the end of the week I get my payslip and I'm like 'is that it again?' . . . lots of people I know, all my mates are on like two hundred and something and I'm thinking I'm working in a big factory and I'm like on that kind of money, it's rubbish . . .

For Sharon, this was something which restricted the type of job that she applied for, because she lived on her own and had calculated that she needed to earn an income above the minimum wage. This meant that there was a 'benefits trap' effect, wherein there was a financial disincentive to accept the minimum wage when compared with her present income from social policy provision. Thus, underpinning the inadequacy of in-work income was the issue of the minimum wage: for those in receipt of it, it was a factor which contributed to their low income and thus a sense of unfairness with regard to their circumstances; for those who did not work, it acted as a disincentive to work.

5.4.2   Household income and family structures

While these findings might on some level suggest the presence of individualised approaches to managing transitions, further analysis of the qualitative material shows that structural factors, and in particular household income, play a central role in shaping labour market experiences.

Almost all participants had received free school meals during their entire schooling, the exception being Larry who had only received it for the last three years, suggesting a general ongoing level of income poverty in their families while growing up. The interviews highlight how this low-income family status was reinforced in the transitions of participants through the youth period, because of their need to provide significant amounts of their own income to supplement the family income. For example, around 50 per cent of Mikealae's income went towards the household, as he was the only person with an employment income. Mikealae stated that the fact his income was the main one in the household did not make him feel pressured, and that 'I'm actually kind of happy ... it's coming out of my pocket': it was something that his brothers before him had done, so it was something he had been expecting to do from an early age. However, there was an underlying pressure on him to have a job, per se:

> ... let's say if I don't have a job that's when I would feel pressure cos I'm thinking how would the whole house run without my kind of input into the house ... [there's pressure] to have a job yes and something that I like because for instance if I lose this job ... I'd have to quickly look for a job even if I don't like it I might have to go into it just for the income for now 'til I look for a stable job that I like and that I want to get into so in terms of that yes I would be pressured.

The overriding emphasis in the above is on having a job, meaning there is an obvious tension with having 'something that I like', and it may well be that this is being overridden by the family income imperative to have a job, and also a reason for his need for a second job as outlined in Table 5.1. This is evident in the way Mikealae also described his feelings towards his new second job, which was in retail:

> ... I am happy that I've found a job and I'm not just doing nothing but it is like not what I want in terms of like retail I don't mind going into retail but there are some shops that I do mind working at and I don't mind working at but you can't you know beggars can't be chooser if you said it ...

This is also possible to observe in relation to Rod, who outlined how the money he had to contribute to the household had recently increased because his father had been made redundant. He described how not contributing had been an important factor in one of his brothers having to leave the family home:

> ...my older brother moved out because he wouldn't get a job, he didn't want to work and don't see him anymore...both of them, my parents said if you don't find a job cos you've got to start paying your way, you know what I mean, when you're an adult if you don't find a job you can't live rent free, nobody can, and then he moved out...he's living with somewhere else now.

5.4.3   Welfare agencies

For some participants, their negative experiences of job-searching also related to the welfare agencies charged with finding them work. Most of the participants had had negative experiences of both job placement schemes, such as the New Deal, and job centres. Criticism was divided into two main groups. On the one hand, participants were critical of the types of jobs that such schemes and centres provided, with Lance in particular stating that their main focus was to 'find me a job, any job, as long as I get a job, that's their job done'; and this was echoed by Mikealae, David and Rod. On the other hand, they were critical of the training provided by these schemes and centres, with Gemma particularly scathing on this point:

> ...like now they said 'we got a college thing for you' and then you'll get a job, pretty much sure I've got five weeks left on mine and they says 'you'll have a job before the end of the five weeks', and I says alright then. So I'm thinking ok, they're going to teach you how to do this this this and this and train you up a bit or something and they sat me at the computer for, what was it, nine til five I was sat at a computer looking for jobs...

Participants' experiences support the ongoing existence of Coffield et al.'s (1986) observation of 'shit jobs and govvy [government] schemes' for young adults, and more recently Furlong and Cartmel's (2004) claim that there is no evidence of skill gains through the New Deal, and were grounded in the fact that such training rarely if ever led to a meaningful job, as shown in Figure 5.1. This shows that for most participants, informal sources rather than formal sources are the main way in which they found jobs, through their networks of friends or family, and this was especially the case for current jobs. Indeed, with the exception of Larry, the usefulness of job centres to find employment was non-existent

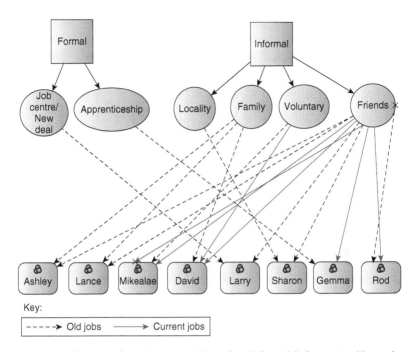

Figure 5.1 Sources of employment – Formal vs Informal Information Networks (designed with NVivo)

for participants, and other research has shown how on a rough count, friends, neighbours and family members account for over two-thirds of all jobs obtained by young people (MacDonald et al., 2005, p. 882).

5.5 The limits of individualised policies

The findings above emphasise that, regarding their work experience, participants showed specific examples of disrupted and fractured experiences in employment status over a short period of time. This suggests that, rather than unemployment, it was market insecurities and the lack of opportunities which were more relevant to participants. Income-wise, there was also evidence that the two prevailing policy assumptions of (a) increased dependence on family members for support and (b) financial independence through labour market were both subverted. There was a general lack of usage of formal welfare agencies, with greater reliance on informal sources, suggesting limited welfare dependency for labour market opportunities. Finally, there was also a general reliance on the locality for labour market opportunities, which reinforced the exclusionary nature of labour market experiences.

In particular, participants' generally fragmented and disrupted labour market experiences suggest that, as per Furlong and Cartmel (2004), while unemployment is an important contributory factor to their excluded status, just as pervasive are the labour market insecurities and the lack of opportunities for a decent quality job which they experience on a daily basis. So, despite the inclination to find work, a lack of availability of work in general was evident as contributing to the unemployment status of participants, suggesting that they were not necessarily less committed to the idea of work than other groupings (Crompton, 2006).

This palpable awareness of their own inability to effect changes in their own unemployment status led to a reliance on other agencies, such as job centres. However, evident from the data and, as argued by Smith (2005, p. 108), 'it is here where clients' lack of power becomes apparent and the façade of working in partnership is revealed'. This is because where participants challenged the obligation to undertake training and employment in tasks and fields they deemed irrelevant, and which proved to be irrelevant as they rarely led to a job, the outcome was sanctions which worked to further intensify their exclusion. Rather, the least troubling course of action was to accede, regardless of such agencies' apparent uselessness and also the frustration that they engendered.

In particular, this research suggests the weakness of seeing young people as actively drawing on their flexible and individualistic circumstances to create positive labour market biographical identities, as notions such as Arnett's (2006) theory of 'emerging adulthood' have claimed. This perspective wrongly attributes changing socio-economic factors to a psychological developmental phase, and neglects the impact of structural constraints in the labour market, particularly on the least well-off. A good example of this is in relation to their employment experiences, where as we saw, employment 'choices' were something that were rather stumbled upon, as a consequence of other more desired options closing off to participants. Echoing Colley:

> Such findings suggest that we need to be cautious in interpreting young people's positive perceptions of choice once they have entered particular career pathways. It may sometimes be a psychological protection they construct retrospectively, having experienced powerful structural constraints upon their choices at an earlier stage.
>
> (Colley, 2005, p. 4)

Concomitantly, the chance of achieving economic independence through work was not something which was really feasible at participants' wage rates. Two ways in which participants tried to overcome this was by working longer hours and/or having multiple jobs, as shown in Table 5.2. This signals a low-pay financial imperative which is indicative of multiple job-holding in the UK as a whole (Wu et al., 2009), especially for those in the early stages of their participation in the adult labour market (Dickey et al., 2011).

Within these different outcomes, however, was a prevailing depowering effect of such low income, wherein it limits both the economic and social opportunities and life chances possible to participants (Bartley, 2004), something of which they were evidently aware. Moreover, it can also serve to reinforce the familial bonds that young people have, as the increasing delay in achieving economic independence redoubles the importance of family relationships to young people's life chances and demonstrates how going from youth to adulthood is 'inextricably bound up' with the lives of others, particularly family members (Scott, 2005). This would seem to subvert prevailing middle-class notions of the 'bank of mom and dad' subsidising children well into adulthood (Knight, 2011), instead illustrating that disadvantaged young people have to make an important financial contribution to the household income, which acts to constrain the opportunities and choices reflected in recent youth policy. While this reliance was important in enabling young people to work, it was something which reinforced their disadvantaged status, as such local jobs were typically in low paid, insecure, temporary and informal employment. Of course, an obvious question to ask is if the opportunities provided by a neighbouring locality are so much better, then why do participants simply not move to such places? Green and White (2007) have highlighted 'bounded horizons' as important in constraining the labour market behaviour of young people, whereby a reluctance to travel outside their immediate locality plays an important restricting role in labour market entry and advancement. This suggests that it is participants' place attachment and aspirations per se which confine their labour market opportunities, and so posits personal agency as the principal factor. But rather, as we have seen above, there are important structural reasons constraining young people's labour market perspectives to their locality, not least of which is that it is here through informal sources that they find most of their jobs.

Thus, what separates those less advantaged from those more advantaged is not a deficit of aspirations, but the means to achieve them (Hey, 2005). This means that the prevailing emphasis on individual responsibility, vis-à-vis individualised/troublesome exclusion from the labour market, works to rationalise failure at the individual level, thereby obviating the fact that social and material constraints are all at work in the processes of choice (Ball et al., 2000). Such an outcome 'may be expected to have an even greater effect on psychological well-being, as individuals may be most likely to blame themselves for a lack of success' (Cassidy et al., 2006, p. 17). Consequently, it is perhaps not surprising that such 'reflexivity losers' (Hey, 2005) adopt strategies and tactics for survival (Thompson et al., 2003) such as drinking, drug-taking and crime, as symptoms of social exclusion, which lead to further, intensified, experiences of social exclusion. This simply reflects the gap between the extent of participants' formal rights and their material ability to exercise them, as there are often overwhelming educational, locality, income and family context constraints on participants' labour market circumstances, and these are more important than their 'reflexive individualisation'. Thus, the emphasis on individualised factors obviates the importance of structural inequality to social exclusion, and in so doing necessitates the adoption of strategies and tactics which lead to the reproduction rather than the transformation of social exclusion.

Notes

1. Connexions was set up by the government as a replacement service for The Careers Service. Its aims were to provide a 'universal and comprehensive' youth support service for those young people leaving compulsory schooling in the form of access to high-quality support and guidance, especially in relation to careers guidance. It worked mainly as a gatekeeper to access to other more specialist forms of support. See Smith (2007) for an outline and critique. The Coalition government in 2010 effectively abandoned Connexions as a universal policy and set up a new National Careers Service in 2012.
2. A scheme introduced to reduce unemployment for young people (18–24 years old) through training, subsidised employment or voluntary work. As an active labour market policy, it had the notion of conditionality at its heart, with young people unemployed for more than six months compelled to go on to the scheme and to take up one of the three options that the scheme provided, under treat of the loss of benefits.
3. This government document was the summary of responses to a consultation that had been undertaken in relation to youth and young people. It was the largest response ever made to a government call for consultation, and it set out the government's responses to the consultation.
4. This was a government scheme to encourage more young people to attain and remain in further education (16–18 years). It was means tested and provided financial incentives for those who had good attendance and also had good grades. In 2010 the Coalition government scrapped EMA in England, although it remains in Scotland, Wales and Northern Ireland.

References

Allard, C. (2005). 'Capitalizing on Bourdieu. How Useful Are Concepts of "Social Capital" and "Social Field" for Researching "Marginalized" Young Women?'. *Theory and Research in Education* 3 (1), 63–79.

Arnett, J. (2006). 'Emerging Adulthood in Europe: A Response to Bynner'. *Journal of Youth Studies* 9 (1), 111–23.

Ball, J., Maguire, M. and McCrae, S. (2000). *Choice, Pathways and Transitions Post-16: New Youth, New Economies in the Global City* (London: Routledge/Falmer).

Bartley, M. (2004). *Health Inequality: An Introduction to Theories Concepts and Methods* (Cambridge: Polity).

Bradford, S. (2005). 'Modernising Youth Work: From Universal to the Particular and Back Again', in Harrison, R. and Wise, C. (eds.) *Working with Young People* (London: Sage Publications), pp. 57–69.

Bullen, E., Kenway, J. and Hay, V. (2000). 'New Labour, Social Exclusion and Educational Risk Management: The case of "Gymslip Mums"'. *British Educational Research Journal* 4, 441–56.

Cassidy, C., O'Connor, R. and Dorrer, N. (2006). *Young People's Experiences of Transition to Adulthood a Study of Minority Ethnic and White Young People* (York: JRF).

Cieslik, M. and Pollock, G. (eds.) (2002). *Young People in Risk Society* (Aldershot: Ashgate).

Cobb-Clark, D.A. and Ribar, D.C. (2009). 'Financial Stress, Family Conflict, and Youths' Successful Transition to Adult Roles', *IZA Discussion Papers*, No. 4618, http:// hdl.handle.net/10419/35924.

Coffield, F., Borrill, C. and Marshall, S. (1986). *Growing Up at the Margins: Young Adults in the North East* (University of California: Open University Press).

Colley, H. (2005). *Do We Choose Careers or Do They Choose Us? Questions about Career Choices, Transitions, and Social Inclusion.* Available from: http://education.exeter.ac.uk/tlc/docs/publications/LE_HC_PUB_%20Vejleder%20Forum%20abstract.doc (accessed on 27 June 2013).

Cooper, C. (2012). 'Understanding the English "Riots" of 2011: "Mindless Criminality" or Youth "Mekin Histri" in Austerity Britain?' *Youth and Policy* 109, 6–26.

Crompton, R. (2006). *Employment and Family: The Reconfiguration of Work and Family Life in Contemporary Societies* (Cambridge: Cambridge University Press).

Crompton, R. (2010). 'Class and Employment'. *Work, Employment, Society* 24 (1), 9–26.

Dickey, H., Watson, V. and Zangelidis, A. (2011). 'Is It All about Money? An Examination of the Motives behind Moonlighting'. *Applied Economics* 43 (26), 3767–74.

France, A. and Wiles, P. (1997). 'Dangerous Futures: Social Exclusion and Youth Work in Late Modernity'. *Social Policy and Administration* 31 (5), 59–78.

Fudge, S. and Williams, S. (2006). 'Beyond Left and Right: Can the Third Way Deliver a Reinvigorated Social Democracy'. *Critical Sociology* 32 (4), 583–602.

Furlong, A. and Cartmel, F. (2004). *Vulnerable Young Men in Fragile Labour Markets. Employment, Unemployment and the Search for Long-term Security* (York: JRF).

Graham, H. and McDermott, E. (2006). 'Qualitative Research and the Evidence of Policy: Insights for the Studies of Teenage Mothers'. *Journal of Social Policy* 35 (1), 21–37.

Green, A. and White, R. (2007). *Attachment to Place. Social Networks, Mobility and the Prospects of Young People* (York: JRF).

Hansard (2011). House of Commons Debates. Vol. 531, col. 1051. (11 August).

Hedidge, D. (1979). *Subculture: The Meaning of Style* (New York: Methuen).

Hey, V. (2005). 'The Contrasting Social Logics of Sociality and Survival: Cultures of Classed Be/Longing in Late Modernity'. *Sociology* 39 (5), 855–872.

Jones, G. (2002). *The Youth Divide – Diverging Paths in Adulthood* (York: JRF).

Jordan, B. (1996). *A Theory of Poverty and Social Exclusion* (Oxford: Polity Press).

Kim, U., Trandis, H., Kağitçibaşi, C., Choi, C. and Yoon, G. (1994). 'Introduction', in U. Kim, H. Trandis, C. Kağitçibaşi, S. Choi and G. Yoon (eds.) *Individualism and Collectivism* (Thousand Oaks, CA: Sage), pp. 1–18.

Knight, J. (2011). 'The Danger of Driving the Bank of Mom and Dad and the Building Society of Gran and Granddad to the Wall'. *The Independent* 10 April 2011.

Levitas, R. (2005). *The Inclusive Society? Social Exclusion and New Labour*, 2nd ed. (Basingstoke: Palgrave Macmillan).

Lindsay, C., McQuaid, R. and Dutton, M. (2007). 'New Approaches to Employability in the UK: Combining "Human Capital Development" and "Work First" Strategies?' *Journal of Social Policy* 36 (4), 539–60.

MacDonald, R. (2000). 'Youth, Social Exclusion and the Millennium', in Macdonald, R. (ed.) *Youth, the 'Underclass' and Social Exclusion* (London: Routledge), pp. 167–97.

Macdonald, R., Shildrick, T., Webster, C. and Simpson, D. (2005). 'Growing Up in Poor Neighborhoods: The Significance of Class and Place in the Extended Transitions of "Socially Excluded" Young Adults'. *Sociology* 39 (5), 873–91.

Maginn, P.J. (2007). 'Towards More Effective Community Participation in Urban Regeneration: The Potential of Collaborative Planning and Applied Ethnography'. *Qualitative Research* 7 (1), 25–43.

McDowell, L. (2001). ' "It's that Linda Again": Ethical, Practical and Political Issues Involved in Longitudinal Research with Young Men'. *Ethics, Place and Environment* 4 (2), 87–100.

Ministry of Justice (2012). 'Statistical Bulletin on the Public Disorder of 6th to 9th August 2011–February 2012 Update', Available from: http://www.justice.gov.uk/downloads/statistics/criminal-justice-stats/august-public-disorder-stats-bulletin-230212.pdf (accessed on 27 June 2013).

ONS (2008a). 'Annual Survey of Hours and Earnings, Table 2.5a', Available from: http://www.statistics.gov.uk/downloads/theme_labour/ASHE_2008/tab2_5a.xls (accessed on 27 June 2013).

ONS (2008b). 'Annual Survey of Hours and Earnings, Table 4.5a', Available from: http://www.statistics.gov.uk/downloads/theme_labour/ASHE_2008/tab4_5a.xls (accessed on 27 June 2013).

Rogers, S. (2012). 'Public vs Private Sector Pay: Who Earns More?'. *The Guardian* [Online] Available from: http://www.theguardian.com/news/datablog/2012/mar/27/public-private-sector-pay#start-of-comments (accessed on 27 June 2013).

Scott, J. (2005). 'Teenagers at Risk: A Prospective Study of How Some Youth Beat the Odds to Overcome Family Disadvantage', Available from: http://www.esrc.ac.uk/my-esrc/grants/L134251027/outputs/Read/394959ee-f705-4c19-8bd3-4e3ab636e932 (accessed on 27 June 2013).

Shildrick, T., MacDonald, R., Webster, C. and Garthwaite, K. (2012). *Poverty and Insecurity: Life in Low-pay, No-pay Britain* (Bristol: Policy Press).

Smith, J. (2005). 'Risk, Social Change and Strategies of Inclusion for Young Homeless', in Barry, M. (ed.) *Youth Policy and Social Inclusion* (Abingdon: Routledge), pp. 161–82.

Smith, M.K. (2007). 'The Connexions Service in England, the Encyclopaedia of Informal Education', Available from: www.infed.org/personaladvisers/connexions.htm. Last update: 10 October 2013 (accessed on 13 February 2014).

Smith, N. (2010). 'Economic Inequality and Poverty: Where Do We go from Here?' *International Journal of Sociology and Social Policy* 30 (3/4), 127–39.

Spence, J. (2005). 'Concepts of Youth', in Harrison, R. and Wise, C. (eds.) *Working with Young People* (London: Sage Publications), pp. 46–56.

Spence, J. and Wood, J. (2011). 'Youth Work and Research: Editorial'. *Youth and Policy*, 107, 1–17.

St Croix, T. (2012). 'If Someone Is Not a Success in Life It's Their Own Fault' What Coalition Youth Policy Says about Young People and Youth Workers', Available from: http://www.indefenceofyouthwork.org.uk/wordpress/?p=2561 (accessed on 27 June 2013).

Thompson, R., Henderson, S. and Holland, J. (2003). 'Making the Most of What You've Got? Resources, Values and Inequalities in Young Women's Transitions to Adulthood'. *Educational Review* 55 (1), 33–46.

Welshman, J. (2004). 'The Unknown Titmuss'. *Journal of Social Policy* 33 (2), 225–47.

Wu, Z., Baimbridge, M. and Zhu, Y. (2009). 'Multiple Job Holding in the United Kingdom: Evidence from the British Household Panel Survey'. *Applied Economics* 41 (21), 2751–66.

Zimmerman, D. and Wieder, L. (1977). 'The Diary: Diary-Interview Method'. *Urban Life (now Journal of Contemporary Ethnography)* 5 (4), 479–97.

6
Young People at Work in Greece before and after the Crisis

Lefteris Kretsos

6.1 Introduction

The unfortunate pioneering role of Greece in the course of the current economic crisis has made the country an international point of reference and analysis. Shock economic therapies implemented after May 2010, when Greece became the recipient of a financial bailout package, had serious social consequences (Kretsos, 2012a). Financial support from the Troika[1] and especially the IMF has been conditional on reductions in public deficits and public spending, thus initiating drastic labour market reform and welfare state retrenchment that is unprecedented in the post-war period (Hall, 2011; Meardi, 2012). Young workers are, among other social groups, heavily affected by the current crisis and the policies that were gradually implemented in Europe after 2008 (European Commission, 2013).

This development reinforced pre-existing labour market inequalities at the expense of youth, especially in Greece where unemployment amongst young workers has hit almost 65 per cent (data for August 2013). To some extent this development has emerged as a consequence of the way that the labour market and employers have responded to these economic difficulties (Kretsos, 2012b; Simms, 2011).

Young people, defined for the purpose of this chapter as people between the ages of 16 and 30, traditionally face more difficulties than older workers in entering the labour market and in finding stable and well-paid jobs.[2] Precarious employment is defined as employment characterised by the absence of security elements associated with the typical full-time, permanent employment that was considered as a major historical achievement of trade unions in the post-war period. Precarious employment is also closely associated with similar concepts such as 'insecure work' (Heery and Salmon, 2000) and 'vulnerability at work' (Pollert and Charlwood, 2008). According to McKay et al. (2012) individuals in precarious work are more likely to be excluded from social rights, such as to decent housing, medical care, pensions and education, while exclusion from these social rights pushes individuals into precarious work. In general, precarious work is characterised by lack of decent wages and loss of stability: in work; in pay; in professional paths; in friends and family ties; and in the protection of social and political rights. Precarious work becomes endemic in an economic context, such as that of Greece, characterised by pressing demands for more flexibility and scarcity of resources available to support the management, regulation and protection of decent individual and collective work biographies.

The aim of this chapter is first to explore the strong roots of young precarious employment in Greece. It is argued that the social and employment disadvantage of youth should be conceptualised not only as a consequence of the current crisis, despite the dramatic rise of youth unemployment and youth precarious employment rates after 2008, but also as part of the historical interplay between social, cultural and economic forces with opposing interests regarding the future regulatory outcomes. This interplay of social and economic forces in Greece involves not only a set of different social actors, such as militant employer groups, right-wing think tanks, the media, successive governments and organised labour, but also other structural factors in the Greek economic and employment system. Such factors include the informal economy and the familistic style of the provision of welfare (Karamessini, 2008). However, this interplay of the above forces and structural factors has been put under strain by the current crisis, deepening further the social and economic inequalities at the expense of younger workers, and especially those young workers with non-standard contracts.

In order to address these issues the remainder of this chapter is organised into three further sections. Section two summarises the explanations that have been advanced in the international literature regarding the phenomenon of precarious employment among young workers and the difficulties in drawing international comparisons. Section three discusses the labour market deregulation dynamics in Greece with an emphasis on young workers. The underlying argument is that the labour market situation for young people has worsened in the last three decades. Section four examines the repercussions of the crisis for the labour market position of the young workforce. It is argued that the crisis has acted as a catalyst for significant changes in the economy and the nature of work that make young people more insecure, precarious and likely to end up worse off than their parents. Section five provides conclusions.

6.2   Comparing and defining national examples of precarious youth employment

A growing literature has been developed on how and why job insecurity and low pay have spread during the last 20 years, affecting a widening spectrum of young workers including young skilled professional workers. Work insecurity is promoted by the expansion of flexible forms of employment and the deregulation of industrial relations, such as part-time and temporary employment, involuntary in the majority of cases, pseudo self-employment contracts, subsidised job placements, undeclared work, low earnings for the current level of living, employment in sectors and organisations with high probabilities of bankruptcy or high levels of dismissals, and insufficient coverage if someone is unemployed.

For example, examining the case of the US labour market, Sweet and Meiskins (2008) have noted that the spread of job insecurity has occurred because of the decline of older, more secure types of work, the changing strategies for organising work and the changing composition of the labour force. Other scholars suggest that the spread of work insecurity is the result of employer strategies to restore low profit rates after the oil crisis of the 1970s. This formula was primarily about the reduction of employees' real wages through several strategies, including direct cuts of wages (and benefits), the shift towards 'contingent' jobs (such as part-time jobs, temporary jobs and so on), and 'two tier' wage systems (in which new employees are hired at much lower starting wages compared with existing employees) (Brenner, 1998; Callinicos, 2003; Dumenil and Levy, 2002; Moseley, 1999; Shaikh, 1999). In a similar vein, Kretsos (2010) has argued that young workers and new entrants in the labour market are among the social groups most affected by this income inequality and wage squeezing process.

The restructuring of employment relations and the decrease in real wages have created, among other things, a deep generational gap in the allocation of income and the allocation of secure jobs in the economy. In all European countries young people appear to have a higher inclination than the rest of the population towards such types of contingent or precarious employment (Biletta and Eisner, 2007). Common traits and also national paths to the labour market marginalisation of young people are observed. Such paths, trends and paradigms of young workers' precarity are hard to compare, as the characteristics that determine insecure employment vary between countries, age groups and/or sectors of economic activity, making difficult a specific definition that takes into account all the different aspects of youth precarious employment.

There is much ambiguity regarding the definition of work and pay disadvantage that may be observed in European youth labour markets (Kretsos and Livanos, 2012). Indicative of this is that there is still no universally accepted definition. Almost all monographs and comparative research analysis on precarious employment highlight the dominance of debates that usually reflect various issues of national interest (Anderson and Rogaly, 2005; Barbier et al., 2002; Broughton et al., 2010; Fudge and Owens, 2006; Kretsos, 2011; McKay et al., 2012; Polavieja, 2005).

Nevertheless, the concept of precarious (youth) employment is wider and more dynamic than other relevant concepts (for example, insecure work, contingent employment, flexible and non-standard work), as it captures changes that are taking place in employment systems and work organisation. In particular, precarious employment is understood here as a functional conceptual device that describes, better than any other relevant term, the global transformations at work and modern youth labour market inequalities (Vosko et al., 2009). In this context, the present study aims to explore the historical roots of precarious youth employment in Greece by examining first the period 1980–2007 and second the period after 2008, when the upsurge of the economic crisis made the situation tougher for many young workers.

6.3 Precarious youth employment in Greece before the crisis (1980–2007)

The employment disadvantage of youth in Greece both in terms of having higher unemployment rates than other working groups and in terms of greater levels of precarious employment is not new. As Biletta and Eisner (2007) have suggested, youth unemployment in Greece does not warrant priority attention among political parties. Nevertheless, the situation is somewhat more complex, as approaches to integration in labour markets, social transfers and public policy have a direct effect on young people's transition to adult life and their interaction with their surroundings (Morena Mingez et al., 2012). According to Blanchard and Portugal (2001), the unemployment rate may reflect or hide realities that are utterly dissimilar in different labour markets. This is partly related to young people's access to material and immaterial resources from the family, civil society and the welfare state.

Southern European countries including Greece are characterised by familism in the provision and distribution of welfare (Esping-Andersen, 1990; Karamessini, 2008; Kretsos, 2011a; Saraceno, 1994). Having family as the main cornerstone of social solidarity results in safeguarding the earnings and career stability of the male breadwinners. Otherwise social cohesion is put at risk, intergenerational solidarity links are broken and young workers are left on their own in an ocean of insecurity and poverty, as either state support or decent job opportunities are limited in the southern European context (Guillén and Matsaganis, 2000).

According to Ferrera (1996), in Greece and the other Mediterranean countries, as well as possessing this social cohesive role the family plays a significant part both in the welfare state and in the labour market. Increased housing and product prices and the deterioration of prospective employment for new labour market entrants have made the role of family more significant for the provision of social protection during the last few decades. For example, for Neugart (2008) there is a politico-economic equilibrium with relatively high employment protection (through legislation) and relatively low unemployment benefits in countries with strong family ties, including Greece.

Not surprisingly, young workers used to cope with and address risks and economic stressors, such as low pay, job insecurity, job loss and underemployment, by mobilising their own family and social networks. Typical examples include the cases of unemployed university graduates who were supported by their families, the creation of many small family businesses funded by members of the family, relatives or friends, and the support in finding a job through informal personal and family networks.

In a similar vein, Sabbatini (2008) commented on Italy that 'it's not what you know, but who you know'. This common aphorism summarised much of the conventional wisdom regarding social capital and came from a widespread sense that close competition for jobs and contracts generally requires the 'right contacts' in the 'right places'. As relevant studies have indicated, social networks and family support are considered to be more significant in alleviating the sorrow of unemployment or the pain caused by low pay and work insecurity that graduates feel in southern Europe (Gentile, 2011). Besides, almost 50 per cent of young adults (18–33) live with their parents in Greece, Italy, Portugal and Spain, while the proportion of their counterparts in United Kingdom, Germany and Scandinavian countries is less than 30 per cent (Giuliano, 2007).

Nevertheless, the squeezing of family income thanks to austerity policies and the effects of economic recession has made the previous model of intergenerational solidarity unsustainable and fragile. Demonstrations and violent confrontations between police and (mainly) young people across those countries have become endemic since 2010, and partly reflect the agony of the younger generation as they try to avoid social exclusion and poverty risks.[3] Among others, the Indignados/Αγανακτισμένοι (Outraged) movement in Spain and Greece, which occupied Puerta del Sol in Madrid and Syntagma Square in Athens, demanded real and direct democracy and have been considered as among the most successful workers' mobilisations since the restoration of democracy in 1975.

The failure of family networks and labour market institutions to provide decent job opportunities for the majority of young people was evident in many relevant studies and surveys even before Lehman Brothers' collapse. For example, according to the outcomes of Euro-Barometer and European Working Conditions surveys, Greek young people were the least optimistic about their future and enjoyed the lowest levels of job satisfaction across Europe. In a similar vein, there were signs of a higher preference for left-wing parties among young people in the national elections of 2008 (especially young people living in urban areas).

In any case, the economic crisis in 2010 found Greek youth already detached from mainstream political parties and social institutions. For example, according to an earlier study by Pascual and Waddington (2000), in Greece 70.1 per cent of young people expressed no trust in mainstream trade unions, compared with only 22.9 per cent who did not trust the army and 40.6 per cent who did not trust the judiciary system. This discontent, anger and mistrust was definitely related to the precarious position of young people in the Greek labour market. In 2008, almost one year before the outbreak of the current crisis and the implementation of sweeping austerity measures, the youth unemployment level was double the national average. Further, young workers represented 40 per cent and 27 per cent of temporary and part-time employees respectively, while young people were represented on a much higher level in the lowest wage deciles (net monthly income up to €750) and on a much lower one in the most well paid (net monthly income more than €1,000) (Κριτικίδης, 2008). In addition, according to data from the OECD, flexible and contingent forms of employment among young workers have risen dramatically over the years despite their involuntary character, while their percentage was lower among older employees (Kretsos, 2010) (Tables 6.1 to 6.5).[4]

Table 6.1 Demographic characteristics of young people (15–29 years old), 1980–2007

	Population		Labour force		Employment		Unemployment	
	Share in 2007 (%)	% change (1980–2007)	Share in 2007 (%)	% change (1980–2007)	Share in 2007 (%)	% change (1980–2007)	Share in 2007 (%)	% change (1980–2007)
EU15	27.31	–22.49	22.83	–29.81	21.64	–24.54	38.58	–36.33
Greece	27.30	–11.84	21.06	–17.45	19.02	–16.14	27.30	–11.84

Source: Eurostat.

Table 6.2 Part-time employment for selected age groups, 1987–2007

	EU15		Greece	
	Share in 2007 (%)	**% change (1987–2007)**	**Share in 2007 (%)**	**% change (1987–2007)**
Total	18.14	39.25	7.82	19.87
15–19	42.79	149.07	15.79	110.72
20–24	19.97	137.49	10.31	42.80
25–29	13.38	38.60	7.32	−2.67
30–34	14.16	14.91	6.73	−7.52

Source: Eurostat.

Table 6.3 Percentage of involuntary part-time employment by age group (2007)

	EU15	Greece
Total	21.0	42.8
15–24	23.6	44.7
15–39	23.9	51.5

Source: Eurostat.

Table 6.4 Temporary employment for selected age groups

	EU15		Greece	
	Share in 2007 (%)	**% change (1987–2007)**	**Share in 2007 (%)**	**% change (1987–2007)**
Total	14.80	28.70	10.90	−34.34
15–24	42.80	32.51	27.00	−10.89
15–39	22.00	37.50	14.20	−19.77

Source: Eurostat.

Table 6.5 Percentage of involuntary temporary employment by age group (2007)

	EU15	Greece
Total	57.4	82.5
15–24	33.6	62.9
15–39	52.3	79.1

Source: Eurostat.

Further, false or pseudo self-employment (or dependent self-employment; that is, employment usually characterised as a 'grey zone' between dependent and independent employment, as far as social security, dismissal and other employment rules are concerned) was quite significant and widespread. The respective figure of false self-employment for the age groups aged 16–34 was as high as 16 per cent in 2007 (GSEE, 2008).

Finally, an important aspect of young people's vulnerability at work was related to their earnings, as income level has a tremendous impact on the security that people gain from their job. Looking at relevant data from the Structure of Earnings Survey (SES), significant differences between the average earnings for all employees compared with those of young workers (aged 15–29) are to be found. In general the risk of youth poverty in the countries of southern Europe, including Greece, becomes more serious owing to underdeveloped labour market policies, the low level of social transfers and pronounced labour market segmentations.

For example, monthly earnings in those countries vary between 50 and 86 per cent of the EU15 average. At the same time the respective figures for the monthly earnings of young employees are much lower and vary between 39 and 66 per cent for young employees. In essence, young workers in Greece not only received lower wages than their EU15 counterparts, but they also had dramatic differences from the rest of the population of their country.

To summarise, precarity among young people was a trademark of the Greek labour market, and despite various experimentations in social and economic policy and the existence of informal social and family networks of support, it has not been eradicated even during periods of economic growth in the last few decades.[5] As discussed next, this difficult situation was exacerbated after the economic crisis in 2008, and the implementation of austerity policies that drastically reduced family incomes and decreased the available job opportunities especially for young people.

6.4   Precarious youth employment in Greece with the outbreak of the crisis (2008–12)

Long before the outbreak of the crisis many European countries implemented neo-liberal youth employment policies mainly oriented towards the flexibilisation of the youth labour markets. This development was consistent with what Greer and Doellgast (2013) consider as marketisation. Marketisation includes a wide range of phenomena, such as outsourcing, privatisation, active labour market policies and the international integration of markets for goods, services, capital and labour, that leads to increasing economic and social inequality. Marketisation forces resulted in, among other things, relaxation of employment protection legislation, a reduction in the benefit period for young people, implementation of means-tested social benefits and the introduction of welfare-to-work programmes. In addition to institutional and policy failures to deal with high unemployment and precarious employment levels, young people have been punished severely by the current economic crisis. For example, it was stressed in a relevant report prepared by the International Labour Organisation (ILO) (Global Employment Trends for Youth, 2010) and the 2010 Joint ILO-IMF Conference that the crisis and consequent mass unemployment have seriously affected the youth population. In a similar vein, the European Commission (2013) has argued that young people are the biggest victims of the current economic crisis, especially those aged 18–24.

Not surprisingly, the scale of youth worklessness is leading to concerns that a 'lost generation' is being generated. Evidence from many countries across Europe suggests that this younger generation will be the first to experience a decline in living standards compared with that of their parents.[6] Similar media narratives are to be found in Greece, especially after 2010 owing to its unfortunate pioneering role in the current crisis. In essence, Greece has become practically a byword for 'structural adjustment' across Europe, and numerous studies have indicated that debt resolution mechanisms and policies promoted by successive Greek governments since 2010 and the Troika have seriously tested the state's commitment to raising human rights standards and stamping out abuses wherever they occur. It could be held as an example of a market leaning towards a more individualised approach to labour market regulation.

The country is stepping back from human rights, and this was reflected in the latest report of the ILO committee of experts regarding the application of ILO conventions (ILO, 2013), as well as the Athens visit report of United Nations experts on foreign debt and human rights.[7] Under the threat of national economic collapse (as well as the specific control rules of the Troika on bailing out Greece twice since 2010), the emphasis of policy and collective bargaining has been on drastically reducing public spending, dismantling labour law and social security systems, and saddling people with insecure jobs.

In this framework, the main youth employment policy initiatives taken by Greek governments as a response to the crisis have resulted in significant wage cuts and the introduction of lower minimum income scales. Indicative of the primary orientations of public policy towards youth was the termination of work-placement contracts of about 50,000 young workers (stagiaires) in the public sector in October 2009 (Clark, 2012). Young precarious workers were also affected by the easing of employers' dismissals requirements: compensation payments have been reduced and justifications required by employers when making redundancies have been relaxed. According to a recent study by Koutentakis (2012), the reduction in the cost of firing resulted in a rapid unemployment rise.

The ILO report (2011), which was published before the conclusion of the second loan agreement, stated with respect to the minimum wage levels for young people:

> Based on statistical information provided by the Hellenic Statistical Authority (EL.STAT) and EUROSTAT, the poverty level in Greece was at €6,000–7,000 per year. On this basis, it was considered that a young person could cover basic needs with a subminimum wage of €584. This amount also corresponded to what was paid in terms of unemployment benefits.

Contrast this with the minimum wage levels for young persons that were set in the light of the second loan agreement, under which young persons receive €510.95.

Such policy and collective bargaining measures have resulted in transferring the burden of the economic crisis onto workers, and especially onto young people, through the widespread use of cheaper, more atypical and temporary contracts, leading to the gradual expansion of a new underclass of low-paid, precarious and more insecure youth. Labour market deregulation became very evident with the report issued by the Labour Inspectorate (SEPE).[8] According to SEPE, during the first four months of 2012 almost 46 per cent of new contracts in the private sector were for flexible forms of work, such as part-time work and work rotation.[9] Compared with the first four months of 2011, the conversion of full-time employment contracts to flexible forms of employment increased by 47 per cent, with 4,909 employment contracts switching to part-time employment. About 7 per cent (513 cases) of work contracts changed to work rotation schemes with the agreement of the employee, whilst 69 per cent (3,328) were imposed unilaterally by the employer (Stamati, 2012). Dedousopoulos (2013) has also argued that there is a rapid and noticeable reduction in the share of full-time jobs (see Table 6.6).

Further, most of those losing their employment during the crisis have been young people under 29 years of age. For example, seven out of ten workers who lost their jobs between 2009 and 2010 were young men (Κρητικίδης, 2010), while four out of ten workers who lost their jobs two years later were young people aged up to 29 (Stamati, 2012). In absolute terms, 333,733 young people aged 15–29 lost their jobs in 2012.[10] Further, six out of ten young workers who lost their job were young male workers (Stamati, 2012). After almost six years of stark economic recession, unemployment and youth unemployment respectively reached 26.8 per cent and 56.6 per cent (of which female youth unemployment is 62.1 per cent) (see Table 6.7).

Table 6.6 Employment changes in Greece, 2009–12

	New contracts	Full-time jobs	Part-time jobs	Job rotation
2009	945,138	746,911	157,738	40,489
2010	875,952	586,281	228,994	60,677
2011	762,544	460,706	233,538	68,300
2012	683,443	375,843	241,985	65,615
Composition of new contracts				
2009	100	79.0	16.7	4.3
2010	100	66.9	26.1	6.9
2011	100	60.4	30.6	9.0
2012	100	55.0	35.4	9.6

Source: LIB, press release 12 March 2013, Tables I, IV and V.

Table 6.7 Unemployment rate by age group, 2007–12

Age group	2007	2008	2009	2010	2011	2012
15–24	22.9	22.1	28.5	34.7	46.7	56.6
25–34	11.6	10.6	13.0	18.9	27.0	34.1
35–44	6.3	6.1	8.3	11.6	15.9	23.3
45–54	4.5	4.5	6.9	9.3	14.1	19.5
55–64	3.1	3.1	4.9	6.8	9.0	15.4
65–74	1.4	0.8	1.0	1.9	3.6	4.9
Total	8.1	7.5	10.0	13.8	19.7	26.8

Source: ELSTAT, Labour Force Survey (LFS).

Nevertheless, the main policy response to the crisis by successive governments since 2009 was the enactment of a special employment regime for young people. This regime is characterised by significant cuts to unemployment benefits by about 25 per cent, even for seasonal workers, and lower wages for young workers.[11] The Greek Trade Unions Congress (GSEE) criticised the government for this initiative and made a formal complaint to the ILO, as deregulation of the existing minimum protective legislative framework, in conjunction with the absence of adequate guarantees and deficient inspection mechanisms, might 'lead to multiple harmful side effects for young workers' especially in the absence of active labour market policies (see the ILO report (ILO, 2011, p. 334)).

The state's Manpower Employment Organization (OAED) recently announced a new scheme for the 'acquisition of work experience'. According to this policy initiative, OAED grants a subsidy corresponding to 100 per cent of the employers' and employees' social security contributions, whereas employers pay a wage corresponding to 80 per cent of the minimum monthly wage or day wage. The work experience programme aims to provide employment for 10,000 16–24-year-old unemployed persons. Nevertheless, the scheme is problematic, as it is addressed only to private sector enterprises. It also has a specified duration (6–12 months), and only those aged 16–24 are eligible to join.[12]

The data on income and living conditions provided by the Statistical Service (EΛΣΤΑΤ) indicate that the population groups that are most vulnerable and exposed to poverty risk are the youngest (aged below 17, 23 per cent) and the oldest (aged over 65, 22 per cent). Nevertheless, unemployed people have the highest risk of poverty among the population (37 per cent). In this context of rising youth unemployment many young and talented people have been forced to emigrate. In a relevant study, Labrianidis (2013) found that since 2010 almost 150,000 young educated people have left the country. It is a concern that this figure represents almost 10 per cent of the workforce with high skills and scientific capabilities.[13] In 2012, emigration, primarily by well-educated young people, increased by 78 per cent, and according to estimates more than 3,000 medical doctors have already emigrated to Germany alone since 2009. Greece is not an attractive place for many young people who want to establish a lifetime project and find a decent job.

In February 2012 the minimum wage (calculated at Purchasing Power Standards), for people younger than 25, became, for the first time, higher in a new EU member (Poland) than in an old EU member (Greece), when Poland increased the monthly minimum wage by 8.2 per cent to 1,500 zlotys (€357), while in Greece the respective wage was reduced by 20 per cent to €586, and by 32 per cent for people under the age of 25, to €510 per month.[14]

The problematic position of young workers in the labour market has serious social consequences, such as a delay in gaining economic independence, the late formation of families and a strong fall in fertility rates, with crucial consequences for both society and the sustainability of the welfare state. To summarise, as we saw in the previous part of the chapter, the issue of precarious employment among young workers in Greece has strong roots and is a structural problem. However, the economic crisis has significantly aggravated the situation of all workforce groups, and especially young people.[15] There are two mechanisms through which the policies put forward after the economic crisis lead to changes in young people's employment prospects: the first is a rise in the unemployment rate; the second is increased rates of precarious employment. Both mechanisms result in making young labour undervalued, cheaper and more dispensable to employers. At the same time eliminating the welfare state and social protection standards results in further weakening of the capability of young workers to cope with the economic stressors of job insecurity, low pay, unemployment and underemployment.

6.5   Discussion

Young workers in Greece cannot be considered as temporarily labour market 'outsiders' because of the recent crisis that has hit the country. The majority of young people have been trapped in persistent unemployment or low-paid, contingent jobs located at the periphery of the labour market for many years, as even in previous times of significant economic growth, both the youth unemployment ratio and other employment indicators have been systematically unfavourable compared with those of the general population, and even more so compared with other European countries. This negative development has been the case since the early 1980s, even if the crisis has acted as a catalyst for further diminishing the working and living conditions of young people. Work precariousness and high unemployment among young people still remain the trademark of the Greek labour market, posing serious risks in young people's lives and in the emancipation process.

The ongoing crisis and the strategic choices made by the Greek government and the Troika further feeds the beast of high and persistent youth unemployment and precarious employment. The available statistical data are alarming, even if official statistics use limited tools to define precarious employment and have very elastic definitions of unemployment. Young people in Greece are exposed to uncertainty at unprecedented levels, as the institutional settings and the family and social structures that used to provide safety from the risk of unemployment and other stressors have severely weakened owing to drastic labour market and welfare state reforms. In essence, the Draconian austerity measures that have been implemented make previous models of intergenerational solidarity unsustainable, because they reduce young people's access to economic resources (squeezed family income, fewer job opportunities) and social transfers (welfare state decline).

The Greek case indicates that austerity policies do not work for young people. It further tells us that historical legacies and traditions still matter in the way that common problems across European societies, such as youth unemployment and precarious employment, are defined and perceived. Finally, it shows us that forced deregulation and structural reforms have their limits and risks. During the last three years and in the midst of the economic crisis young workers in Greece have been engaged in hard fights for the protection of workers' rights from the consecutive waves of lay-offs and salary cuts, and even for the very right of organising. Part of that struggle was driven by radical unions and strong networks of rank-and-file activists, many of them young. Those networks left their mark in all forms of resistance to austerity and labour market deregulation policies, and in certain cases they acted as a catalyst for the organising and mobilisation of broader groups of the workforce. Young people frustrated by austerity have expanded social unrest and public anger at the mainstream political institutions. The numerous protests that have taken place since 2010, the impressive actions of the Greek Indignados Occupy Movement in 2011 and the meteoric rise of SYRIZA (radical left party) in the general elections of 2012 are simply parts of an ongoing youth revolt and resistance to neo-liberalism that may bring about or inspire more radical political and institutional changes in the near future.

Notes

1. Troika is the acronym for the financial lenders of European troubled economies in the European Union 15. Troika is composed of the European Commission (EC) on behalf of the European Union, the European Central Bank (ECB) and the International Monetary Fund (IMF).
2. Despite young people having higher, in comparison to older employees, levels of educational attainment. As the second edition of the Employment and Social Developments in Europe (ESDE) Review (European Commission,

2013) accepts, '[T]he young tend to be more often overqualified than other age groups...The over-qualification of the young in the Mediterranean countries, known for their labour market segmentation and high unemployment rates, has risen much more sharply than in other countries in the last decade.'

3. See, for example, the analysis by Mason (2012).
4. With the exception of the rate of temporary employment that was no higher than those observed in other EU countries and the EU15 average level. Nevertheless, involuntary temporary employment is much greater than the average level of EU15, indicating a stronger desire of young people in Greece for permanent employment than in other countries. This development may in turn be related to the lower, in relation to international comparisons, levels of unemployment benefits across the OECD area (Kretsos, 2011a).
5. It is worth mentioning that in 1994–2008 Greece had the highest (after Ireland) rates of economic growth across the EU. See the analysis in Ioakimoglou and Milios (2005) and Ioakimoglou (2011).
6. See, for example, the studies by Standing (2011) and Ainley and Allen (2010) that explore the dynamics and mechanisms of this trend.
7. See http://www.ohchr.org/RU/NewsEvents/Pages/DisplayNews.aspx?NewsID= 13281&LangID=E.
8. See also the analysis in the study on Precarious Work and Social Rights coordinated by Sonia McKay et al. (2012).
9. See Lampousaki (2011) and http://www.tovima.gr/finance/article/?aid= 462019. See also http://tvxs.gr/news/ellada/sepe-kakos-ergodotis-sxedon-1-stoys-3.
10. In percentage terms this corresponds to a 39.2 per cent reduction in the youth employment level. See the analysis by Stamati (2012).
11. The law provides for a reduction of the minimum wage paid to workers aged under 25 to 84 per cent of the minimum wage and to minors aged 15–18 to 70 per cent of the minimum wage.
12. In January 2013 the government announced a national action plan to combat youth unemployment and to promote youth entrepreneurship. The new plan aims to benefit 350,000 young people aged 15–24 and 25–35 with a total budget of €600 million. The plan has not managed to reduce unemployment rate rises at the time of writing.
13. Budget cuts have created a hostile environment to research and development in the country's universities. See, for example, http://www.tovima.gr/science/research/article/?aid=508842 (accessed 20 April 2013).
14. According to Meardi (2012) the Polish minimum wage in 2012 has also overtaken the Portuguese one.
15. Further, almost all economic forecasts indicate a further rise of youth unemployment.

References

Λαμπριανίδης Λ. Επενδύοντας στη φυγή: Η διαρροή επιστημόνων από την Ελλάδα την εποχή της παγκοσμιοποίησης. Κριτική: Αθήνα. 2011.

Ainley, P. and Allen, M. (2010). *Lost Generation? New Strategies for Youth and Education* (London: Continuum).

Anderson, B. and Rogaly, B. (2005). *Forced Labour and Migration to the UK* (London: Trades Union Congress).

Barbier, Jean-Claude (2013). 'A Conceptual Approach of the Destandardization of Employment in Europe since the 1970s'. in Koch, M. and Fritz, M. (eds.) *Non-Standard Employment in Europe: Paradigms, Prevalence and Policy Responses* (Basingstoke: Palgrave Macmillan), pp. 13–29.

Biletta, I. and Eisner, M. (2007). *Youth and Work* (Dublin: European Foundation for the Improvement of Living and Working Conditions).

Blanchard, O. and Portugal, P. (2001). 'What Hides Behind an Unemployment Rate: Comparing Portuguese and U.S. Labor Markets'. *The American Economic Review* 91(1), 187–207.

Brenner, R. (1998). 'The Economics of Global Turbulence'. *New Left Review* 229, 1–264.

Broughton, A., Biletta, I. and Kullander, M. (2010). *Flexible Forms of Work: 'Very Atypical' Contractual Arrangements* (Dublin: European Foundation for the Improvement of Living and Working Conditions).

Callinicos, A. (2003). 'Feature Review: The Boom and the Bubble: The US in the World Economy, Robert Brenner'. *New Political Economy* 8 (3), 419–25.

Clark, N. (2012). *Training, Jobs and Decent Work for Young People* (Brussels: European Public Service Unions).

Dedousopoulos, A. (2013). 'Promoting a Balanced and Inclusive Recovery from the Crisis in Europe through Sound Industrial Relations and Social Dialogue: The Case of Greece'. ILO High-Level conference on 'Tackling the jobs crisis in Greece: which ways forward?', 25 June, Athens.

Dumenil, G. and Levy, D. (2002). 'The Profit Rate: Where and How Much Did It Fall? Did It Recover? (USA 1948–2000)'. *Review of Radical Political Economics* 34 (4), 437–61.

Esping-Andersen, G. (1990). *The Three Worlds of Welfare Capitalism* (Cambridge: Polity Press).

European Commission (2013). *Employment and Social Developments in Europe 2012 (ESDE) Review* (Luxembourg: Publications Office of the European Union).

Ferrera, M. (1996). 'The "Southern Model" of Welfare in Social Europe'. *Journal of European Social Policy* 6 (1), 17–37.

Fudge, J. and Owens, J. (2006). *Precarious Work, Women and the New Economy: The Challenge to Legal Norms* (Oxford: Hart Publishing).

Gentile, A. (2011). 'Labour Market Instability and New Patterns of Transition to Adulthood: Spanish Young Adults in Times of Crisis', paper presented at the Causes of Precarious Work amongst Young People, 23 September 2011 Warwick, UK.

Greer, I. and Doellgast, V. (2013). 'Marketisation and Its Effects'. Unpublished paper, University of Greenwich.

GSEE (2008). *Labour and Trade Unions: Quantitative Research Results* (in Greek) Athens: VPRC.

Giuliano, P. (2007). 'Living Arrangements in Western Europe: Does Cultural Origin Matter?' *Journal of the European Economic Association* 5 (5), 927–52.

Guillén, A. and Matsaganis, M. (2000). 'Testing the "Social Dumping" Hypothesis in Southern Europe: Welfare Policies in Greece and Spain during the Last 20 Years'. *Journal of European Social Policy* 10 (2), 120–45.

Hall, D. (2011). 'Greece: Cuts Watch November 2011'. PSIRU University of Greenwich. Available from: http://www.psiru.org/sites/default/files/greece-cwbrief-Nov2011.pdf (accessed 12 April 2013).

Heery, E. and Salmon, J. (2000). *The Insecure Workforce* (London: Routledge).

ILO (International Labour Organisation) (2010). *Global Employment Trends for Youth*, International Labour Organization, Geneva.

ILO, Report of the Committee of Experts on the Application of Conventions and Recommendations: General Report and Observations concerning Particular countries, Report III (Part 1A), International Labour Conference, 100th Session, Geneva, 2011.

Ioakimoglou, E. (2011). *Labour Costs, Profit Margins and Competitiveness in Greece, 1995–2009* (Athens: Institute of Labour GSEE/ADEDY).

Ioakimoglou, E. and Milios, J. (2005). 'Profitability and Accumulation of Capital in Greece (1964–2004)'. *Theseis* 91, 33–60 (in Greek).

Karamessini, M. (2008). 'Still a Distinctive Southern European Employment Model?' *Industrial Relations Journal* 39 (6), 510–31.

Koutentakis, F. (2012). 'Unemployment Dynamics in the Greek Crisis'. Working Papers 1205, University of Crete, Department of Economics.

Kretsos, L. (2010). 'The Persistent Pandemic of Precariousness: Young People at Work', in Tremmel, J. (ed.) *A Young Generation under Pressure?* (New York: Springer), pp. 3–22.

Kretsos, L. (2011). 'Union Responses to the Rise of Youth Precarious Employment in Greece'. *Industrial Relations Journal* 42 (5), 453–72.

Kretsos, L. (2012a). 'Greece's Neoliberal Experiment and Working Class Resistance'. *Working USA* 14 (4), 517–27.

Kretsos, L. (2012b). 'Young Precarious Workers in Greece: An Old and On-going Story'. *Construction Labour Research News* 3, 13–22.

Kretsos, L. and Livanos, I. (2012). 'Precarious Youth Employment in Europe: A Quantitative Analysis'. Paper presented at the 24th SASE Annual Meeting, Global Shifts: Implications for Business, Government and Labor, Cambridge, June.

Κρητικίδης, Γ. (2008). 'Νέοι και Μισθωτή Απασχόληση' [Young Workers and Employment]. Ενημέρωση 148, 15–22 (in Greek).

Κρητικίδης, Γ. (2010). 'Απασχόληση και Ανεργία στο τρίμηνο του 2010' [Employment and Unemployment in the first quarter of 2010], Ενημέρωση, issue 174, July–August (Athens: INE/ γσEE – AδEδΥ), 2–25.

Lampousaki, S. (2011). 'Sharp Increase in Flexible Forms of Labour', Available from: http://www.eurofound.europa.eu/ewco/2011/05/GR1105029I.htm (accessed on 4 October 2013).

Mason, P. (2012). *Why It's Kicking Off Everywhere: The New Global Revolutions* (London and New York: Verso).

McKay, S., Jefferys, S., Paraskevopoulou, A. and Keles, J. (2012). 'Study on Precarious Work and Social Rights', Available from European Commission website: ec.europa.eu/social/BlobServlet?docId=7925&langId=en (accessed on 18 December 2013).

Meardi, G. (2012). 'Flexicurity & State Traditions: The Europeanisation of Employment Policies before and after the Economic Crisis'. Paper presented at the European Sociological Association's Conference, Geneva, September.

Minguez, M.A., Peláez, A.L. and Sánchez-Cabezudo, S.S. (2012). *The Transition to Adulthood in Spain. Economic Crisis and Late Emancipation* (Barcelona: 'la Caixa' Welfare Projects).

Moseley, F. (1999). 'United States Economy at the Turn of the Century: Entering a New Era of Prosperity?' *Capital & Class* 23 (1), 25–45.

Neugart, M. (2008). 'The Choice of Insurance in the Labor Market'. *Public Choice* 134 (3/4), 445–62.

Pascual, S.A. and Waddington, J. (2000). 'Young People: The Labour Market and Trade Unions', Report prepared for the Youth Committee of the European Trade Union Confederation, Brussels: ETUC.

Polavieja, J.G. (1999). 'How Do Labour Market Experiences Affect Political Attitudes?' Center for Advanced Study in the Social Sciences Working Paper 1999/142, Madrid, Instituto Juan March de Estudios e Investigaciones.

Polavieja, J.G. (2005). 'Flexibility or Polarization? Temporary Employment and Job Tasks in Spain'. *Socio-Economic Review* 3, 233–58.

Pollert, A. and Charlwood, A. (2008). 'Vulnerable Workers and Problems at Work: Who Experiences Problems at Work, What Problems Do They Experience, What Do They Do about Them and What Happens as a Result', UWE Working paper, no. 11. Available from: http://www.esrc.ac.uk/my-esrc/grants/R000239679-A/outputs/read/3f4fc1ca-7e38-401b-af5d-c9805f1f2471 (accessed on 15 November 2013).

Sabbatini, F. (2008). 'Social Capital as Social Networks: A New Framework for Measurement and an Empirical Analysis of its Determinants and Consequences'. *Journal of Socio-Economics* 38 (3), 429–42.

Saraceno, C. (1994). 'The Ambivalent Familism of the Italian Welfare State'. *Social Policy* 1 (1), 60–82.

Shaikh, A. (1999). 'Explaining the Global Economic Crisis'. *Historical Materialism* 5 (1), 103–44.

Stamati, A. (2012). 'Continuity and Discontinuity in Employment Policy for Young Workers after the Crisis: The Greek case', paper presented at the ESRC Seminar, Policy Reactions to the Rise of Precarious Employment among Young Workers, University of Greenwich-London.

Standing, G. (2011). *The Precariat: The New Dangerous Class* (London: Bloomsbury).

Simms, M. (2011). 'Helping Young Workers during the Crisis: Contributions by Social partners and Public Authorities', Available from: http://www.eurofound.europa.eu/eiro/studies/tn1101019s/uk1101019q.htm (accessed on: 18 May 2013).

Sweet, S. and Meiksins, P. (2008). *The Changing Contours of Work* (London: Pine Forge Press).

Vosko, L.F., MacDonald, M. and Campbell, I. (2009). *Gender and the Contours of Precarious Employment* (London: Routledge).

7
The Impacts of Employment Instability on Transitions to Adulthood: The *Mileuristas* Young Adults in Spain

Alessandro Gentile[1]

7.1 Introduction

Given the high rates of unemployment and lack of secure jobs, combined with a weak system of activation policies and a shortage of access to social assistance, Spanish young adults aged between 20 and 30 are more dependent on family support and remain in the parental home for longer than their European counterparts (Aassve et al., 2010). As many scholars outline, employment instability affects the long-standing sustainability of youth biographical projects and, as a consequence, exerts a negative influence over generational replacement (Blossfeld and Mills, 2005; De Singly, 2005). Studying young people's working conditions provides us with an important means of understanding structural constraints over their life trajectories and helps us better attend to their demands (Roberts, 2007).

Specific questions can be formulated in order to analyse how they perceive job uncertainty during their process towards full emancipation.[2] How do they describe their working conditions? How does job precarity influence their definition of independence and autonomy? What strategies and attitudes do they develop when faced with the pressures that labour market insecurity places on their transitions and social integration? To answer these questions, the author has carried out in-depth qualitative research on the interpretation of employment instability by young adults who are dealing with their transitions to adulthood.[3]

The *mileuristas* constitute a useful category for such analysis because of their main characteristics. This expression was coined in Barcelona by a graduate student who wrote a letter to the newspaper *El País* in 2005 deploring her job situation as representative for her generation: people around 30 years old, with high skills and academic degrees who were surviving with precarious jobs and were earning a gross monthly salary not exceeding €1,000. This chapter presents the results of 40 interviews with young adults from Barcelona whose characteristics fit this profile. The kind of flexibility and security they look for, the influence of the labour market on their emancipation and the role their families play as social shock absorbers of job uncertainty are all explored.

The findings suggest that the strategies formulated by *mileuristas* can be organised into eight types of responses, which are linked to their socio-economic background, family context, professional career, housing situation and biographical prospects. The interpretation of and responses to employment instability vary greatly across each type, from the experience of job flexibility as an opportunity, a 'trampoline' or a challenge, to the experience of job precarity as a trap. In these terms, the study underlines how structural factors interact with individual professional projects to shape different patterns of emancipation.

7.2   Spanish young adults in a segmented labour market

During the last two decades the so-called 'new social risks' related to deep demographic changes (an ageing population, an increase in the participation of women in the labour market and new household forms) and to cyclical economic downturns have been weakening permanent employment and public protection schemes – the main pillars of the traditional welfare institutions in Europe (Taylor-Gooby, 2004). As a consequence, we observe greater job volatility and unpredictability than in the past (Gallie and Paugam, 2003). Since the mid-1990s a new set of welfare and labour market configurations has been developed in the European Union with the aim of reinforcing jobseekers' responsibility to adapt to this employment instability (Moreno and Serrano, 2007). With such impetus given to this paradigm of activation, through the combination of individual rights and obligations, new entrants to the labour market – especially young people – have been repeatedly called upon to deal with employment uncertainty by adopting a strong attitude of personal commitment and flexibility.

In Spain, prior to this change, education to work transitions for young people were more linear, quite easy and mainly respectful to an adequate correspondence between high qualifications and job integration (García Montalvo et al., 2006). Since then, these transitions have become more and more unfavourable, owing to:

- The increase in labour segmentation: during the last two decades the Spanish labour market has been characterised by a strong division between permanent workers (*insiders*) and flexible workers (*outsiders*) that concerns the different distribution of benefits, salary and career opportunities between these two categories of employees (Polavieja, 2003). Young people are more exposed to intermittent unemployment caused by economic recession (Aragón et al., 2011);
- The lack of an adequate correlation between their educational degrees and their job placement, with limited opportunities of professional promotion resulting in the overqualification or undervaluation of their human capital (Toharia et al., 2008);[4]
- The cultural emphasis on work as a fundamental tool for consolidating their autonomy, social participation and material welfare, while at the same time facing lower salaries and inconsistent job experiences, making it more difficult to plan life projects (Antón, 2006).

In the last few years, growing unemployment and temporary work among young people in Spain has strengthened the connection between employment instability and delayed transitions to adulthood (Aassve et al., 2010; Golsch, 2003; Requena, 2007). Between 2004 and 2006, employment grew considerably through the extraordinary spread of temporary contracts (34.4 per cent compared with 14.5 per cent in the European Union), most of them for workers under the age of 25 (73.4 per cent). From 2007, temporary contracts fell slightly among youth but the number of permanent contracts began to lower in 2011. Unemployment increased with the depletion of permanent jobs and also the many flexible jobs that were not renewed: this was especially the case for those positions that were held by youth in the construction sector and in low-qualified services, and in many administrative areas of the public sector (Aragón et al., 2011). According to data from the Spanish National Statistics Institute (INE), in the third trimester of 2012, the proportion of 20–24-year-old unemployed surpassed 50 per cent, while the unemployment rate for those aged 25–29 reached 31.1 per cent. The highest peaks in unemployment came from those youth who only had compulsory education, while those who held higher education grew at a slower rate. However, when comparing 2007 and 2011, we observe an increase of 18 per cent in the number of unemployed people aged between 25 and 29 with university degrees.

The term *mileurista* has been adopted by many Spanish newspapers with the aim of providing a flash portrayal of those highly educated young adults without a job or with a precarious one. They are mainly middle-class urbanites, still living in their parents' home or just at the beginning of their independent life away from home. After graduating, their positions did not significantly improve; on the contrary, they register higher underemployment than their European peers, as well as a higher rate of fixed-term contracts and lower wages (Eurostat, 2009). Spanish graduates are very likely to avoid marginal sectors of the labour market: they do not usually experience long periods of unemployment or work in manual jobs, and their salaries increase more than those of the lesser-qualified workers (Wolbers, 2007). Even so, the length of time needed for achieving job stability has become prolonged and more uncertain,[5] which means that their emancipation is often not as readily achievable as they expected (Casal et al., 2011). Since the current financial crisis began, the proportion of 'independent' young adults in Spain (those who have left their parental home) has not maintained the same growth registered at the end of the 1990s: the last increase in emancipation for those aged between 16 and 34 was in 2005 (40.7 per cent) and 2007 (44.8 per cent), which dropped slightly in 2011 (44.1 per cent) owing to the decrease of available work (from 75.4 per cent in 2005 to 63.1 per cent in 2011) (Moreno Mínguez et al., 2012).

From an institutional point of view, Spain belongs to a family-oriented welfare system (Naldini, 2003), with a marked generational bias in social policy benefits for the adult population and permanent workers (Marí-Klose and Marí-Klose, 2006). Families compensate for the lack of public welfare for young adults, and this is based on micro-solidarity among its members. Public issues which are not covered by public monetary transfers and welfare services are considered to be 'private matters' (Moreno and Marí-Klose, 2013). Therefore, negative aspects originating from employment instability are, in part, absorbed by parents, who support their children and protect them from the risks related to their transitions towards emancipation.

This 'familism' is an ideological and cultural reference that shapes social cohesion through this intergenerational pact between family members, according to a descendent line of monetary transference and strong mutual aid (Kohli et al., 2007). For this reason, young people's capacity to set secure patterns of emancipation is greatly influenced by their family context and background. Spanish *mileuristas*, as graduates and young adults from middle-class families, feel particularly disappointed with respect to their failed expectations of upward social mobility after studies, by their extended length of stay in the parental home and continued family dependence. Their professional and biographical trajectories are being cut even shorter by the economic crisis that has hit Spain since 2008 (Casal et al., 2011).

7.3 Analytical model and interpretative typologies

Employment instability influences three spheres of one's life. These spheres can be made up of six dimensions (two for each sphere):

- The *instrumental sphere*, which refers to the salary dimension (intermittent and limited income) and the strategic dimension (uncertain life planning);
- The *identity sphere*, built around the professional dimension (difficulty in developing a career consistent with the qualifications acquired) and the personal dimension (weak definition of an unequivocal and long-standing self-definition in society);
- The *institutional sphere*, containing the social dimension (few or inadequate benefits related to the occupational and working conditions) and the citizenship dimension (no trade union representation, high risk of exclusion and social deprivation).

If employment instability means that workers are unable to consolidate at least one of these dimensions, they consider their life conditions to be precarious. On the contrary, if they perceive it does not weaken their instrumental, institutional and identity assets, they will not see themselves in problematic conditions.

Because of this distinction, this study focuses on the meaning that *mileuristas* attributed to each dimension of employment instability as they described their experiences of the following transitions, each part of the process of emancipation:

1. From living with their parents to leaving home, outside the family. This change involves a variety of cost-opportunity decisions for youth in achieving and sustaining their independence. They balance different options between *what they want to be* (personal identity) and the desirability of their families' beliefs and expectations that advise them about *what they should do* (or would advise them to do) in order to be recognised as socially integrated adults (De Singly, 2005).
2. From a dependent way of life to personal autonomy as self-determination. Autonomy refers to the discretionary choice of the young adults, depending on *what they want to do* (professional identity) and *what they can be* (the *functioning* dimension as a 'strategic

capacity') (Sen, 1985), referring to the alternatives they have (for example, consolidating a relationship, taking up residency on their own or starting a family).
3. From family support to economic independence. This dimension deals with the monetary aspect and indicates what they *can do* (salary dimension) in terms of consumption, savings, spending and investing, and what they *should be able to do* (the social protection dimension), depending on the amount of private resources which will allow them a certain level of security, in the case that public welfare programmes cannot cover their risks (Requena, 2007).

The emancipation process of every *mileurista* is developed through these transitions: if one of these is not accomplished, we are dealing with an incomplete emancipation. The correspondence between these three transitions and the six dimensions which define the identity, instrumental and institutional spheres of employment instability is used in this research for understanding the relationship between employment instability and individual experiences of precarity. The extent to which employment instability affects the three spheres is mediated by: cost-opportunity calculations on the part of young people, the capacity to pursue employment that is consistent with their professional goals and the familial resources that they have access to (Figure 7.1).

To organise the information gathered from the interviews, the *mileuristas* were divided into eight groups, creating a typology according to whether they: belong to upper-middle class or lower-middle class families, with reference to the declared highly sufficient or insufficient resources (economic, patrimonial, symbolic and relational) that can be employed for their life transitions; have a coherent (or incoherent) professional project that is in line with their high educational qualifications; live with their parents or by themselves. This typology, set out in Table 7.1, sets out eight groups of *mileuristas* based on their circumstances and the way in which they make sense of them.

This typology provides us with a detailed framework for understanding how *mileuristas* perceive their employment instability. Drawing on this framework, we outline young people's different interpretative discourses according to their abilities in facing structural constraints and to their specific life transitions.

7.4   The social representations of employment instability

The interpretative framework for the *mileuristas'* experiences of employment instability is defined by two intersecting axes. The first one

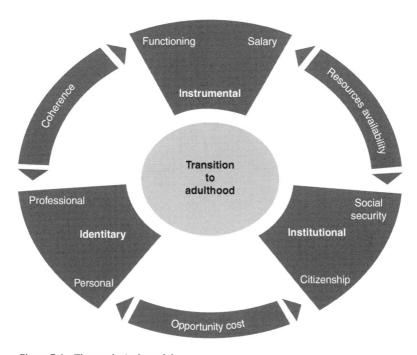

Figure 7.1 The analytical model

Table 7.1 A typology of *mileuristas* young adults

		Professional trajectory	Social background	
			High-middle class	Low-middle class
Still live at home	YES	Coherent	I CAREER-BUILDERS (4)*	II UPRIGHTS (5)
		Incoherent	III OPPORTUNISTS (4)	IV BLOCKED (6)
	NO	Coherent	V NAVIGATORS (6)	VI BELIEVERS (4)
		Incoherent	VII ACROBATS (5)	VIII BORDER-RIDERS (6)

Note: *Number of interviewees for each group.

indicates their status with regard to flexibility, distinguishing between those who voluntarily accept job insecurity to enhance their career opportunities and to improve their social position (the 'flexible'), and those who have to cope with it against their will because it makes them unsatisfied about their labour and life conditions (the 'flexibilised'). The second axis corresponds to the young adults' perception of job flexibility in a continuum running from the positive pole, in which they can find alternatives for social mobility and personal satisfaction, to the negative pole, related to the risks they can face and, in light of these, their vulnerability. Each group of interviewees is inserted within this framework. The information gathered from them has been summarised into four theoretical categories, or discursive structures, that have been constructed according to the similar contents of each participant. Using these tools, their accounts of employment instability have been defined as a 'trampoline', a 'resistance', a 'trap' or a 'challenge' (Figure 7.2).

Following this logic, I present the eight types of *mileuristas* and the four theoretical categories defining employment instability and its impact on their process of emancipation.

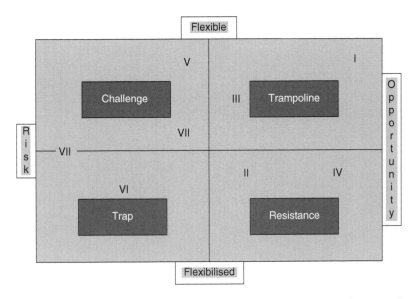

Figure 7.2 The representation of employment instability by each type of *mileuristas*

7.4.1   Employment instability as a trampoline

The *career-builders* and the *opportunists* come from upper-middle class families. It is possible to distinguish them by their consistent (the *career-builders*) or inconsistent (the *opportunists*) professional trajectories. They voluntarily assume temporary jobs, despite their over-qualifications, but only if these working options provide them with some material independence or with concrete prospects of career development. In the meantime, they combat labour insecurity by drawing on family support and keeping their residence at the parents' household. Their condition as *mileuristas* would not allow them to maintain the level of consumption they are accustomed to if they left home: their jobs just allow them to cover basic needs or have some small savings. Although they consider their salaries to be inadequate for the achieved university education, they trust that their incomes will grow in the future.

> My parents pay for just about everything. This makes me feel at ease because it allows me to focus on what I need, such as studying or looking for a better job. Right now this is good for me.
>
> (25-year-old female, BA and MA in Psychology, secretary in a consulting agency)

Flexibility creates a delay in reaching their aspired income level, but they justify it as a strategic option. Employment instability is slowing down their trajectories but it will not prevent the increase of their social status in the long term following a sequential social integration. Job security is achieved by acquiring experience in the same profession, which also strengthens their skills. Therefore, fixed-term contracts are not a problem, but rather an asset for increasing their opportunities. This is a central approach for the *career-builders*, while the *opportunists* grant work a more instrumental value.

> Entering the labour market is a long process. If you accumulate experience you can stand out among the rest. I want to get a good job in my field. This requires time. Meanwhile, it is convenient for me to stay at home.
>
> (27-year-old male, BA in Engineering, research fellow in an ICT company)

For the *career-builders*, higher education represents the beginning of a vocation and professional path to follow with a cumulative logic, and they explore valuable training and job offers. They accept overqualification as an inevitable step in the labour market, believing it can turn into a formative experience in accordance with their academic degrees. The *opportunists* will recognise themselves as emancipated adults only once they are able to count on enough resources to be self-sufficient. At the moment, they settle for jobs that motivate them less (for example, call-centre operators or secretaries), but still leave them free time for social or leisure activities (hobbies, sports and so on), or for searching for better jobs. *Career-builders* and *opportunists* place more emphasis on emancipation while living at home. In their opinion, it is normal to rely on the family if their jobs do not allow them to preserve their level of consumption and well-being. The security given by their parents does not make them feel that employment instability could interfere with their plans. They are oriented towards the future, deploying a defensive and 'wait-and-see' strategy (the *opportunists*) or an attitude based on a progressive accomplishment of professional objectives (the *career-builders*).

> I hope to live on my own. I am still young and I don't want to just throw myself into living away from home because I would lose lots of things, security, comfort . . . and without having a good job, why would I leave home?
>
> (26-year-old male, BA in Political Science, administrative assistant in a HR company)

For both of them, leaving home is a secondary issue to be taken into consideration. The *opportunists'* declared priority is to keep all comforts they currently enjoy at home, without being a burden on their families. They do not stigmatise their position because job insecurity does not encourage them to take risks in unpromising situations: this would be neither practical nor convenient; therefore it is neither logical nor desirable. The *opportunists* pay little attention to the implications of employment instability with respect to welfare rights. For the *career-builders*, such questions will be solved when they stabilise their professional careers. Once their occupational status is consolidated, they will have access to the social protection which corresponds to their professional category. Until that stage is reached, the families will keep covering their personal and daily needs.

7.4.2   Employment instability as a resistance

The *mileuristas* defined as *believers* and *uprights* come from the lower-middle class, and represent the first generation of university graduates in their families. The former have already left home, while the latter live with their parents. They both describe employment flexibility as unwanted and involuntary. Their current job situation is making it difficult to follow the conventional patterns of emancipation. According to their ideal expectations (in the traditional life-course sequence of study, work, leave home) they would like to have a permanent job in order to collect the resources necessary to form a new family.

Salary is the most problematic aspect for them. Those who live at home do not ask their parents for money; they usually contribute a small amount for domestic expenses. They cannot reach a suitable standard of living with the current prices of goods, services and housing in Barcelona. The intermittence or expiry of their incomes, in the form of scholarships, grants or temporary contracts, do not allow them to put in place any long-term planning for independence. The shared residence with their parents represents (or represented, as in the case of the *believers*) an asset while they are preparing for definitive emancipation. Employment instability is a form of resistance to all the strategies that should guide them towards this goal. There is a strong clash between their jobs and their 'functioning' since they consider their expectations legitimate, owing to their efforts at university and to the parental aid they have received.

The *believers* and the *uprights* insist on acquiring better qualifications and skills in order to gain labour stability and upward social mobility. Balancing professional success with their private circumstances tests the coherence of their trajectories. This tension becomes even more explicit after they have accumulated working experience with no prospect of contractual stabilisation, or after having invested time, money and personal dedication to their training without achieving any significant career improvement. They feel ready to match the offers of the market, even if they are disappointed by the few qualified employment opportunities available.

> I believe in what I have studied, that is why I aspire to have a dignified job. There aren't any offers that are really good now. It seems as though the companies don't even consider you, and the crisis is complicating everything. It is not easy but I don't want to give up.
>
> (28-year-old female, BA in Architecture, enrolled in an MA, designer in an architectural studio)

Their life plans are consistent with their parents' expectations of desirable itineraries of social insertion. That is why their parents motivate them to profit as much as possible from their studies and not to be disillusioned by insecure emancipation options. The commitment of *believers* and *uprights* is to keep defending their employability, strengthening their perseverance and confidence.

> My parents taught me that in order to be integrated into society, you need to work. I want to work in my profession...my parents have helped me a lot, but they aren't there to help out all the time nor will they always be there.
>
> (28-year-old male, BA in Engineering, front-desk receptionist in a customer service centre)

To rely on the family home is convenient from a short-term point of view but can easily become a source for impatience and nervousness. The parents will always be their main support, but they know that the achievement of independence is exclusively in their own hands: they want to stop resorting to mum and dad for support as soon as they can. In this respect, the limited availability of economic and social resources accentuates the ascribed asymmetries that exist when compared with their peers from families of upper social classes. For this reason, they also denounce the social barriers which prevent their stabilisation in the labour market, paying for these with the delay in emancipation and with low-quality jobs or unsatisfactory careers.

> If you know someone or if you are someone's child, then you can get a job and you just stay in that position or you have everything already solved. That's why some people, like me, have fewer advantages than others. This is unfair...but no one says anything about it.
>
> (27-year-old male, BA and MA in Law, apprentice in a law office)

In their contributions I detect disappointment more than a sense of victimisation, which is also influenced by their perception of opaque recruitment and selection practices. As they point out, the lack of meritocracy and the nepotism which discriminates against them in the labour market increases their precarity.

Those who have a training contract and those who pursue postgraduate studies feel that they are getting closer to achieving better jobs, while at the same time regretting that Spain invests too little in innovation and quality job offers.

7.4.3   Employment instability as a trap

The *blocked* and the *border-riders* describe employment instability as a trap, with little or few available solutions. Young adults from lower-middle-class families are gathered in these two typologies. They lack any satisfaction or confidence about better opportunities in the Spanish labour market, despite their high qualifications. Their studies do not provide them with any specialisation that could be used as a comparative advantage in a stable process of career-building. They have long-standing work experiences in less qualified sectors (mainly in personal and commercial services), with flexible contracts that allow them to combine several jobs.

The *blocked* still stay at the parental home, while the *border-riders* have recently begun to live on their own but in precarious economic conditions. The *border-riders* are used to saving money but often do not reach the monthly income threshold of *mileuristas*. They merely meet their personal expenses and try to minimise parental aid, partly because family finances were interrupted when they left home. They place an emphasis on the practical difficulties of paying monthly rent, and are often forced to resort to loans from friends or other relatives. These two types of interviewees have no strategy either to enhance or improve their situation. They follow conventional patterns of transition to adulthood but their current jobs will not allow them to enjoy a minimal amount of security. Consequently, their biographical prospects stand below their original expectations.

The *blocked* are not comfortable with their dependence on their families. They primarily believe in employment stability as the unique prerequisite for a real adult life. Even though the *border-riders* have not consolidated financial security, they have left home mainly owing to personal circumstances (such as conflicts with parents or their mere desire for autonomy), or just because they do not want to be a burden on their parents' economy. The training courses they take (mainly information technology and foreign languages) allow them to accumulate useful credentials in order to be more competitive in the labour market and to better explore new job opportunities. However, at the time of the interview, all their attempts at finding another occupation or of stabilising their current one had failed. They realise that many companies are not interested in them because their qualifications are considered too high or because they do not have enough practical experience. The *blocked* do not want to live on their own without the resources to do so. The *border-riders* have tried to get a 'real' job, managing not to rely on their families; they assume the risks of leaving home despite being aware of all the problems they have to cope with. 'Living from day to day' is the main characteristic feature of their lifestyle, with the possible eventual failure of their emancipation, the constant risk of social marginalisation and the consequent return to the parental home against their wishes. This residential reversibility is an option that stresses them, increases conflict with parents and reinforces the vulnerability of their life prospects.

> You are an adult if you have a respectable job ... a full adult is a person with a family, as well. I am not an adult because I don't yet have a job providing me security. If I can't find anything better, I will have to move back in with my parents or go abroad.
>
> (26-year-old male, BA in Biology, bartender)

They feel trapped in an unfavourable environment, 'exposed to the mercy of avid business owners who want to take advantage of their availability to work at low cost' (direct quotation). They cannot do anything to improve the few social protection ties and poor quality of their jobs. As such, they feel trapped in a paradoxical position, with their hopes unfulfilled, achievements incomplete and a growing personal frustration. It is when compared with those who are already emancipated and settled in stable employment that their individual insecurity is seen as social vulnerability. That is why the *blocked* and the *border-riders* outline the impossibility of any certain form of future life planning and the disappointment with political institutions which should guarantee their social integration. Their main difficulties are an incapacity to pay into the welfare system with any continuity, the limited formal recognition of their capabilities and the complete absence of stable salaries that would give them real independence and a social defence against the current economic crisis.

7.4.4   Employment instability as a challenge

The *navigators* and the *acrobats* are *mileuristas* from upper-middle-class families and have already left the parental home. The difference between them derives from those with coherent (the former) and incoherent (the latter) professional trajectories. These young adults see employment instability as an intrinsic challenge to their life projects. They declare to be dealing with the risks of job insecurity by relying on the economic resources from their social position, which allow them to maintain personal well-being and look for professional improvement.

The *navigators* are orientated towards social and personal success through consistent transitions from education to the labour market. The *acrobats* seek other life routes that either interest or stimulate them, considering a large range of specialisations or job alternatives in different fields. It is fundamental for both groups to update their abilities in order to be professionally and socially more competitive.

They mainly complain about the intermittency of their salaries and about the variance in the payment deadlines that are often arranged directly with their employers. Nevertheless, they benefit from important monetary transfers from their parents, and this makes it possible to sustain their standard of living. The *navigators* consider themselves fully emancipated, while the *acrobats* prefer to consolidate their autonomy by collecting high-valued formative and professional credentials. The challenges that stem from their unstable working situation are considered opportunities for gaining job experience.

Their patterns of emancipation are less structured than those who represent employment instability as a *resistance* and as a *trampoline*. The *navigators* are open to new life experimentation and changes in the professional sphere by enhancing their social and relational capital. According to this, they maintain the lifestyle they used to share with friends and colleagues who hold the same degrees and are from the same social background.

> My parents have had the same job their whole lives. Now there is a lot of insecurity but there are also lots of possibilities for changing your life. It's up to you. Today you may work in one job, tomorrow in another...For me it's fundamental to do what you like and be OK with that.
>
> (28-year-old female, BA in Anthropology, freelance photographer)

The *navigators* are accustomed to job flexibility. In their opinion, job uncertainty is an unavoidable element of the Spanish labour market, especially in this period of crisis. They firmly state that everybody must accept this fact and should learn to cope with this reality. *Navigators* and *acrobats* feel responsible for their social integration: insecurity is a source of encouragement for them to develop their independence and seek better job opportunities.

> You need to know how to sell yourself well. This means you need to do things the best way you know. For me, this means always playing the game. This is the norm, in life and with work.
>
> (27-year-old male, BA in IT, webmaster for different companies)

The perception of the risks attached to employment instability allows them to know what their limits are and therefore deploy more efforts for the future. That is why the participants from these two groups insist on proving their merits and abilities all the time. Employment instability is a normal part of their emancipation, and they want to take advantage of it. They always look for a positive balance in their favour when they get a job. In addition, they tend to work simultaneously on different commitments so that if something should fail, they always have a job alternative, just in case. Their aim is to adapt themselves to the structural uncertainty rather than avoiding it.

The *acrobats* do not shut themselves away from things which could stimulate their curiosity; their self-realisation takes place in activities that develop parallel to their work, as in the case of the *opportunists*. They seek out profitability from their personal initiatives, with stimulating experiences such as events, social happenings, cultural proposals and creative groups, just for fun or for the pleasure of sharing common interests.

> To be precarious is to be constantly at risk. I've learned to live with the uncertainty so that it doesn't affect my life too much. I've got a clear idea about what I enjoy doing, while maintaining my lifestyle, and still being able to go to the cinema, take trips, go out with friends, have fun ... But when I work, I like to do it well ... even if it may not be forever.
> (26-year-old male, BA in Economy, assistant fellow for a multinational company)

The *navigators* are geared towards strengthening their position in the labour market, so they need their skills to be valued in their respective professional categories. Social welfare benefits are limited owing to their job insecurity, as is the case with all the participants in this research. However, the *navigators* declare to be able to resolve this issue without major problems. They claim dissatisfaction regarding the welfare institutions but, unlike the *blocked* and the *border-riders*, this attitude is more dependent on their autonomy than an explicit complaint about the lack of social policies. The *acrobats* expect a basic safety net that ensures their security in the course of their professional trajectory. In other terms, they demand concrete support from public institutions in order to manage the risks posed by the current socio-economic climate, making the *mileurista* condition compatible with their lifestyle.

7.5   Conclusion

In the last decade the analysis of the impact of employment instability on young adults' emancipation has acquired increasing importance among social scientists and policymakers in Spain. More specifically, life and working experiences of *mileuristas* provide interesting evidence for the understanding of employment instability as a complex social phenomenon, and for the analysis of new patterns of transitions to adulthood that are influenced by it.

This research has outlined the aspects of job uncertainty that are acceptable or not for *mileuristas*, how they adapt to this uncertainty, and the social or family resources they can rely on. The research has revealed the importance of family backgrounds and social policies in allowing young adults to mitigate the risks of job insecurity and associated social exclusion. Parental help in particular is a decisive factor in the development of their emancipation, particularly in such a family-oriented welfare system as the Spanish one. Hence, from one side, the new patterns of youth independence are embedded in a framework of structural insecurity, a high risk of social marginalisation, and greater individualisation; from the other side, this situation coincides with the slight increase in social inequality between who can and who cannot manage job uncertainty on their own or with the help of his/her basic safety net (the parents).

Among those *mileuristas* who have already experienced living away from home, whether they are upper-middle or lower-middle class, employment instability is an established characteristic of their life. They learn to take advantage of this instability (as in the case of *navigators*) or are resigned to the insecurity it brings (as with the *border-riders*). Those who see this instability as a *challenge* put traditional patterns of job placement aside. Their aim is to strengthen their professional position and collect new experiences, even though their transition to adulthood has been prolonged and has become less linear than in the recent past. Their lifestyle is indicative of this shift: they rent apartments, frequently go in and out of the training system, plan to travel or live abroad, and do not complain about the discontinuity of their jobs.

On the contrary, those who represent employment instability as a *trampoline* or as a *resistance* are more closely attached to the 'conventional' path to emancipation. For the latter, the conventional trajectory is a misleading one, because they are unable to achieve their expectations of upward social mobility, welfare and forming a family. For the former, the challenge lies in taking advantage of or coping with labour market flexibility and its potential to open new personal and professional opportunities. The *navigators* and the *acrobats* recognise that current job insecurity is very different from their parents' work experiences. As a consequence, they understand that their biographical transitions require personal commitment as well as a deep change in terms of beliefs, values and priorities. They face job uncertainty not only when entering the labour market but also during their process of career consolidation. In the best cases, they can reach independence by maximising their high qualifications and proactive attitudes in a very competitive context.

In general, as the interviewees remarked, social policies should help them adjust to changes in the labour market, without renouncing concrete returns on their investment in higher education. They mainly ask for support in order to maintain their income, to pursue easier transitions from one job to another and accumulate professional skills. The *mileuristas* who see employment instability as a *resistance* and as a *trap* ask for institutional intervention focused on guided counselling and individual training that allow them to keep following their desired professional pathways. The criterion by which they feel they will be considered as adults corresponds to a full-time permanent job consistent with their professional skills. That is why they are looking for a stable job as a definitive solution that leads to independence. This is the case for the *blocked* and the *border-riders*, who outline that the lack of job security frustrates their efforts and their motivation.

In contrast, the *navigators* and the *acrobats* demand support in generating innovation and individual sustainability in their life planning. In these terms, an indispensable step for them is to overcome the socio-cultural anchors related to traditional pathways of emancipation (the 'standard biography') and to encourage new pathways between training and employment, according to their preferences, vocations and life circumstances (the 'choice biography') (Furlong et al., 2006).

The interpretations of employment instability made in this study serve an important portion of the youth in Spain, but not all youth. For this reason, research about other groups of young people are needed to include further variables that are not included in this analysis (for example, with regard to gender issues or to different educational levels). The typology presented in this research may be useful for further research exploring how structural factors interact with individual professional projects to shape patterns of emancipation among other groups of young people.

Notes

1. This chapter has been written during the research activities of the SOLFCARE project ('Family Solidarity, Attitudinal Change and Reform of the Welfare State in Spain: Familism in Transition'), financed by the Spanish Ministry of Science and Innovation (2012–13), CSO2011-27494.

2. Labour uncertainty and job precarity are descriptors for the uneasy life conditions of people with low-quality jobs in terms of contractual continuity,
salary, career development, personal satisfaction and social protection (Gallie
and Paugam, 2003).
3. The data used in this chapter is from the first PhD research on this social category, carried out in 2008 (Gentile, 2012). Barcelona offered a very suitable
context for this study owing to the dynamics of labour and residential emancipation in its young adult population, which at the time was – and still is –
more pronounced (a high proportion of flexible workers among young graduates from university, and a high rate of rental housing by young people) than
other large cities in Spain (Merino and García, 2007).
4. The adults have blocked access to permanent positions in the labour market
and young people mostly compete for temporary jobs requiring lesser qualifications, despite having higher education than older workers. The competition
amongst younger workers for the available labour market opportunities ends
up forcing some with a higher educational level into jobs that require lower
qualifications (Toharia et al., 2008).
5. The requirements of having higher education combined with the lack of an
adequate match between supply and demand in the Spanish labour market –
which invests less in innovation than many other European countries and
generates few job offers for highly qualified workers (Walther, 2006) – are no
guarantee of quality job insertion. For this reason, the prospects of a return
on the investment made in education and training are often neglected in the
transition from university to the labour market.

References

Aassve, A., Arpino, B. and Billari, F.C. (2010). 'Age Norms on Leaving Home: Multilevel Evidence from the European Social Survey'. *DONDENA Working Paper
n.32.*

Antón, A. (2006). *Precariedad laboral e identidades juveniles* (Madrid: Fundación
Sindical de Estudios).

Aragón Medina, J., Martínez, A., Cruces Aguilera, J. and Rocha Sánchez, F. (2011).
Las políticas de empleo para jóvenes en España. Una aproximación territorial,
Informes y Estudios n.22 (Madrid: Ministerio de Trabajo e Inmigración).

Blossfeld, H.P. and Mills, M. (2005). 'Globalization, Uncertainty and the Early
Life Course. A Theoretical Framework', in Blossfeld, H.-P., Klijzing, E., Mills, M.
and K. Kurz (eds.) *Globalization, Uncertainty and Youth in Society. The Losers in a
Globalizing World* (London: Routledge).

Casal, J., Merino, R. and García, M. (2011). 'Pasado y futuro del estudio sobre la
transición de los jóvenes'. *Papers. Revista de Sociología* 96 (4), 1139–62.

De Singly, F. (2005). 'Las formas de terminar y de no terminar la juventud'. *Revista
de Estudios de Juventud* 71, 111–21.

Eurostat (2009). *Youth in Europe. A Statistical Portrait* (Luxembourg: Official
Publications of the European Communities).

Furlong, A., Cartmel, F. and Biggart, A. (2006). 'Choice Biographies and
Transitional Linearity: Re-conceptualising Modern Youth Transitions'. *Papers.
Revista de Sociología* 79, 225–39.

Gallie, D. and Paugam, S. (2003). *Social Precarity and Social Integration* (Luxembourg: Official Publications of the European Communities).

García-Montalvo, J., Peiró, J.M. and Soros, A. (2006). *Los jóvenes y el mercado de trabajo de la España urbana. Observatorio de Inserción Laboral 2005* (Valencia: Fundación Bancaja).

Gentile, A. (2012). *Inestabilidad laboral y emancipación. Jóvenes-adultos en el umbral del mileurismo en Roma y Barcelona* (Berlin: Editorial Académica Española).

Golsch, K. (2003). 'Employment Flexibility in Spain and its Impact on Transitions to Adulthood'. *Work, Employment and Sociology* 17 (4), 691–718.

Kohli, M., Albertini, M. and Vogel, C. (2007). 'Intergenerational Transfers of Time and Money in European Families: Common Patterns, Different Regimes?' *Journal of European Social Policy* 17, 319–33.

Marí-Klose, P. and Marí-Klose, M. (2006). 'Edad del cambio. Jóvenes en los circuitos de solidaridad intergeneracional'. *Centro de Investigaciones Sociológicas n.226* (Madrid: Siglo XXI).

Merino, R. and García, M. (2007). *Itineraris de formació i inserció laboral dels joves a Catalunya* (Barcelona: Fundació Jaume Bofill).

Moreno, L. and Marí-Klose, P. (2013). 'Youth, Family Change and Welfare Arrangements. Is the South Still so Different?'. *European Societies* 15 (4), 493–513.

Moreno, L. and Serrano, A. (2007). 'Welfare Europeanization and Activation'. *Política y Sociedad* 44 (2), 31–44.

Moreno Mínguez, A., López, A. and Segado, S. (2012). *La transiciones de los jóvenes españoles en un contexto de crisis económica*, Colección Estudios Sociales n.34 (Barcelona: Fundación La Caixa).

Naldini, M. (2003). *The Family in the Mediterranean Welfare States* (London: Frank Cass).

Polavieja, J. (2003). 'Estables y precarios. Desregulación laboral y estratificación social en España'. *Centro de Investigaciones Sociológicas n.197* (Madrid: Siglo XXI).

Requena, M. (2007). 'Familia, convivencia y dependencia entre los jóvenes españoles'. *Panorama Social* 3, 64–77.

Roberts, K. (2007). 'Youth Transitions and Generations: A Response to Wyn and Woodman'. *Journal of Youth Studies* 10 (2), 263–69.

Sen, A. (1985). *Commodities and Capabilities* (Amsterdam: North Holland).

Taylor-Gooby, P. (ed.) (2004). *New Risks, New Welfare*: *The Transformation of the European Welfare State* (Oxford: Oxford University Press).

Toharia, L., Davia Rodriguez, M.A. and Verdú, A. (2008). 'To Find or Not to Find a First *Significant* Job'. *Revista de Economía Aplicada* 16 (46), 37–60.

Walther, A. (2006). 'Regimes of Youth Transitions. Choice, Flexibility and Security in Young People's Experiences across Different European Contexts'. *Young: Nordic Journal of Youth Research* 14 (2), 119–39.

Wolbers, M. (2007). 'Employment Insecurity at Labour Market Entry and Its Impact on Parental Home Leaving and Family Formation. A Comparative Study among Recent Graduates in Eight European Countries'. *International Journal of Comparative Sociology* 48 (6), 481–507.

Part II

Changing Transitions, Welfare Sources and Social Policies

8
Labour Market Risks and Sources of Welfare among European Youth in Times of Crisis

Lara Maestripieri and Stefania Sabatinelli[1]

8.1 Introduction

Tackling youth unemployment has long been a key priority in Europe. In the European context, particularly in the last quarter of a century, the fragile position of the unemployed, and especially the young unemployed, has for the most part been considered to be the result of individual failings, such as weak competencies, unattractive CVs or poor motivation or adaptability (Crespo and Serrano Pascual, 2004). Consistent with this, European institutions have promoted supply-side policies aimed at dealing with youth unemployment by improving the *employability* of the young, and young people have become one of the primary targets of the activation policies which developed as a key policy approach (Barbier, 2005; Lødemel and Trickey, 2001; Serrano Pascual, 2007; van Berkel and Hornemann Møller, 2002).

Over the years, supply-side labour market policies have been criticised for several reasons. First (and beyond the scope of this chapter), they have been challenged for their failure to make a real impact on employment. The rise in unemployment and inactivity rates, especially among young people (Dietrich, 2012) in the current recession, has drawn attention to the insufficiency of supply-side policies alone. This has brought back onto the European and national agendas the need for policies to stimulate the creation of more jobs, and of a better quality. Second, the activation approach has been criticised for the coercive and stigmatising character it often shows, as opposed to a more empowerment-oriented approach (Serrano Pascual, 2007; Torfing, 1999). A third source of criticism concerns the contradictory nature of the individualisation process that has accompanied the development of these policies. There is a tendency towards the individualisation of responsibility for unemployment (blaming individuals for the reasons already mentioned). Paradoxically, though, while the personalised character of these programmes has long been described as their key strength, the measures are often standardised in their contents, based on the application of common rules, incentives and sanctions, and targeted at broad categories – such as 'young unemployed people' – that are understood to be internally undifferentiated (Sabatinelli and Villa, 2011; van Berkel and Valkenburg, 2007).

This chapter challenges the assumption underpinning supply-side labour market policies that young people at risk of unemployment are a homogenous group. Over the last few decades, transitions to adulthood have become prolonged and destandardised. This trend, coupled with the diversification of pathways in and out of the workforce, has increased the group of young people at risk of unemployment, blurred its boundaries and increased its inner differentiation (Billari, 2004; Bynner, 2005; Guillemard, 2005). The group is not only differentiated by individual features such as skills, motivation and experiences, but also by the type of resources that they do or do not have access to. The resources that young people have access to through the welfare state depend largely on the context they are embedded in, including the welfare model and the way that young people's citizenship status is understood in the country where they live (Walther, 2006). Yet, they also depend on the features of their previous labour market participation, in some countries more than others. The diversification of pathways in and out of work and the varying implications for social rights has led to increasing differentiation in young people's experiences of labour market risk.

Drawing on interviews with vulnerable European young people, this chapter aims to deepen our understanding of the conditions of social vulnerability in young people at risk of unemployment. By social vulnerability we do not mean a state of material deprivation, but rather a multidimensional condition of instability in one or more of the main systems of social integration: family, welfare or labour market (Ranci, 2010). The analysis looks at the subsequent steps in the personal history of the interviewees, exploring the factors that form the basis of work instability among young people, and the resources to which they have access that can act as protective factors. In doing so, it draws out both individual features and structural factors, and their relationship. It also explores the impact on their well-being and their strategies for coping with labour market precarity.

The rest of the chapter is organised into four sections. In the next section, the research objectives and design are presented. In the third section, we present five 'profiles' of work precarity that emerged from our interviews; we explore the ambivalence of their work instability and investigate the interrelations between their agency, the constraints they face and the resources they rely on. In the fourth section, we discuss the impact of unemployment on the well-being of our young interviewees, and their strategies to cope with it. In the final section, we draw some conclusions and implications for policy-making.

8.2   Research objective and design

The results presented in this chapter are drawn from a wider research project, the European FP7 project WILCO,[2] which set out to examine, through a cross-national comparison, if and how local welfare systems promote social cohesion in European cities. The project focused on three vulnerable groups (young precariously employed, single mothers with pre-school-aged children, and first-generation migrants) and three policy areas (passive and active labour market policies, early childhood education and care, and housing). The comparison included ten European countries, covering all geographical areas and welfare models: Sweden for the Nordic model, Germany and France for the continental model, the UK for the Anglo-Saxon liberal model, Italy and Spain for the Mediterranean model; Poland and Croatia for the eastern European countries, plus two hybrid cases: Switzerland, considered a mix of the continental and liberal model, and the Netherlands, a mix of the Nordic and continental model with strong insertions of the liberal approach in the last few decades (Esping-Andersen, 1999; Ferrera, 1996; Van Oorschot, 2006).

This chapter focuses on one of the three cited vulnerable groups that were the subject of the research project, young precariously employed, and aims to address the consequences of occupational instability for social vulnerability in this group. It draws on the qualitative analysis of 120 in-depth interviews carried out in 20 European cities: two cities in each of the above-mentioned countries, namely one large regional town and one middle-sized city.[3] In order to target vulnerable young people, the sample was selected on the basis of the following criteria: aged between 18 and 33;[4] either jobless or in unstable employment; with a low educational level (maximum ISCED 3[5] and not studying at university); and either living autonomously, or eager to live autonomously but living with family of origin because of insufficient economic means.

The rationale was to try to capture young adults at the time they exit, or strive to exit, their family of origin. Interviewees were recruited through a large range of employment, orientation and training services, youth centres and other agencies.

The study set out to understand the interviewees' education and labour market trajectory, the resources they mobilised or accessed to cope with unemployment, and the impact of unemployment on their personal well-being and strategies for the future. The next two sections present the findings of the interviews. In particular, the following section identifies and compares five profiles of work precarity, while the subsequent one analyses the impact of unemployment on the well-being of interviewees.

8.3   Findings: Profiles of labour market risk and sources of welfare among European youth

The interviews revealed that the labour market experiences of the young interviewees did not conform to a 'standard' profile of unemployment. Rather, they represented a 'grey' state of weak integration into the labour market. Young people's working biographies were discontinuous and unstable and their stories were made up of episodes of unemployment followed by occasional jobs, temporary contracts and failed efforts to start apprenticeships or university. Often, unemployment was the result of the expiration of a temporary contract. The persistence of the current global economic crisis has intensified some of the labour market disadvantage experienced by these young people, particularly for some categories, such as first- or second-generation migrants (a finding particularly evident in Germany, Sweden and The Netherlands) and women (seen in Italy).

The interviewees' weak integration into the labour market was the result of several factors. While education was perceived by most to be a key factor to ease the transition to a permanent position in the labour market (as research confirms, see for instance Isengard, 2003), for many, their education level and/or their specialisation did not make them competitive in the labour market. In most cases, this was a result of two processes. The most fragile cases dropped out of school early; others had a professional qualification but it was inadequate, either because it was in a sector that was too specialised or in crisis or because it lacked a clear vocational route to meet labour market demands.

Although characterised by low levels of education and inadequate qualifications, the unstable labour market integration of the interviewees was often the result of a combination of vulnerabilities, of which low education was just one. Fragile familial circumstances, a chain of unstable biographical steps, and the opportunities and constraints offered by local labour markets and welfare systems influenced their stories of precarity. Many of them had experienced difficult family situations, some of them had a criminal record and some of the women had experienced a teenage pregnancy. Their complex biographies suggested that young people's vulnerability stems from an individual fragility in a range of mutually reinforcing domains (family, labour market, welfare system) (Ranci, 2010).

While all the young people in our study were weakly integrated into the labour market and shared similar experiences of work instability, they were characterised by different biographical and work trajectories, and had access to different resources that protected them to varying degrees from work instability. Among our 120 interviewees, we identified five different 'profiles' of work instability or labour market risk, based on a multifaceted combination of features such as education and skills, labour market trajectories and aspirations. The main elements considered in the analysis were: the age at which they obtained their first job (excluding occasional and seasonal work), if they had ever had one; their educational achievements or failures; the number and duration of employment experiences accumulated; the number and duration of spells of unemployment or inactivity; and whether interviewees pursued clear individual professional goals (such as establishing their own business, obtaining a permanent job in a specific sector, or becoming a film-maker). On the basis of these indicators, taking into account similarities and differences, a qualitative construction of different profiles was carried out.

For each of the identified profiles we then examined which resources were available to the interviewees to help them cope with and overcome their condition of instability. Their access or lack of access to resources is central to understanding the degree to which labour market risks precipitated social vulnerability. Drawing on Polanyi's (1944) spheres of socio-economic integration, we classified resources according to three pillars: the (labour) market, redistributive public welfare, and support from close primary networks, such as family. We also took into account the role of solidarity networks (non-governmental organisations, neighbourhood associations and the like). Resources stemming from third sector bodies were classified as 'public welfare' where organisations were – entirely or partly – implementing publicly financed programmes. We explored how the resources varied in their generosity, continuity and their actual impact on individual welfare, but we also assessed the balance between contributions from different pillars, as access to resources in more than one pillar can offer greater protection should resources in another dry up. Most interviewees reported having at least some support from all three welfare pillars. However, as expected given our sampling process, the market was significantly less prominent than public and family resources.

The next section sets out the five profiles of work precarity, describing the distinctive features of each one, as well as outlining the challenges facing those in each group. Among the oldest interviewees, some had had a stable job in the past, while several had chained together a long series of short-term jobs; the youngest appeared confused about their possible careers, and rather passive; only a few interviewees were guided by a specific professional project, while others had already been long excluded from the labour market. The analysis also sets out the different configurations of resources (or 'resource packages') from the three pillars available to each group of young people. The research did not reveal a strong association between any precarity profile and socio-demographic characteristics such as gender or migrant background. In addition, no clear pattern emerges in the way that the five precarity profiles appear across countries and welfare regime models.

8.3.1 Interrupted careers

The individuals in the first profile were typically among the oldest of the interviewees (aged 27 and over). This group (made up of 15 interviewees) had experienced a more 'traditional' form of unemployment. After initially experiencing strong labour market integration, resulting in a coherent professional profile, they were pushed out of the labour market and had remained unemployed for quite a long time.

The reasons for which they were unable to find another job were differentiated on the basis of gender. Men typically interpreted their exit from the labour market as a consequence of the business cycle: quite often male interviewees blamed the economic crisis for their situation, particularly since neither their motivation, nor their experience, nor activation measures seemed enough to find another job. In contrast, many female interviewees, who were aged around 30 at the time of the interview, felt discriminated against either because they had a young child or because there was the potential for them to have a baby and thus take maternity leave during an employment contract. Age was an issue for both men and women: as they grew older, they could no longer benefit from financial incentives for employers to hire younger workers. In other cases, temporary contracts were not renewed because public regulation required that they be transformed into permanent ones after a certain number of extensions, a stipulation with which their previous employer was reluctant to comply.

> I've been a hairdresser for 11 years but now I've been unemployed for about two years. I didn't want to change jobs, it's just that I couldn't find a job anymore, also because I'm beyond the age for apprenticeship contracts. This is very limiting for me and it's one of the reasons why I'm doing other courses to try and change jobs.
>
> (Female, 31, Italy)

As a result of their relatively strong labour market integration in the past, these individuals had built up a greater entitlement to public support than their peers. In most cases, they were accessing contribution-based income support payments for unemployment that were more generous than the means-tested social assistance schemes, and which were often accompanied by retraining and reorientation services. These interviewees were also more connected with public employment services, and were more aware of their social rights. More than half of this group combined this public support with help from their families, either their parents or their partners, making their 'resource package' balanced and sound. But more than a quarter of these individuals, a larger proportion than in the whole sample, relied entirely on public welfare. They received monetary transfers (mainly unemployment benefits but also child allowances, housing benefits or others), they lived in public housing, and their children were enrolled in public day-care facilities. The information they could access about available jobs or training opportunities all came through their contacts with public welfare agencies.

The soundness of the resources they could access, including the relative generosity of public resources, supported the individuals in this group to continue to actively pursue labour market reintegration, despite challenges associated with the length of their unemployment, the poor economic conditions in their localities, having young children or other family members to care for, and the outdated nature of their professional skills. The major challenge for these young people was overcoming the scarring effect of their long period of unemployment. For those relying exclusively on public welfare, an additional risk was that they had little to fall back on if their entitlement to public support ceased or there were public policy changes which reduced their access to support schemes, for instance because of austerity programmes.

8.3.2   Precarious with fragmented paths

The largest group in our sample (48 interviewees) included individuals who had had more or less continuous, but transient, labour market opportunities. Accepting the best offers they received in the short term, they managed to achieve income continuity while never achieving stable employment. Even though they experienced the shortest unemployment spells among our interviewees (less than six months on average), these were sometimes only spaced out by very short contracts of a few weeks or even days. As a result, at the time of interview, they were trapped in a 'grey' condition of unstable labour market integration, which might deteriorate over time, since their fluctuation did not allow them to accumulate enough consistent professional experience to be competitive in any sector or profession. As they grew older, their CVs became increasingly fragmented and it became more difficult for them to achieve a permanent job contract and forge a successful career:

> If I had to write a CV now, I think I could fill up 3 pages at least … My parents always told me: 'make sure you have an income' … so at some point I was just too easy in accepting anything that I was offered […] And whether that helped me in my career? Well, if I look at where I was when I was 18 and where I am now, then no.
>
> (Male, 30, the Netherlands)

The lack of employment stability also jeopardised their future prospects of achieving independence by leaving their family of origin and establishing a new household.

The interviewees with this profile can be described as 'mid-siders'; that is, those workers with atypical contracts, a group that has increased significantly in the last few decades owing to the flexibilisation of labour markets (Jessoula et al., 2010). 'Mid-siders' are not entirely excluded from the labour market, but are only entitled to part of the welfare protection that those with permanent contracts are granted. Not only was their access to social protection limited, but many young people in this group reported being forced to accept jobs with low wages. The drastic deregulation of job contracts over the last few decades has increased the incidence of precarious and fragmented career paths, increasing the vulnerability of young workers. This is particularly true in southern European countries, where the new social risks created by labour market deregulation were not compensated for by reforms of social protection systems (Bonoli, 2007).

Two-thirds of the *precarious with a fragmented* path reported having very limited resources across all three pillars. They had few opportunities to draw resources from the labour market, and their relatives were for the most part as economically disadvantaged as they were (which partly explained the pressure to accept short-term jobs). They had limited entitlement to public welfare because of the low degree of social protection associated with atypical job contracts and the meagre nature of residualist social assistance-style income support payments, particularly in southern and eastern countries. Hence, in spite of their ongoing participation in the labour market, the degree of social vulnerability experienced by this subgroup was the highest of all five groups, since they could barely make ends meet and their integration into basic social spheres was extremely weak.

For this group, the chain of short-term experiences fostered a general mistrust of the labour market as a sphere of social integration. Only a minority in this group declared that finding a new job would be the solution to their precarious situation. Most did not view it as a solution, as none of their many past occupational experiences had been and they felt that any new job they were likely to get would probably be similarly short and lacking in career prospects. Confronted with the reduced availability of jobs brought about by the enduring economic crisis, many appeared to have no idea of what the future held for them, both in the short term and in the medium to long term.

8.3.3   Flexible with a professional project

The smallest group we identified was made up of nine young adults (around 24 years old on average), characterised by being highly motivated to pursue a professional career. Interestingly, most of them were involved in creative and artistic fields, such as theatre, dance or filmmaking. Their passion nourished the determination with which they pursued their professional goals. Each had a strategy for pursuing a successful career that involved alternating between employment and training initiatives with the aim of developing a set of competencies highly sought after in their field of interest. Many of them were involved in new educational projects in order to improve their chances of obtaining attractive positions.

These interviewees had access to a wide package of resources, made up of entitlements to public welfare, some attachment to the (labour) market and family support. Their strong motivation guided them in pursuing resources that made their end goal more achievable: they sought out specialised training courses and public funds for cultural projects, they submitted bids for start-up funding, and they used their contacts to locate interesting employment opportunities which expanded their professional networks. These resources helped to keep them highly motivated and able to invest financially in their careers. While the training that these interviewees participated in was often expensive (particularly when the fees were combined with the opportunity costs of study), some of them had a temporary, instrumental job to cover their basic needs while they studied and some relied on additional support from their family and primary networks to supplement their basic income. Parents often covered their housing costs or supported them with monetary transfers. Some of these interviewees avoided living with family by pooling resources and cohabiting with friends or colleagues with similar professional pursuits.

Their strong resource packages meant that these interviewees were in a position to cope with periods of unemployment. Except for the instrumental jobs that some undertook to supplement study, they were more selective about the jobs they accepted, seeking out work and training experiences that contributed to the development of their desired occupational profile. Often they were young enough to access contracts aimed at easing the first entrance in the labour market, making them competitive with older workers even if they lacked experience. Their selective labour market strategy was often rewarded by obtaining longer job contracts than those acquired by individuals in the other four groups (17 months on average):

> I have a precarious lifestyle. Probably, it is due to the fact that in Italy there aren't many opportunities for young people. You have the chance to learn a job at school, but it's hard to do it in practice afterwards. Many young people have good ideas to contribute to the creative sector, but it's hard to establish a real career, particularly in my field [film-making].
>
> (Male, 28, Italy)

These interviewees seemed to cope better than others with the flexibility of their labour market involvement, which was perceived by these interviewees as typical not only of their generation, but also of the field in which they are interested. The most serious risk this group of young people faces is the failure of their professional project. Despite their high motivation, this may occur not only because of contingent economic cycles, but also because competition is intense in creative sectors and because the skills they accumulated are so specialised that they may not be easily transferred to other sectors.

8.3.4   Young and fragile

The fourth profile we identified was made up of young people who had just left the educational system at the time of the interview, quite often without achieving a basic qualification. Many of these 14 interviewees had limited and fragmented work experience, mostly temporary (for example, seasonal work in retail, personal services or tourism, sometimes without a contract) or attached to youth activation programmes. They were the youngest group in our sample (under 20 on average) and they had not yet developed a clear idea of their future. They exhibited little sense of agency to achieve self-determined goals; none spoke of passions or talents which they wanted to pursue; nor had they been motivated by any work experience in the past to pursue a career in a specific field. None actively pursued paid employment, and during unemployment spells they seldom underwent training or retraining. Some waited for someone to offer them 'something to do'. Their main aspiration was to access an apprenticeship. Although poorly paid or even unpaid in some countries, it was the only option they cited as a prospect for gaining some professional experience and improving their chances for labour market integration.

> I was doubting a little, whether I should continue studying or not, so I didn't do anything for two or three months, just thinking if I was going to go back to school or look for a job. And then I decided to get a job because I wanted to earn money, help my parents and stuff, and then I started looking for a job.
>
> (Male, 25, the Netherlands)

Two-thirds of those with a *fragile* profile had access to a variety of resources from the three welfare pillars. Still being young, many were supported by their families. Others had unstable family backgrounds and limited labour market attachment, and as a result of the accumulation of social disadvantage some of these interviewees were supported entirely by public welfare agencies. However, the remaining third had scant access to resources from any pillar, including public welfare. This sub-group, alongside the group identified in the next section, was the most vulnerable to the risk of social exclusion.

Occurring at such an early stage of life, this vulnerability is particularly dangerous. For this group, the most insidious risk was the passivity with which they approached their condition of unemployment. This lack of motivation, combined with their limited familiarity with the labour market, has the potential to turn their current NEET situation (not in employment, education or training) into a longer-lasting condition, jeopardising their medium- or long-term professional prospects and leading to ongoing exclusion from education and employment. This is a particular risk for those who are not adequately supported by their family or formal services.

8.3.5   Marginal and weak

The individuals with this final profile (34 in total) are arguably the most fragile of all the interviewees and they are quite often at risk of social exclusion. Besides a weak school record, including failures and dropping out, they also have a difficult personal and family background. Many had experienced parental illness, death or imprisonment, or a difficult parental separation. Some had difficult migration trajectories, or they had early contact with the criminal justice system (for illegal drug use or trafficking).

> I started [lower secondary general schooling], but I failed and I went to a lower level [...], eventually dropping out, because of absence and fighting. I ended up in drugs-related crime, earning hundreds of euros a day. Finally, police caught me and I went to prison for a few months. With a record, I cannot apply for a job now, but I'm thinking of taking over a shop.
>
> (Male, 22, the Netherlands)

In some cases, disability and illness made their integration into the labour market more difficult than that of their peers. In other cases, interviewees had caring responsibilities for dependent family members, which decreased the possibility of being employed full time, and positions with flexible hours were difficult to find. For many young women, early pregnancy became an obstacle to labour market integration, especially if they had few options for sharing caring responsibilities (for instance after separation from the child's father) or if childcare options were lacking in the area where they lived.

With these particularly precarious backgrounds, coupled with fragmented experiences in the labour market, most of these young people were long-term unemployed at the time of interview (on average, more than 18 months had passed since their last contract). They did not yet have clear ideas about what to do in the future. Some of the interviewees reported having been encouraged by their public employment services tutors to use the months of unemployment in order to get trained or retrained, so as to be better equipped and more competitive once the economy started to recover. However in most cases, the interviewees reporting this had not acted on the suggestion.

Almost half of the interviewees in this group had access to scant or unbalanced resources, depending on one pillar alone, most commonly public welfare. Some received a wide range of supports from social services, including protected labour market experiences, income and housing support, and access to information. However, the quality of these initiatives depended on the generosity of the national and local welfare systems, and thus varied from country to country. In southern and eastern countries in particular, social assistance benefits are either meagre or lacking completely, labour market programmes are limited, except for some local project-based exceptions, and housing provision or support are residual, so the overall impact of the all-welfare resource packages was limited.

Poorly integrated into the labour market and scarcely supported by their family and primary networks, this sub-group of interviewees suffered a high level of social vulnerability. The fact that they relied heavily on public welfare resources exposed them to an additional risk: that their entitlements may expire or be reduced.

8.3.6 Work precarity of the young: Different profiles, differentiated needs

Our analysis has identified five different profiles of labour market precarity, evident across each of the ten European countries studied and across welfare regimes. The findings highlight the complex and varied nature of work instability, showing the differing constraints facing young people with different profiles. Interviewees with *interrupted careers* experienced a traditional form of unemployment: after initially experiencing stable labour market integration, they found themselves outside the labour market; those who were *precarious with fragmented paths* had completed one short contract after another, achieving neither stabilisation nor professionalisation; in contrast, the *flexible with a professional project* included their multiple experiences in a coherent path guided by a strong orientation and motivation; the *young and fragile* seemed stuck in a long and difficult transition from education to work; and the *marginal and weak* combined difficult biographies and family background with a weak education and labour market integration.

Across the five profiles the young interviewees had access to different sets of resources. For approximately half of our interviewees, these resources were rather well balanced, deriving from the market, the family and public programmes. This sound 'package' protected them from a shift into impoverishment or at least kept them on the verge of subsistence. A quarter of our sample had access to an unbalanced set of resources, stemming mainly or exclusively from public welfare or family-based support. These individuals are particularly at risk because if their only source of support should disappear (their entitlement to a measure could expire, or their parents may no longer be able to support them), they would be left with no other buffer. The remaining quarter only had access to a scant set of resources. Although they wanted to access more secure support through, for example, applying for welfare measures, they were either not entitled or lacked the relevant information about their rights. Others did not even try to apply, discouraged by previous stigmatising experiences.

In some instances, profiles of precarity and resource packages combined to leave the interviewees with weak relationships to all three spheres: weak attachment to the labour market and limited support from family or the welfare state. Those in the *precarious with fragmented paths* and in *the marginal and weak* groups who – at the same time – had only one source of support (all welfare or all family) or little support at all, were most at risk of becoming economically deprived and socially excluded. These young unemployed people bear the greatest level of social vulnerability in our sample, exposed to a large extent to market contingencies. Most of these cases were concentrated in the cities of southern Europe, which supports existing research that finds – when the family is absent or unable to provide support – little other social buffering is available in the Mediterranean welfare systems (Ferrera, 2005; Leibfried, 1992).

The comparison of these profiles reveals that the impact of employment instability on social vulnerability is filtered by different configurations of resources. In the next section, we discuss the impact of employment instability on the well-being of the interviewees, and the strategies they had to cope with it.

8.4   Coping with unemployment

8.4.1   Managing the insufficiency of economic resources

Although characterised by diverse profiles of work precarity, the young Europeans that we interviewed shared similar strategies to cope with their conditions of instability that cut across welfare regimes and countries. The most common strategies involved changes in or a reorganisation of their life expectations and plans, something that has also emerged from previous research (Blossfeld et al., 2005), as well as reducing expenditure, both for consumption and for investment.

For many interviewees, a reorganisation of life plans typically meant the postponement of steps towards autonomy and adulthood (such as moving out of their parents' home, cohabitation and having children) or even, for some of them, taking a step backwards and going back to live with their family of origin (see Berrington and Stone in this volume for a detailed analysis of this phenomenon in Britain). Among those who did live outside the parental home, many relied heavily on their family. In some instances, all available resources in the family (including the extended family) were put together in income-pooling strategies. This lifted these young interviewees beyond a threshold of dangerous social exclusion. Nevertheless, dependence on family stressed and depressed the young adults, who felt as if they were 'late' developers, compared with an ideal of full autonomy that they believed they should have achieved at their age. Those who had returned to live with their parents after a period of autonomy complained of a sort of personal regression, and of not feeling treated as an adult by their relatives.

> I moved back with my parents. They've always helped me, but the relationship is strained since I moved back, because they treat me as a child, not as an adult.
>
> (Female, 24, Spain)

Even more widespread was the severe reduction of expenditure. This not only meant relinquishing everything that was not indispensable (such as leisure, sports and holidays), but also cutting back on basic goods (such as reducing health expenses or food quality). Some incurred debts on expenses such as utilities, rent and car insurance. Many dropped out of training courses or gave up plans to start new ones because they lacked the money to do so. Only those *with a professional project* viewed training as a basic good or 'fundamental expense' and cut back on other essential goods – such as clothes or housing – or took out loans in order to pursue relevant courses.

Interviewees also developed a number of methods for increasing their income. Many borrowed money from relatives and friends or from social services where possible; some reported selling family goods (such as second real estate properties or the car) or finding room-mates in order to share the housing costs; several undertook minor illegal activities (such as selling drugs on the street). Some were developing migration plans, or even thinking about extreme solutions such as 'selling ovules', or 'having children' in order to receive family allowances and have priority for social housing.

The interviewees who reported having access to resources that they could 'fall back on', such as family support, said that while this helped to overcome their present difficult situation, it did not allay their concerns about the future. However, the interviewees facing the strongest challenges were those without resources to fall back on. For these young people, the severe reduction of expenditure had a significant impact on their basic quality of life, both in terms of food and housing.

> Now I go to the food bank once a week. In the beginning, I was ashamed by this, but now I can see that there are also people coming who have a job, but even for them it is not enough. My children also learned to buy cheap items like cheap chocolate or to look at the kg-price [and] that it is better to buy at the discount shop than at the supermarket just around the corner.
>
> (Female, 28, Germany)

8.4.2   Well-being and strategies for the future

Across all European countries in this study, young people reported the negative impact of labour market instability on their overall well-being. The documentation of the relationship between labour market attachment and well-being has a long history (see Jahoda et al., 1971). However, the sociological analysis of this relationship has regained momentum in recent years as the labour market has become precarious (Standing, 2011) and a flexible model of work has come to predominate (Castel, 2003; Sennett, 1998). In an increasingly flexible and unstable labour market, being a fully integrated member of the workforce remains of great importance both for people's financial stability and for their sense of identity (Strangleman, 2007).

As a result of their precarious labour market attachment, our interviewees reported feelings of distress, anxiety, a loss of confidence, a negative outlook, and the absence of a strategy for the present and of plans for the future. These feelings simultaneously lead to and were reinforced by strained family relations, and/or psychological and other health problems, such as depression and rapid changes in weight. Some interviewees reported making an effort to maintain a routine: waking up early, carrying out everyday activities, and doing (cheap) sports or volunteer work. Others, on the contrary, had lost their daily routine, often remaining inactive all day, feeling worthless and useless, or even plunging into despair.

> It's been very stressful, I stayed at home, and only the need to walk my dog forced me to get out of my apartment. I lost contact with most friends.
>
> (Male, 20, Spain)

In this sense, having a concrete 'project' or strategy for the future had an important impact on the well-being of some of the interviewees: these projects (most commonly including searching for a job, getting additional training or emigrating) helped many to avoid the sense that they were 'surrendering' to their situation of distress, by finding new motivation and becoming 'active'. Having no concrete plans for the future had a negative impact on their self-esteem, even among those with access to a reasonable level of resources.

> Unemployment has taken away a lot of my pride. You always feel you are not good enough. It really gets you down.
>
> (Male, 25, UK)

Several young people reported that being engaged in activation programmes such as training courses and protected jobs was fundamental to restoring their motivation, their self-esteem and their daily routine. This was particularly important for those who were not pursuing an autonomous concrete professional project:

> At first I felt really bad. Now, since I am in the programme, I don't feel like an unemployed person anymore, and it's getting much better.
>
> (Female, 21, Switzerland)

However, other interviewees reported disappointment in and suspicion towards public programmes. Some took an instrumental approach to the activation programmes, reporting actions such as sending the exact number of applications the rules required (no less and no more), because they felt the programmes were just a baseless instrument to justify the provision of income support.

These findings suggest that the rigidity of activation measures may (further) reduce the trust that young recipients have towards public welfare and activation services, especially when they feel compelled to accept jobs that do not match their skills, or that are of short duration and/or very low pay in order to protect their entitlement to support.

8.5   Conclusions

In this chapter we have analysed the conditions of social vulnerability of poorly educated and precariously employed young people living in ten European countries. We have examined their education and labour market pathways and the resources available to help them manage financially and plan for their future. The analysis has showed how similar degrees of work instability can result in varying degrees of social vulnerability, depending on diverse combinations of *individual factors*, such as personal skills and motivation, *structural factors*, such as the labour market context and social policy system, and the support available from *family* and other sources. Reconstructing the pathways of interviewees through education and work allowed us to explore the effects of education and work history on the type of public welfare protection that they could access (in some countries in particular), and on their motivation and strategic agency.

Youth unemployment has long been considered a consequence of individual shortcomings, to be tackled through supply-side measures aimed at increasing individual employability. However, this approach has been criticised because it is no substitute for programmes that increase labour demand and improve job quality. The need for labour market policies to be 'tailor made' to the characteristics and needs of the individual recipients has gained wide consensus over the last few decades (van Berkel and Valkenburg, 2007). Yet, these policies do not recognise the heterogeneity of young people at risk of unemployment and are based on a dichotomous understanding of 'employability', in which individual skills and attitudes are considered as being either fit for the existing or potential jobs, or not fit and in need of adaptation to those jobs through additional education or training.

Our results show, instead, a more complex picture. Individuals have diverse combinations of strengths and weaknesses that change over time (for instance, some skills can be acquired, while others become obsolete; motivation can be strengthened thanks to positive experiences, or eroded through inactivity). At the same time, similar strengths or weaknesses in skills acquisition or labour market experience may have different outcomes depending on a person's motivation, the strength of their professional project, the local labour market opportunities and the resources they have available to them.

This heterogeneity among young people who are unemployed or at risk of unemployment points to a need for differentiated policy responses. Interviewees with an *interrupted career* have had stable work in the past and therefore had strong 'employability skills', or the 'soft skills' (such as familiarity with work routines and cultures) that make the transition back into the labour market a smooth one. However, their 'hard' skills or qualifications had often become outdated. They are entitled to mainstream income support measures, but there is a risk that their entitlements may expire before they find a new job. To find stable employment opportunities, the young with this profile need support in identifying opportunities for retraining or updating their skills. On the contrary, for our *young and fragile* interviewees the main risk is that the transition from school to work may become too long and may result in a slide towards a NEET status. For these individuals, even short-term work experiences may be a useful way of allowing them to develop their skills, build some experience and enhance their CVs. In contrast, continuing to accumulate short-term work experiences would not ameliorate the career trajectory of the *precarious with fragmented paths*. What these individuals need is the opportunity to identify a pathway towards a more stable position. This means training and targeted work experiences, but it also requires income support to free them from the immediate need to pursue any salary whatsoever. Those *flexible with a professional project* do not need labour market orientation, as they have a definite vocational ambition and a well-defined professional plan, but rather specific counselling to identify and access targeted resources in order to be able to afford specialised training or start-up funds to pursue their project. Finally, the *marginal and weak*, the most exposed to commodification and at risk of exclusion among our young, need more robust and encompassing help, providing social support as well as orientation, training and (possibly protected) work experiences.

The findings from our interviews suggest that relevant and targeted activating programmes could make a significant difference to the experiences of unemployment and instability, though the rigid rules often prevented individuals from obtaining the type of support they required. The impact of austerity measures on such programmes risks further limiting their scope, especially in contexts where they were already comparatively less developed, such as in southern and eastern countries, and where cuts are particularly sharp, as in the British and Dutch context. However, in order to be effective and contribute to reducing the social vulnerability of young people at risk of unemployment, activation measures need to be better adapted to their differing sets of circumstances.

Notes

1. We warmly thank Manuel Aguilar Hendrickson and Annalisa Murgia for their valuable comments.
2. 'Social innovations at the local level in favour of cohesion' (www.wilco project.eu).
3. The cities included: in Spain, Barcelona and Pamplona; in Italy, Milan and Brescia; in Switzerland, Bern and Geneva; in France, Nantes and Lille; in Germany, Berlin and Münster; in the Netherlands, Amsterdam and Nijmegen; in the UK, Medway and Birmingham; in Poland, Warsaw and Płock; in Croatia, Zagreb and Varaždin; and in Sweden, Stockholm and Malmö. Our warm thanks go to all the researchers who contributed to the fieldwork (www.wilcoproject.eu/who-are-we/partners/), and to all the young people who agreed to be interviewed and entrusted us with their experience of work precarity.
4. Individuals aged under 18 were excluded from the sample as they would typically still be in compulsory schooling in all the countries included in the study. However, we included people just over 30 in order to include young adults in countries such as the southern ones whose exit from the parental home is comparatively delayed. For the same reason, we included in the sample interviewees living with their parents, as long as they did so for economic reasons.
5. Level 3 of the ISCED (International Standard Classification of Education) scale makes reference to upper secondary education, usually providing education in preparation for tertiary education or qualified employment. The main reason was to observe young adults with a weak educational profile, who have the highest probability of being jobless, long-term unemployed or in unstable employment (Baranowska and Gebel, 2010).

References

Baranowska, A. and Gebel, M. (2010). 'The Determinants of Youth Temporary Employment in the Enlarged Europe: Do Labour Market Institutions Matter?' *European Societies* 12 (3), 367–90.

Barbier, J.C. (2005). 'The European Employment Strategy, a Channel for Activating Social Protection?' in Zeitlin, J., Pochet, P. and Magnusson, L. (eds.) *The Open Method of Co-ordination in Action: The European Employment and Social Inclusion Strategies* (Bruxelles and New York: P.I.E.-Peter Lang).

Billari, F.C. (2004). 'Becoming an Adult in Europe: A Macro(/Micro)-Demographic Perspective'. *Demographic Research*, SC3(2), 15–44.

Blossfeld, H.-P., Klijzing, E., Mills, M. and Kurz, K. (2005). *Globalization, Uncertainty and Youth in Society* (London and New York: Routledge).

Bonoli, G. (2007). 'Time Matters: Postindustrialization, New Social Risks, Welfare State Adaptation in Advanced Industrial Democracies'. *Comparative Political Studies* 40 (5), 495–520.

Bynner, J. (2005). 'Rethinking the Youth Phase of the Life-course: The Case for Emerging Adulthood?' *Journal of Youth Studies* 8 (4), 367–84.

Castel, R. (2003). *L'insécurité Sociale. Qu'est-ce qu'être Protégé?* (Paris: Éditions du Seuil).

Crespo, E. and Serrano Pascual, A. (2004) *The EU's Concept of Activation for Young People: Towards a New Social Contract?* Unpublished.

Dietrich, H. (2012). 'Youth Unemployment in Europe. Theoretical Considerations and Empirical Findings', Available at: library.fes.de/pdf-files/id/ipa/09227.pdf (accessed on 16 July 2012).

Esping-Andersen, G. (1999). *Social Foundations of Postindustrial Economies* (Cambridge: Polity Press).

Ferrera, M. (1996). 'The "Southern Model" of Welfare in Social Europe'. *Journal of European Social Policy* 6 (1), 17–37.

Ferrera, M. (2005). *Welfare State Reform in Southern Europe. Fighting Poverty and Social Exclusion in Italy, Spain, Portugal and Greece* (London: Routledge).

Guillemard, A.M. (2005). 'The Advent of Flexible Life Course and the Reconfiguration of Welfare', in Andersen, J.G., Guillemard, A.M., Jensen, P.H. and Pfau-Effinger, B. (eds.) *The Changing Face of Welfare Consequences and Outcomes from a Citizenship Perspective* (Bristol: The Policy Press).

Isengard, B. (2003). 'Youth Unemployment: Individual Risk Factors and Institutional Determinants. A Case Study of Germany and the United Kingdom'. *Journal of Youth Studies* 6 (4), 357–76.

Jahoda, M., Lazarsfeld, P. and Zeisel, H. (1971). *Marienthal. The Sociography of an Unemployed Community* (Chicago, IL–New York: Aldine, Atherton).

Jessoula, M., Graziano, P.R. and Madama, I. (2010). ' "Selective Flexicurity" in Segmented Labour Markets: The Case of Italian "Mid-Siders" '. *Journal of Social Policy* 39 (4), 561–83.

Leibfried, S. (1992). 'Towards a European Welfare State: On Integrating Poverty Regimes in the European Community', in Ferge, Z. and Kolberg, J.E. (eds.) *Social Policy in a Changing Europe* (Boulder: Westview Press).

Lødemel, I. and Trickey, H. (eds.) (2001). *An Offer You Can't Refuse* (Bristol: Policy Press).

Polanyi, K. (1944). *The Great Transformation. The Political and Economic Origins of Our Time* (Boston, MA: Beacon Press).

Ranci, C. (2010). *Social Vulnerability in Europe. The New Configuration of Social Risks* (London: Palgrave Macmillan).

Sabatinelli, S. and Villa, M. (2011). 'Individualisation without Personalisation? The Paradoxical Logic of the Quasi-Market Based Employment Services in the Lombardy Region'. Paper presented at the 9th Annual ESPANET Conference 'Sustainability and transformation of European Social Policy', Valencia, 8–10 September 2011.

Sennett, S. (1998). *The Corrosion of Character. The Personal Consequences of Work in the New Capitalism* (New York and London: Norton & Co).

Serrano-Pascual, A. (2007). 'Activation Regimes in Europe: A Clustering Exercise', in Serrano Pascual, A. and Magnusson, E. (eds.) *Reshaping Welfare States and Activation Regimes in Europe* (Brussels: P.I.E. Peter Lang), pp. 275–316.

Standing, G. (2011). *The Precariat: The New Dangerous Class* (London and New York: Bloomsbury Academic).

Strangleman, T. (2007). 'The Nostalgia for Permanence at Work? The End of Work and Its Commentators'. *The Sociological Review* 55 (1), 81–103.

Torfing, J. (1999). 'Workfare with Welfare: Recent Reforms of the Danish Welfare State'. *Journal of European Social Policy* 1 (9), 5–28.

van Berkel, R. and Hornemann Møller, I. (eds.) (2002). *Active Social Policies in the EU. Inclusion through Participation?* (Bristol: Policy Press).

van Berkel, R. and Valkenburg, B. (2007). *Making It Personal. Individualising Activation Services in the EU* (Bristol: The Policy Press).

Van Oorschot, W. (2006). 'Dutch Welfare State: Recent Trends and Challenges in Historical Perspective'. *The European Journal of Social Security* 8 (1), 57–73.

Walther, A. (2006). 'Regimes of Youth Transitions: Choice, Flexibility and Security in Young People's Experiences across Different European Contexts'. *Young* 14 (2), 119–39.

9

Have Nordic Welfare Regimes Adapted to Changes in Transitions to Adulthood? Unemployment Insurance and Social Assistance among Young People in the Nordic Welfare States

Anna Angelin, Timo Kauppinen, Thomas Lorentzen, Olof Bäckman, Pasi Moisio, Espen Dahl and Tapio Salonen

9.1 Introduction

Entering adult life consists of several transitions that are related to finding a source of income, establishing an independent household and creating new family formations. This stage of 'becoming' entails a move from needing others to living as an autonomous and economically independent citizen (France, 2008; Smeeding and Philips, 2002). This key life stage, where several major transitions and life-course events take place concurrently (Anxo et al., 2010; Müller and Gangl, 2003), results in increasing vulnerability to poverty (Moore, 2005). In the Nordic countries (Finland, Sweden and Norway), economic autonomy has become quite difficult to obtain for many young people; continued financial support from either parents or social assistance is a reality for many. Poverty is central in understanding if and how young people can transition effectively into adulthood. Within the populations of the Nordic countries today, young people are among those most likely to be economically vulnerable.[1] Despite being relatively affluent compared with young people in many eastern and southern European countries, it is evident that this life phase is associated with increasing vulnerability in the Nordic countries.

How can this be explained when these countries belong to the Nordic cluster of institutional welfare states that are recurrently described as universalist (Esping-Andersen, 1990; Vogel, 2002) and when general Nordic poverty rates are among the lowest in the OECD area (OECD, 2008)? This chapter presents results from our research project, 'Youth trajectories: a longitudinal study of risk factors for marginalisation in Finland, Sweden and Norway'.[2] The aim of the project is to shed light on the transition from adolescence to adulthood in these three Nordic countries, with a focus on the risks of marginalisation.[3]

This chapter explores the function and development of unemployment benefits and social assistance as indicators of how the Nordic welfare regimes are responding to the life trajectories of younger citizens, based on our analyses of longitudinal national datasets. The chapter reveals that means-tested payments have become more central in meeting the needs of out-of-work young people, and that there has been a simultaneous decrease in young peoples' reliance on earnings-related social insurance benefits. It argues that social background and certain life-course events are particularly strong predictors of receipt of social assistance among young people. The consequence is that – in a system characterised by 'universality' – young people, particularly the most vulnerable, are exposed to insecurity during their transition to adulthood.

9.2 Nordic youth poverty and marginalised trajectories

How the transition from youth to adulthood evolves cannot be solely perceived as an individual pathway, since societal and cultural norms formulate desired trajectories. The risk of poverty during young adulthood can depend on the prevailing 'transition regime' (Vogel, 2002) that creates economic, institutional and cultural norms and patterns that affect and structure this life-phase and outline a 'climate of normality' (Walther, 2006). The Nordic countries have been considered as belonging to a 'universalistic transition regime' supported by social rights, such as social assistance and linked to citizenship status regardless of family situation (Walther, 2006).

Young people's transitions are highly individually differentiated and can be understood as classed, gendered and culturally diverse (Bottrell and Armstrong, 2007; Tolonen, 2008). It is therefore misleading to discuss young people as a homogenous group. Despite this, there are some quite apparent features that characterise Nordic young people's transitions, such as late labour-market entry and leaving the parental home early, factors that often increase financial vulnerability. Previous comparative research reveals that the main explanatory factor for the high youth poverty in this age group in the Nordic countries in comparison to other European countries is the pattern of leaving home very early (Mendola et al., 2009). Finland, and even more so Sweden, also struggle with high youth unemployment rates exceeding 20 per cent (Nordic Council of Ministers, 2011), and almost a quarter of all households in Sweden needing social assistance are young adults who have left the parental home (SKL, 2011).

During the last few decades, the transition between youth and adulthood has evolved into a prolonged, de-standardised and more unstable life phase for young people in the Nordic countries (Salonen, 2003), characterised by a high level of mobility as well as temporary jobs (du Bois-Reymond and Lopez Blasco, 2003; TemaNord, 2010, p. 515) and where education often constitutes a substantially extended life-period. The extensive structural changes in the Nordic labour market has led to less secure conditions for those with low formal competence or skills, often resulting in precarious trajectories.

In the Nordic countries, remaining outside employment and in receipt of various public benefits is often perceived as a major welfare risk for youths and a predictor of disadvantaged individual trajectories. Spatial metaphors, where this group are defined as 'excluded', 'outside' or 'on the margins' of society and welfare state arrangements are frequently expressed, often within a context where more deterministic and permanent scenarios are presented in relation to young people who lack education, income and employment (Angelin, 2009; Nord 2012: 005, 2012).

The next section will examine the policy context in which young people in the Nordic countries undergo such transitions before then analysing longitudinal register data on receipt of social assistance and inclusion in unemployment benefit schemes.

9.3   Policy context: Social assistance and unemployment insurance in three Nordic countries

The general trend in the Nordic countries after the Second World War was to move away from residual social assistance and towards social insurance as the main element of income protection for unemployed people (Johansson and Hvinden, 2007). The Nordic countries faced economic recession in the early 1990s, which had a severe impact on Sweden and Finland. Norway was less affected, one explanation being

Norway's access to oil revenues (Drøpping et al., 1999; Jonung et al., 2009). This period is often referred to as 'the welfare crisis': the recession prompted a shift towards increased legal regulations that enforced compliance to work obligations and participation in activation schemes as a condition for receipt of social assistance (Lødemel and Trickey, 2001; Scarpa, 2009). Since the 1990s, there has been an increasing connection in welfare-to-work programmes between eligibility for receipt of social assistance and behavioural conditions and sanctions related to non-compliance, not least targeted towards young citizens in Sweden, Norway and Finland (Thorén, 2008; Ulmestig, 2007). All three countries subsequently experienced a strong economic upturn during the late 1990s. Nevertheless, receipt of social assistance among young adults remained at quite high levels in Finland and Sweden.

Every country has been affected by the global economic crisis that began in 2008, yet again, Sweden and Finland stand out and specifically with regard to high youth unemployment. The Nordic Council of Ministers (Nord 2012:005, 2012) expressed great concern in relation to marginal inclusion of young citizens and what they define as a substantial and increased 'exclusion' from education and work among young people in the Nordic countries, where around 10 per cent of young people between the ages of 15 and 24 are defined as at risk of permanent exclusion.

The structure of unemployment protection differs in the Nordic countries: Finland and Sweden follow the so-called Ghent system (voluntary membership in unemployment insurance funds) while Norwegian unemployment protection is compulsory (Sjöberg, 2011). Although universal welfare benefits and services are considered characteristic of the Nordic welfare model, unemployment benefits rely predominantly on previous employment in order to qualify for benefits (Timonen, 2003). The financial turbulence and crisis of the 1990s brought about extensive restructuring, with substantial retrenchment and tightening up of social protection systems, and unemployment benefits became increasingly dependent on previous employment, which excluded many young adults from earnings-related benefits (Scarpa, 2009; Timonen, 2003).

In all three countries, social assistance is a last-resort form of means-tested economic support for all citizens, including those who need additional economic support even when eligible for unemployment benefits. However, support is only available when all other options have been exhausted. The countries' systems are characterised by a high level of discretion on the part of the local authorities that administer and finance the social assistance system. In 2010 Norway had the lowest level of social assistance: around 3.5 per cent of the population aged over 18 were recipients. Finland was the Nordic country with the highest proportion: above 6 per cent and Sweden was located in the middle with receipt of benefits close to 4 per cent (Nordic Council of Ministers, 2011). A common pattern in all three countries is a substantially higher uptake of social assistance benefits among young adults.

According to Kuivalainen and Nelson (2012) Finnish and Swedish social assistance benefit levels have been heavily eroded since the 1990s. Since the turn of the century the levels have been too low to lift recipients above the EU 'at-risk-of-poverty rate' (60 per cent of median disposable income). Benefit levels have remained stable in Norway, but even this Norwegian level has been too low to be adequate in terms of the 'at-risk-of-poverty rate' (Kuivalainen and Nelson, 2012, p. 78).

Based on this information, we set out to present our longitudinal analyses of the trends in coverage and development of unemployment insurance and determinants of social assistance for young people in the countries studied.

9.4 Method

The Nordic countries have the rare opportunity of merging, for research purposes, the individual level data[4] on demography, social security benefits, social assistance, work activity, unemployment, education and so on from different population-based registers. All data in this research project were delivered by national unemployment services or collected from national statistics offices. Use of register-based data collected from official public sources ensures comparability between countries.[5] The analyses we present on unemployment insurance benefits are based on age-specific unemployment numbers compiled for all three countries covering the last 10–20 years (presented in full in Lorentzen et al., 2014). The analyses related to determinants of social assistance (presented in full in Kauppinen et al., 2014) were based on longitudinal register-based datasets and cross-tabulations. Generalised ordinal logistic regression was applied as statistical methods. In Sweden ($N = 669,027$) and Norway ($N = 362,959$), we used the whole population, but in Finland we used a 25 per cent sample of the population ($N = 109,374$). The populations consisted of persons belonging to the birth cohorts from 1978 to 1984, living in a family in the respective country at the age of 16. We measured the person's total number of months of receipt of social assistance when aged 18–24.

9.5   Findings from the studies

9.5.1   The development of unemployment insurance in three Nordic countries

Nordic countries are often perceived as providing generous unemployment benefits and extensive labour market intervention with capacity to protect young adults who are only loosely connected to the labour market. In this part of our research project,[6] we investigated whether this perception was adequate and whether there has been a displacement in the type of welfare services available for unemployed young people in Norway, Finland and Sweden. Young adults in the Nordic countries are specifically vulnerable to tightening up of benefit regulations and policy changes relating to unemployment protection, not only because they are more likely to be unemployed, but also because they are often barely entitled or not entitled at all to receipt of unemployment insurance benefit owing to eligibility criteria that predominantly bases the right to social welfare protection on previous employment.

The net replacement rates in earnings-related unemployment insurance corresponds to the compensation rate of 53 per cent in Finland, 63 per cent in Norway and 48 per cent in Sweden for a single average wage earner (Nososco, 2011). The structures of unemployment protection in these countries have many similarities but the main differences are compulsory membership of Norwegian unemployment insurance funds, in contrast to voluntary membership in the Finnish and Swedish unemployment insurance funds. In addition to earnings-related benefits, Finland and Sweden also have a flat-rate benefit for qualified unemployed people who are not members of an unemployment fund. Finland has also implemented a third form of means-tested unemployment support.

9.5.1.1   *Finland*

Finland has a three-tier system and is the only one of the three countries to have this third form of means-tested unemployment support. The tiers include an earnings-related daily allowance, a flat-rate basic allowance and a means-tested labour market subsidy. Since the early 1990s, insurance-based unemployment benefits, especially in relation to young unemployed persons, have been characterised by cutbacks and the tightening up of eligibility criteria (Aho and Virjo, 2003). Means-tested labour market subsidies were targeted towards those without previous employment experience. The earnings-related unemployment benefit in Finland is now only available for unemployed persons who have been a member of an unemployment fund for at least eight months preceding unemployment and who also meet various prescribed conditions regarding previous employment history. The unemployed persons who meet the conditions regarding previous employment history, but are not members of an unemployment fund (or who have received the earnings-related benefit for the maximum time period) can apply for a flat-rate basic allowance. The basic benefit is a flat-rate sum amounting to about €698 (around €579 after tax). Unemployed jobseekers in Finland with no employment history (or those who have exceeded the maximum benefit time period) can apply for the means-tested labour market subsidy, payable over an indefinite period.

The insurance-based benefits of young unemployed persons living with their parents can be reduced by a maximum of 50 per cent, based on parental income. In addition, unemployed persons aged less than 25 with no vocational degree are obliged to apply for a student place leaving thousands of young adults denied this subsidy each year because of their failure to receive or refusal to seek a student place (Kananen, 2012). This leaves social assistance as the only financial support available for this particular group of young adults in Finland. Major reforms in the social assistance system took place at the beginning of the 2000s, bringing about a successive tightening up of work testing and sanctions. Social assistance now contains much stricter work testing, sanctions and means testing than 15–20 years ago (Kananen, 2012).

Figure 9.1 depicts the coverage rates of the earnings-related daily allowance, flat-rate basic allowance and the means-tested labour market subsidy for unemployed persons in Finland aged 24 and under for the period 1988–2008. Earnings-related benefits were relatively less prevalent for young people in Finland over the whole period: the coverage rate went from 25 per cent to less than 10 per cent for the youngest age group. The means-tested labour market subsidy quickly replaced the flat-rate basic unemployment benefit, since coverage of this benefit increased for the 24 and under age group; the level had exceeded 80 per cent by the end of 2008. By 2008 the means-tested unemployment benefit had taken over as the most important form of unemployment protection for all age groups in Finland.

9.5.1.2 Norway

Norway has a one-tier unemployment benefit system where the only alternative for unemployed persons who do not qualify for unemployment benefits is means-tested social assistance. There have been several changes to unemployment benefit eligibility over the last two decades,

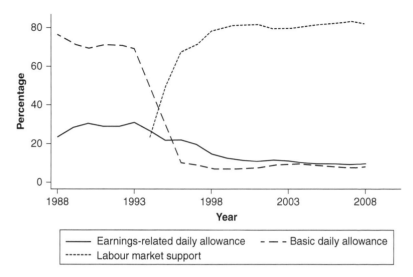

Figure 9.1 Unemployment benefits coverage for unemployed persons aged less than 25, Finland, 1988–2008
Source: Social Insurance Institution of Finland and Supervisory Authority of Finland.

characterised by a tightening up of eligibility regulations, shorter benefit periods, and stricter behavioural requirements with the intent of curtailing entitlement to unemployment benefits and getting claimants back into employment more quickly (Andreassen, 2003). Benefit levels, however, have remained unchanged. The overall percentage of those entitled to earnings-related benefits has decreased over the last two decades. The coverage rate of young unemployed persons was already substantially lower than that of older unemployed persons in the late 1980s. By 2010, it had decreased to roughly 45 per cent (Figure 9.2).

Despite the decreased coverage rate, unemployed young adults in Norway are included within unemployment benefit protection to a substantially higher degree than in Sweden and Finland.

9.5.1.3 *Sweden*

In Sweden unemployment protection comprises a two-tier system. In addition to earnings-related benefits, Sweden has a flat-rate benefit for qualified unemployed persons who are not members of an unemployment fund. Since the early 1990s, the general trend has been towards lower levels of remuneration and increasing demand for entitlement to

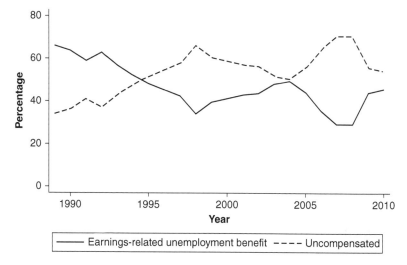

Figure 9.2   Unemployment benefits coverage for unemployed persons aged less than 25, Norway, 1989–2010

Source: The Norwegian Labour and Welfare Services.

various social security and unemployment benefits. The issue of unemployment insurance in Sweden has been the subject of intense debate as the government has implemented several policy changes that dramatically increased premiums paid by members into unemployment funds. The reform also saw the abolition of the opportunity to earn rights to receive unemployment benefits for students by studying, which primarily affected young adults in higher education. Over the period of 2006–08, 498,000 persons ended their membership of unemployment insurance funds, 40 per cent of these were young people aged between 16 and 34 (Kjellberg, 2010). Over the relatively short period of 2007–08, one in four members aged between 16 and 24 years left the unemployment insurance system, presumably largely due to drastically increased membership fees and changed conditions. Persons under 20 years of age are not entitled to basic unemployment benefit in Sweden. The maximum compensation for those only entitled to the flat-rate basic insurance component is the equivalent of €33 daily.

Unfortunately, our Swedish data only cover the period after 1999. We therefore have no information covering the economic downturn of the mid-1990s. The percentage of unemployed young people in 1999 who qualified for the basic allowance or the earnings-related unemployment benefit was 45 per cent. By the end of the period, the total

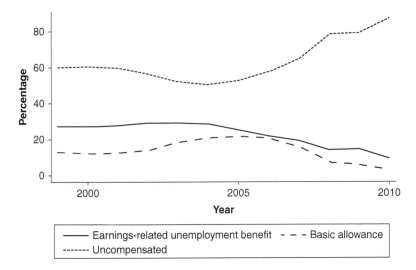

Figure 9.3 Unemployment benefits coverage for unemployed persons aged less than 25, Sweden, 1999–2009
Source: The Swedish Unemployment Insurance Board's unit of analysis.

coverage rate for young people had fallen to just 10 per cent. Most of this decline took place over the relatively short period of 2004–10. The combined developments in earnings-related unemployment benefits and the basic allowance led to the situation where, by 2010, almost 90 per cent of unemployed people below the age of 25 were not receiving unemployment benefits (Figure 9.3).

Based on these analyses, we assume that, as a complement to the developments in unemployment protection in the three countries, the function of means-tested social assistance has become more central in providing basic living expenses for unemployed young people. Earnings-related unemployment benefits for those aged 24 or below include 45 per cent of unemployed Norwegians; in Sweden and Finland, however, this comprises a figure as low as 10 per cent of the group.

9.5.2 Determinants and the development of receipt of social assistance

Our analyses that stated the increasing importance of social assistance for young people motivated our interest in a more thorough analysis of determinants and distribution. What factors can explain which young people need social assistance and which young people become long- or short-term recipients? The high youth unemployment levels and the increasingly marginal inclusion in unemployment insurance benefits are obviously highly correlated to young people's receipt of social assistance in the countries studied. At the same time, the extended period of transition to adulthood is perceived as a central risk factor for poverty in the Nordic countries, which are characterised by a high prevalence of new social risks owing to young people leaving home at a young age, low familial obligations (to support their young people) and increasing educational demands that further increase the risk of young persons needing public financial support.

These life-course events during young adulthood can have an effect on receipt of social assistance. Their importance is emphasised in theories of individualisation and the 'democratization of poverty' (see, for example, Pintelon et al., 2013). Critical phases and transitions during the life-courses of young adults, such as leaving school or the parental home and establishing a family (especially for single providers), might lead to short-term financial difficulties where receipt of social assistance could be seen as a temporary solution to acute economic hardship for young adults from all social strata (Lorentzen et al., 2012).

Equally, it is evident that extensive financial vulnerability and applying for social assistance are not evenly distributed or 'democratised' since socio-economic background continues to have an effect on the likelihood of receiving social assistance. An overview of research studies on the intergenerational reproduction of disadvantage reveals that young people from less privileged socio-economic backgrounds are more likely to become recipients since they more commonly lack resources and capital that would help them navigate transitions or exercise choice in managing their lives, which can result in long-term receipt of social assistance (Bourdieu, 1986; Furlong, 2006; Kauppinen et al., 2014; Roberts, 2009). Our hypothesis, therefore, was that life-course events mainly lead to short-term receipt of social assistance, while coming from a less favourable social background is probably more related to long-term need for social assistance. We therefore focus on analysing the central relevance of social stratification and life-course factors, asking the following questions. How important are changing transition patterns and the related life-course risks? Are the 'old' socio-economic factors still the most important factors determining social assistance receipt? And can the same factors explain the causes that lead to short-term and long-term social assistance receipt?

Table 9.1 shows the incidence of receipt of social assistance in the cohorts studied when aged 18–24. Finland is the country with the highest uptake – 35 per cent had social assistance during the follow-up

Table 9.1 Distribution of the months of social assistance receipt by country

	Social assistance months during the follow-up						N
	0	1–6	7–18	19–36	37+	Total (%)	
Sweden	77.3	9.9	6.3	4.2	2.3	100	669,027
Norway	83.7	8.4	4.3	2.3	1.3	100	362,959
Finland	64.8	18.1	8.9	4.8	3.4	100	109,374

Source: Kauppinen et al. (2014).

period – while in Norway it was far less common, with 16 per cent having been recipients. However, the profiles among the young people who received social assistance are more similar across all countries; the short-term receipt category (less than seven months) makes up around half of all recipients, while the long-term category (at least 37 months) consists of 8–10 per cent of recipients.

Table 9.2 shows receipt of social assistance in extreme categories of selected variables.[7] Social background was clearly associated with receipt of social assistance, since all social background variables were associated with the risk of receipt of social assistance in all the countries: lower parental income, lower parental education, parental unemployment, and also parents having received social assistance themselves predicted a higher probability of uptake among the young people studied. Sweden is the country where differences in parental income and parental receipt of social assistance were most prominent. Differences in other variables were smaller between the countries. The largest differences were related to parental receipt of social assistance, but in Finland there were also differences with regard to parental unemployment.

Social background variables were related to the number of months of receipt of social assistance. However, none of the categories of social background variables specifically predicted long-term receipt. Short-term receipt was more common than the longest-term receipt in all countries in all the categories of these variables. Our hypothesis that less favourable social background largely increases long-term receipt of social assistance was not valid. The Finnish results, however, were partly in accordance with this assumption: there were no large differences between the social background categories in the probability of short-term receipt of social assistance.

Receipt of social assistance determined by two life-course variables is also illustrated in Table 9.2. As expected, leaving the parental home at a

Table 9.2 Social assistance receipt (%) by selected social background life-course variables

	Months of social assistance (categories 7–18 and 19–36 have been omitted)											
	Sweden				Norway				Finland			
	0	1–6	37+	N	0	1–6	37+	N	0	1–6	37+	N
Social background												
Parental income when 17												
Low[i]	59	13	6	65,669	69	14	4	36,243	57	19	6	10,938
High[ii]	93	4	0	134,005	92	5	0	72,485	80	13	1	21,874
Parent(s) received social assistance when 17												
No	83	9	1	613,595	86	7	1	337,528	69	17	2	99,149
Yes	22	19	14	55,432	47	21	7	25,431	23	25	15	10,225
Life-course												
Age on leaving the parental home												
18	40	14	14	22,231	43	22	8	3,584	35	24	10	10,240
23–24	84	8	1	98,519	86	8	1	53,735	78	14	1	12,598
No. of children when 24												
0	80	9	2	571,062	85	8	1	274,505	68	17	3	94,136
3+	44	14	13	3,680	74	13	2	2,752	38	23	11	1,131

Notes: [i] Lowest decile (equivalised disposable income); [ii] Highest quintile.
Source: Kauppinen et al. (2014).

young age was a strong predictor, with pronounced long-term receipt of social assistance in all countries and especially in Sweden. Becoming a parent was also associated with receipt of social assistance in Sweden and Finland, while this association was much weaker in Norway. Again long-term receipt of social assistance was more pronounced in Sweden. Severe health problems, measured as becoming a disability pensioner during the follow-up, were strongly associated in all countries with receipt and duration of social assistance.

In addition to social background and life-course variables, we also used demographic variables as control variables in the multivariate analyses. Of these control variables, country of birth and family type had the strongest associations with receipt of social assistance. Young people coming from one-parent households, for example, had 1.9–2.6 times higher risk of receiving social assistance themselves when compared with young people who have married parents.

We also assessed in multivariate analyses whether both social background and life-course variables are still relevant as predictors of receipt and duration of social assistance when both groups of variables are simultaneously taken into account. The analyses indicated that both groups of variables are essential in understanding receipt of social assistance by young adults in the three countries. The importance of social background is evident as it continues to be a significant determinant of poverty risk. However, the life-course variables also had an effect. Having parents who themselves received social assistance as well as the establishment of their own household at an early age were especially strong predictors. Both of these also predicted a longer duration of poverty, and had effects independent of each other. As previously described, we aimed to investigate the possible distinction between short-term and long-term receipt of social assistance. Our hypotheses that social background variables predict mostly long-term receipt and life-course factors predict mostly short-term receipt were not confirmed in the analysis. The risk of poverty does not seem to be 'democratised' (see Pintelon et al., 2013). Long-term receipt of social assistance is not merely based on having an unfavourable social background and the effects of life-course factors are not limited to short-term receipt. However, the results vary slightly across the countries with regard to these patterns. Sweden seems to conform least to our hypothesis, especially concerning life-course factors, which had long-term effects, while several life-course variables only had short-term effects in Norway. Short-term recipients are also less differentiated by social background in Finland.

9.6 Discussion and conclusion: How universal is the Nordic welfare model for vulnerable young people?

A longer and more reversible transition to adulthood has become a life phase that covers several years, in some cases up to a decade. Therefore it is worthwhile to reflect on the welfare state capacity to provide social protection during this period. Have the welfare states of Finland, Sweden and Norway shielded young adults from financial vulnerability? Can one conclude that they have adjusted their social protection to the recent challenges of young adults' loose connection to the labour markets that constitute the basic link to and precondition of universal welfare access?

We cannot present any conclusive answers here but will instead shed light on dimensions of this complex issue. Our quantitative analyses, for instance, omitted the potential impact of modifications in the countries' education and labour market structures on social and unemployment protection for young people and instead focused upon policy changes and determinants of social assistance. The conclusions that can be reached from these analyses illustrate how unemployment protection for young adults in these Nordic countries has developed in a direction that substantially differs from the perception of a Nordic model that ensures inclusive and comprehensive welfare state protection. Goul Andersen (2012) states that the Social Democratic transformation of the Ghent model to an almost universalist system has turned out to be reversible to quite a large extent. Our findings from Finland and Sweden certainly seem to substantiate this conclusion. Our analyses demonstrate a development, starting from the early 1990s, where the most important form of income protection for young people is means-tested unemployment and social assistance benefits. As means-tested remuneration has become less and less generous, the risk of poverty for young adults has increased (Kuivalainen and Nelson, 2012). This development in the countries studied, primarily in Sweden and Finland, indicates the central link between policy changes and unemployment benefit coverage, as policy adjustments have resulted in far-reaching changes including increased selectivism with regard to unemployment benefits. Social protection for unemployed young people has progressed towards a situation where conditioned poverty relief has increased and to a substantial extent also replaced rights-based unemployment protection schemes.

Furthermore, our analyses also demonstrate that social background continues to be a significant determinant of poverty risk and also that life-course events have to be taken into account as determinants of social assistance. In conclusion, we found leaving the parental home at a young age and parental receipt of social assistance to be especially strong predictors, confirming earlier findings of the significance of these factors for the risk of poverty during early adulthood in the Nordic countries, and noting that both of these factors also predict a longer duration of poverty, and that they have effects independent of each other.

Understanding patterns of receipt of social assistance among young adults in the countries studied demands a complex and multivariate approach since policies change and social background and life-course events are highly relevant. Long-term receipt of social assistance could be attributed both to social background and to life-course factors, indicating that our hypothesis of short-term social assistance as primarily the result or requirement of temporal relief during the unstable youth phase is not valid. Risks associated with life-course events may have become further pronounced because the patterns of establishment of adult life are taking longer, which can result in welfare exclusion. The looser connection to the labour market constitutes a risk factor for the increased requirement of social assistance, but again our analyses indicate that it is relevant both in relation to short- and long-term receipt of social assistance.

Is it reasonable, then, to interpret young people's relatively greater need for social assistance and lower inclusion in unemployment insurances as indicators of inadequate social policies to meet the social protection challenges that have emerged from changed youth trajectories?[8] This may be partially correct judging from our analyses. However, it is also essential that we state that young people have experienced more extensive unemployment and receipt of social assistance than adults in the Nordic countries for several decades. It is also important to keep in mind that unemployment is the major explanation of fluctuations in the receipt of social assistance. The development that does seem to be relevant in relation to our results is that young adults have experienced less inclusion in rights-based unemployment insurance and that means-tested social benefits are therefore becoming the major remaining form of social protection. Unemployment insurance clearly has a decreased capacity to protect young adults from financial vulnerability, and this contributes to increasing dependence on social assistance as a provider of welfare during periods outside the labour market. It is also evident that life-course events such as having a child or becoming ill at a young age are associated with greater receipt of social assistance, indicating that national social insurance protection schemes are not fully sufficient or adjusted to prevent young people requiring means-tested municipal support.

In conclusion, our research suggests that the redistributive Nordic welfare states seem to have a gap in their comprehensive welfare protection during the critical school to work transition for this specific segment of the population. This could lead to a further discussion on whether the Nordic welfare states lack adequate social policies in relation to this group and if previous requirements in social insurance, for instance employment as an eligibility criterion for inclusion, have become obsolete and less adjusted to the prevailing trajectories of young people in the Nordic countries. The dual categorisation of unemployed citizens in the social protection system creates a division between earnings-related national social insurance (for those previously employed) and means-tested social assistance, resulting in a marginal or non-included position for many young adults in the Nordic welfare states. Young people often express stigmatising experiences because they are not viewed as legitimate recipients of social welfare in the Nordic countries. Young long-term recipients of social assistance often experience shame, powerlessness and deprivation in connection to being dependent on this means-tested benefit (Angelin, 2009).

Notes

1. Although Nordic youths consistently have higher poverty rates than the adult population, it is central to state that their poverty is primarily related to low income and rarely to substantial material deprivation or persistent financial vulnerability throughout the life-course (see Fahmy, in this volume; Halleröd and Westberg, 2006).
2. Funded by The Joint Committee for Nordic Research Councils in the Humanities and Social Sciences (NOS-HS).
3. The results presented in this chapter have been published in the *International Journal of Social Welfare*, 'Unemployment and economic security for young adults in Finland, Norway and Sweden: From unemployment protection to poverty relief' (Lorentzen et al., 2014) and in the *Journal of European Social Policy* in the article 'Social background and life-course risks as determinants of social assistance receipt among young adults in Sweden, Norway and Finland' (Kauppinen et al., 2014).
4. We only used individual register data in the multivariate analyses. In the analyses on unemployment insurance coverage most of the data was aggregated.
5. Although the data are comparable between countries, it is important to keep in mind when reading the numbers that different institutional characteristics and economic conditions might complicate the direct comparison of benefit recipients across countries.
6. See Lorentzen et al. (2014) for a more extensive presentation.

7. Duration categories 7–18 and 19–36 months have been omitted for brevity.
8. By this we mean in relation to the older population of the studied countries.

References

Aho, S. and Virjo, I. (2003). 'More Selectivity in Unemployment Compensation in Finland: Has it Led to Activation or Increased Poverty?', in Standing, G. (ed.) *Minimum Income Schemes in Europe* (Geneva: International Labour Office), pp. 193–218.

Andersen, J.G. (2012). 'Universalization and De-universalization of Unemployment Protection in Denmark and Sweden', in Anttonen, A., Häikiö, L. and Stefánsson, K. (eds.) *Welfare State, Universalism and Diversity* (Cheltenham, UK: Edward Elgar Publishing), pp. 162–87.

Andreassen, J. (2003). *Må vi ta den jobben? Aetats praktisering av mobilitetskravene i dagpengeregelverket* (Oslo: Fafo).

Angelin, A. (2009). *Den dubbla vanmaktens logik. En studie om långvarig arbetslöshet och socialbidragstagande bland unga vuxna.* Lund Dissertations in Social Work no. 38 (Lund: Lund University).

Anxo, D., Bosch, G. and Rubery, J. (eds.) (2010). *The Welfare State and Life Transitions: A European Perspective* (Cheltenham: Edward Elgar Publishing).

Bottrell, D. and Armstrong, D. (2007). 'Changes and Exchanges in Marginal Youth Transitions'. *Journal of Youth Studies* 10 (3), 353–71.

Bourdieu, P. (1986). *Distinction: A Social Critique of Judgements of Taste* (London: Routledge & Kegan Paul).

Drøpping, J.A., Hvinden, B. and Vik, K. (1999). 'Activation Policies in the Nordic Countries', in Kautto, M. and Hvinden, B. (eds.) *Nordic Social Policy, Changing Welfare States* (London: Routledge), pp. 131–58.

du Bois-Reymond, M. and López Blasco, A. (2003). 'Yo-yo Transitions and Misleading Trajectories: Towards Integrated Transition Policies for Young Adults in Europe', in López Blasco, A., McNeish, W. and Walther, A. (eds.) *Young People and Contradictions of Inclusion: Towards Integrated Transition Policies in Europe* (Bristol: The Policy Press), pp. 19–41.

Esping-Andersen, G. (1990). *The Three Worlds of Welfare Capitalism* (Cambridge: Polity Press).

France, A. (2008). 'From Being to Becoming: The Importance of Tackling Youth Poverty in Transitions to Adulthood'. *Social Policy & Society* 7 (4), 495–505.

Furlong, A. (2006). 'Not a Very NEET Solution: Representing Problematic Labour Market Transitions among Early School-Leavers'. *Work, Employment and Society* 20 (3), 553–69.

Halleröd, B. and Westberg, A. (2006). 'Youth Problem: What's the Problem? A Longitudinal Study of Incomes and Economic Hardship among Swedish Youth'. *Acta Sociologica* 49 (1), 83–102.

Johansson, H. and Hvinden, B. (2007). 'Re-activating the Nordic Welfare States: Do We Find a Distinct Universalistic Model?' *International Journal of Sociology and Social Policy* 27 (7/8), 334–46.

Jonung, L., Kiander, J. and Vartia, P. (2009). *The Great Financial Crisis in Finland and Sweden: The Nordic Experience of Financial Liberalization* (Cheltenham: Edward Elgar Publishing).

Kananen, J. (2012). 'Nordic Paths from Welfare to Workfare: Danish, Swedish and Finnish Labour Market Reforms in Comparison'. *Local Economy* 27, 558–76.

Kauppinen, T.M., Angelin, A., Lorentzen, T., Bäckman, O., Salonen, T., Moisio, P. and Dahl, E. (2014). 'Social Background and Life-course Risks as Determinants of Social Assistance Receipt among Young Adults in Sweden, Norway and Finland'. *Journal of European Social Policy* 24 (3), 273–88.

Kjellberg, A. (2010). *Vilka 'hoppade av' a-kassan eller avstod från att gå med? En studie av a-kassornas medlemsras* (Lund: Lund University).

Kuivalainen, S. and Nelson, K. (2012). 'Eroding Minimum Income Protection in the Nordic Countries? Reassessing the Nordic Model of Social Assistance', in Kvist, J., Fritzell, J., Hvinden, B. and Kangas, O. (eds.) *Changing Social Equality: The Nordic Welfare Model in the 21st Century* (Bristol: The Policy Press), pp. 69–88.

Lorentzen, T., Angelin, A., Dahl, E., Kauppinen, T., Moisio, P. and Salonen, T. (2013). 'Unemployment and Economic Security for Young Adults in Finland, Norway and Sweden: From Unemployment Protection to Poverty Relief'. *International Journal of Social Welfare* 23 (1), 41–51.

Lorentzen, T., Dahl, E. and Harsløf, I. (2012). 'Welfare Risks in Early Adulthood: A Longitudinal Analysis of Social Assistance Transitions in Norway'. *International Journal of Social Welfare* 21 (4), 408–21.

Lødemel, I. and Trickey, H. (2001). *An Offer You Can't Refuse: Workfare in International Perspective* (Bristol: Policy Press).

Mendola, D., Busetta, A. and Aassve, A. (2009). 'What Keeps Adults in Permanent Poverty? A Comparative Analysis Using ECHP'. *Social Science Research* 38 (4), 840–57.

Moore, K. (2005). *Thinking about Youth Poverty through the Lenses of Chronic Poverty, Life-course Poverty and Intergenerational Poverty.* CPRC Working Paper 57 (Manchester: The University of Manchester Chronic Poverty Research Centre).

Müller, W. and Gangl, M. (eds.) (2003). *Transitions from Education to Work in Europe. The Integration of Youth in EU Labour Markets* (Oxford: Oxford University Press).

Nord 2012:005 (2012). *Unge på Kanten. Om inkludering av utsatte ungdommer* (Nordisk ministerråd).

Nordic Council of Ministers (2011). *Nordic Statistical Yearbook 2011* (Copenhagen: Nordic Council of Ministers).

Nososco (2011). 'Erstatningsniveu i typetilfelde i forbindelse med arbeidsløshet for forsikrede 2009', Available from http://nososco-da.nom-nos.dk/ (accessed on 9 December 2011).

OECD (2008). *Growing Unequal?: Income Distribution and Poverty in OECD Countries* (Paris: OECD Publishing).

Pintelon, O., Cantillon, B., Van den Bosch, K. and Whelan, C.T. (2013). 'The Social Stratification of Social Risks: The Relevance of Class for Social Investment Strategies'. *Journal of European Social Policy* 23 (1), 52–67.

Roberts, K. (2009). 'Opportunity Structures Then and Now'. *Journal of Education and Work* 22 (5), 355–68.

Salonen, T. (2003). *Ungas ekonomi och etablering – En studie om förändrade villkor från 1970-talet till 2000-talets inledning* Ungdomsstyrelsens skrifter 2003:9 (Stockholm: Ungdomsstyrelsen).

Scarpa, S. (2009). 'The Scalar Dimension of Welfare State Development: The Case of Swedish and Finnish Social Assistance Systems'. *Cambridge Journal of Regions Economy and Society* 2, 67–83.

Sjöberg, O. (2011). 'Sweden: Ambivalent Adjustment', in Clegg, D. and Clasen, J. (eds.) *Regulating the Risk of Unemployment: National Adaptations to Post-Industrial Labour Markets in Europe* (Oxford: Oxford University Press), pp. 208–32.

SKL Sveriges kommuner och Landsting (2011). 'Results From Survey Conducted by SKL', Available from http://www.mynewsdesk.com/se/sveriges_kommuner_och_landsting/news/arbetsloeshet-ofta-bakom-socialbidrag-till-unga-18800 (accessed on 8 November 2013).

Smeeding, T.M. and Phillips, R.K. (2002). 'Cross-National Differences in Employment and Economic Sufficiency'. *Annals* 580, 103–33.

TemaNord (2010). *Labour Market Mobility in Nordic Welfare States* (Copenhagen: Nordic Council of Ministers).

Thorén, K.H. (2008). *Activation Policy in Action: A Street-Level Study of Social Assistance in the Swedish Welfare State* (Chicago: University of Chicago).

Timonen, V. (2003). *Restructuring the Welfare State: Globalization and Social Policy Reform in Finland and Sweden* (Cheltenham: Edward Elgar Publishing).

Tolonen, T. (2008). 'Success, Coping and Social Exclusion in Transitions of Young Finns'. *Journal of Youth Studies* 11 (2), 233–49.

Ulmestig, R. (2007). *På gränsen till fattigvård: En studie om arbetsmarknadspolitik och socialbidrag.* Lund Dissertations in Social Work no. 27 (Lund: Lund University).

Vogel, J. (2002). 'European Welfare Regimes and the Transition to Adulthood: A Comparative and Longitudinal Perspective'. *Social Indicators Research* 59 (3), 275–99.

Walther, A. (2006). 'Regimes of Youth Transitions. Choice, Flexibility and Security in Young People's Experiences across Different European Contexts'. *Young* 14 (2), 119–39.

10
The Dualisation of Social Policies towards Young People in France: Between Familism and Activation

Tom Chevalier and Bruno Palier

10.1 Introduction

The mass expansion of higher education, the extension of the typical duration of studies and growing difficulties in entering the labour market have changed the transition from youth to adulthood. For these reasons some authors refer to youth as a 'new age of life' (Galland, 1993) or, in psychological terms, as 'emerging adulthood' (Arnett, 2000). In the literature on youth and the transition to adulthood, many typologies have been proposed in order to analyse the various possible institutional national arrangements that shape this transition (Breen and Buchmann, 2002; Van de Velde, 2008; Wallace and Bendit, 2009; Walther, 2006). They all rely on the seminal three-term typology of 'welfare regimes' developed by Esping-Andersen (Esping-Andersen, 1990) and further modified by Gallie and Paugam (Gallie and Paugam, 2000), who added a fourth type following the insights of Ferrera (Ferrera, 1996).

France is always categorised into the continental regime type, labelled 'employment-centred' (Walther, 2006), together with Germany and the Netherlands. However, regarding some outcomes (such as youth unemployment rates: 8.6 per cent in Germany against 22.9 per cent in France in 2011, Eurostat) or institutional features (such as the place of vocational education and training) (Busemeyer, 2009), France does not fit well into this category. Some authors have shown that, regarding youth, familism is particularly important for the French transition to adulthood, but not so in the German or Dutch systems (Van de Velde, 2008; Walther, 2006). This feature brings France closer to the Mediterranean regime type. This leads us to reconsider the usual characterisation of

France, which cannot be associated with the same model as the German one when considering social policies dealing with the transition to adulthood (which we will call 'youth social policies').

This chapter analyses the social policies targeted at young people in France. By 'young people', we mean those individuals between the end of compulsory schooling and entry and stabilisation in the labour market (access to standard employment). Thus, they can either be in higher education or trying to enter the labour market (they may be unemployed or in non-standard employment contracts, and not yet integrated into the labour market). This functional (and not biological) definition of young people excludes those in secure work: they are not in transition any more, so they are not 'young' any more, according to our definition. Accordingly, young people in these different positions may claim different kinds of social benefits: student aids, unemployment benefits, social assistance, family policy benefits, tax relief or housing benefits. Our aim is to understand how these social policies from which young people can benefit are structured in France.

In this chapter, we claim that youth social policies typically contribute to the process of dualisation analysed in Emmenegger et al. (2012). By dualisation, they mean treating different social groups differently in terms of policy, and we will underline how French youth social policies differentiate (and reinforce the differences between) two different types of young people, depending on their situation.

In the new post-industrial economy, skills have become crucial to enter the labour market (Abrassart, 2011). With the extension and the development of education, the norm is no longer to enter the labour market soon after the end of compulsory school, but to continue into higher education (Nicole-Drancourt and Roulleau-Berger, 2001). This has led to a growing importance of skills in the production of inequalities. Some authors even say that this trend has produced 'two different youths' (*'deux jeunesses'*) in France (Galland, 2012). The general trend of dualisation between skilled and unskilled individuals, which particularly affects young people (Emmenegger et al., 2012), is reinforced by a dualisation of youth social policies in France. The French youth policies are indeed quite different for those attending higher education, whose parents can benefit from the extension of family policies, and for those unskilled youth who, having difficulties entering the labour market, are subjected to specific active labour market policies.

Our chapter will analyse in detail the content of such dualisation. Taking an historical perspective, we will show how successive answers to social problems met by young people have built a system of dual solutions. First, from after the Second World War to the 1990s, France decided to help families support their young members' continuing education. Second, starting in the 1980s, specific employment policies were developed for those young people not continuing education and having difficulties entering the labour market. In the next section, we will show that there has been a familialisation of public aids directed towards young people in higher education. In Section 10.3, we will analyse the development of specific active labour market policies (ALMP) aimed towards the most vulnerable (low-skilled) young people, with the so-called 'insertion' policy towards young people (*politique d'insertion des jeunes*). In our conclusion, we show that this dual answer to the problems met by young people has contributed to a dualisation of youth in France.

10.2   The familialisation of benefits towards young people

The social problem of 'youth' emerges when there is a misfit between the compulsory school-leaving age, entry into the labour market and the access to full social citizenship, since it raises the problem of the financing of this period. What kind of support can young people benefit from? In France, social policies have been 'familised' in order to address this issue, which means that their purpose is to help families to take care of their children without providing any direct support to the children themselves. With this approach, youth is treated as an extended childhood, either with the biological criterion of age or with the functional criterion of status (such as enrolment in higher education): in this respect, young people are fundamentally seen as 'social minors', or 'dependants' who rely on their parents' support.[1] This familialisation translates into three institutional characteristics regarding social policies: social benefits are directed towards parents since young people are considered as 'dependent'; benefits depend on parental income; and they for the most part take place within the family policy area.

10.2.1   The rise of familialisation towards young people in higher education: 1945–70s

The 'familialisation' of social policies concerns above all young people in higher education: it is the typical pattern of subsidies to higher education in France (Blaug and Woodhall, 1978). There are different types of aid towards students in France: grants (*bourses*) and loans;[2] 'pre-employment contracts'; food and housing subsidies; medical subsidies to healthcare; tax relief to students' parents; family allowances for children in full-time education (Blaug and Woodhall, 1978); and housing benefits (Chevalier, 2012; Van de Velde, 2008).

The familialisation of youth social policies in France was first visible in the grant system for students. The entry of greater numbers of young people into higher education after the Second World War was accompanied by the introduction of means-tested grants based on parental income. In this case, students were not considered as independent households (as they are, for instance, in Nordic countries) (Eurydice, 2009). They are part of their family household and, as article 203 of the civil code states,[3] the parents have to take care of their children until the latter finish their studies. As a result, grants are not supposed to directly help students become independent; they are meant to help the family support the cost of the child pursuing higher education (Orivel, 1975, p. 16). This familism is present in all administrative documents with the 'principle of aid to the family' (*'principe de l'aide aux familles'*). The amounts given through grants are particularly low in France (around €400 a month for the poorest families): they are only supposed to complement the aid of the family to their children, not to replace it.

Starting as a mere grant system, the familialisation of benefits for the young has developed within family policies, especially through tax relief and family allowances. French family policy aims not only to sustain a high birth rate (Lenoir, 1991) but also to encourage children to continue education beyond compulsory school: 'the payment of family benefits is conditioned by educational attending, and their payment beyond compulsory school is conditioned by attending higher education' (De Foucauld and Roth, 2002, p. 114).[4] These benefits are then complemented by fiscal aids to families.

This familialisation of youth also means that young people are considered as 'dependent' regarding social security, and therefore cannot claim social benefits on their own. Social benefits are targeted at families who have a child either under a certain age or enrolled in higher education. When the school-leaving age was raised from 13 to 14 in 1936, the upper age limit to benefit from family allowances was also raised from 16 to 17 years old for young people in full-time education or apprenticeship (Ceccaldi, 2005, p. 67). This age has regularly risen since the Second World War to accompany the extension of education, especially concerning students in higher education.

Income tax relief also forms a fundamental part of the familialisation of youth policy. In France, income tax is not individualised. The fiscal unit is the family, all the incomes of all earners are gathered and fiscal authorities take the number of family members into account when calculating taxable income. Taxable income is divided by a certain number of 'shares' (*parts*), each adult being attributed one share, the first and second child half a share, and each next child a full share (calculation: taxable income/number of shares). As a result, the more children are in the family, the less (proportionally) the family pays in income tax. Since young people in France are considered as children as long as they are in education, they can constitute half a share (or *demi-part*) for the first and the second child, and then one share starting from the third child. The assumption is that the amount of money that parents do not pay in tax goes towards the maintenance of their children's education (Orivel, 1975). By 1974, tax relief for students' parents represented one-third of all public spending towards students – the most important form of public support for young people in education.

Public spending on family policy increased sharply after the Second World War, responding to the expansion of education (both secondary and higher education) and the increase in student enrolment. The number of young people in higher education increased from 159,035 in 1949 to 309,700 in 1960, 850,500 in 1970 and 1,181,100 in 1980 (Galland and Oberti, 1996).

10.2.2   The expansion of familialisation between the 1970s and the 1990s

With a rising number of young people entering higher education, family policy was increasingly used to both accompany this expansion and to deal with students facing specific social problems. The payment of family allowances was extended to children aged up to 19 in 1998, and to those aged up to 20 in 1999, regardless of any educational requirement (CNAF, 2012, p. 100). Housing allowances were also available until the children were 21. Young adults up to 25 years old who are in higher education can be attached to the fiscal household of their parents, and therefore provide 0.5 or 1 share, thereby diminishing the parental income tax (see above) (the attachment limit is set at 21 years of age for young people not in higher education). Parents can also choose not to attach their child to their fiscal household, and instead deduct from their taxable income a maintenance allowance (up to €5.495 per year) to be delivered to their child.[5] In 1993, tax relief for school fees was also made available for parents. In 2012, the relief available for a high school student was set at €153 and at €183 for a higher education student. In 1995, tax relief represented 30 per cent of all aid for students.

The familialisation of aid to young people in France is not only visible through the importance of family allowances and parents' tax relief, but also through young people's exclusion from access to the French basic income. In 1988, a general income-tested basic income, RMI (*revenu minimum d'insertion*: minimum income for insertion), was introduced (Palier, 2005). RMI was not only income-tested, but also age-tested, and only those above 25 could claim it. To be entitled to RMI before 25, one needed to have at least one child.

Analyses of debates at the time of its adoption show that young people under the age of 25 were excluded from access to the RMI in their own right for two main reasons. First, consistent with the familist principle, it was argued that it is the role of the family to take care of their children, and providing young people with access to this kind of welfare support would go against familial solidarity. This, it was argued, would encourage young people to leave the parental home too early, which could carry the risk of isolating them from society (for an analysis of this argument, see Lima, 2004). Second, as Lima has shown, some argued that giving access to this benefit before 25 would discourage young people from studying or working, because they could access some kind of revenue without having to do anything in return (Lima, 2012a). In order to avoid such 'welfare dependency', young people hence could not have access to the RMI.

In France, the age of political citizenship is 18 years old (the right to vote starts at 18), but the legal social citizenship age seems to start at 25. This legal age of adult social citizenship is the symbol of French familism (Chevalier, 2012; Lenoir, 1991; Prost, 1984). However, it raises problems when young people sever their relationships with their family, or when they do not have a family. For this reason, despite the refusal of the RMI to young people, another assistance scheme was adopted in 1988: the *Fonds d'aide aux jeunes*, or FAJ (Fund for Youth Support). However, this scheme does not represent a right for young people. It is not made available to all 'poor' isolated young persons, but the delivery of benefits is based on specific conditions assessed locally by social workers. It is a kind of 'ultra-residual' assistance scheme, with discretion largely in social workers' hands, since they decide if the young people who claim the aid 'deserve' it; this is accomplished through an evaluation of candidates' economic situation and behaviour (Lima, 2008).

In 1992, while the access to unemployment insurance was tightened (Palier, 2005), the specific allowance for young unemployed people (*allocation d'insertion*) was repealed. The aim was to replace passive benefits with active programmes: young people were to be directed towards vocational training programmes or jobs in the public sector instead of relying on social benefits (Palier, 2005). In the meantime, the principle of maintaining the age entry for the RMI at 25 years was affirmed (Palier, 2005). These measures altogether meant that young unemployed people had to rely even more on their families for their maintenance.

Because of French familism, the family's role in supporting children remains important even after they have reached the age of 25. The centrality of family obligations towards its members (which is the basis of French familism: see Damon, 2006) is expressed in the French civil code regulation concerning the obligation of support (*'obligation alimentaire'*): all family members have the duty to support their relatives when the former can and the latter need it. Hence, even for young people over the age of 25 years old, the family is deemed to be the primary source of support, and public assistance is considered only subsidiary (Sayn, 2005). The granting of RMI is delivered if the claimant's parents have fulfilled their legal duties towards their children (Van de Velde, 2007). This follows the legal obligations of parents to take care of their children until they find stable employment (articles 203, 295, 371–2 and—373-2-5 of the Civil Code).

In 2008, the social assistance payment (RMI) was replaced by the RSA (*revenu de solidarité active, or income for active solidarity*), which integrated more working conditions within the scheme, and more generous income tax relief for those with some activity in the labour market. Young people below 25 continued to be excluded from the scheme unless they had children. In 2010, a change was introduced that allowed young people under 25 to benefit from the RSA provided they be 'independent' from their families – meaning that they had worked two full years out of the last three (this specific income-tested basic income for the young was called 'RSA *jeune*': RSA for the young). But only a few thousand young people actually benefit from this programme.

Those young people who are not entitled to social assistance in their own right can still benefit indirectly from the RSA as dependent children when their parents claim for it. In France, 8 per cent of young people aged 16–24 benefit from the RSA, against 6.8 per cent for the whole population; 66.4 per cent of them are covered as dependants and the rest by the 'RSA *jeune*' (Labadie, 2012).

Since the late 1990s, however, state support for young people has progressively changed, providing students with more opportunities for autonomy from their parents thanks to housing benefits, while those not in education have increasingly been targeted with specific inclusion policies.

10.2.3 Housing benefits against familialisation? From the 1990s onwards

Through the development of specific housing benefits, the centrality of the family in supporting its members in higher education has started to be eroded. Despite the central role of parents, France is characterised by the comparatively early age (around 23) at which young people leave their parental home (Van de Velde, 2008). This is mainly owing to the development of housing benefits. In fact, these benefits are open to young people over 18, and are income-tested on the basis of young people's own income without regard for their parents' income. As full-time students are either inactive in the labour market or have characteristically low incomes, many of them can claim for these housing benefits, which provide them with some sort of residential independence. However, if they do claim this housing aid, their parents can no longer benefit from tax relief associated with having dependent children.

Housing benefits do partly operate against familism. This is an unintended effect of the expansion of aid policies originally aimed at other groups. When the housing benefits were created in 1971 and 1977, they were not supposed to be used by young people in higher education. They were means-tested benefits targeted towards the most vulnerable individuals, in order to reduce inequalities and promote access to home ownership. In 1993, the government decided to open some of them to all inactive young people, including students. This was conceived as a technical procedure supposed to make the benefits available to all adults. Unlike grants and family benefits, housing benefits carry no reference to parental income, and therefore became available for most young people regardless of their familial situation. The financial consequences of this reform were not entirely foreseen by the government. As a result of the change in policy, public spending steeply increased from 1993 onwards: instead of the two billion francs planned, the programme cost more than four billion in the first year (Vallat, 2002, p. 491).

In 2006, 42 per cent of all households under the age of 30 received a housing benefit (against 16 per cent for the rest of the population), representing 30 per cent of total recipients of housing benefits (Kesteman, 2010, p. 118). In 2010, out of €16 billion targeted to young people by the family benefits agencies (*Caisses d'allocations familiales* – CAF), €8.5 billion concern family benefits, €2.6 billion concern social assistance, and €5.1 billion concern housing benefits (Nicolas, 2010). Housing benefits have become one of the main benefits available for young people. In 2011, they represented 29 per cent of total student

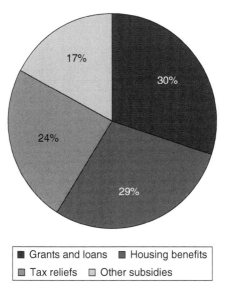

Figure 10.1   Distribution of student support, 2011 (per cent)
Source: Ministère de l'Education Nationale (2012).

support (compared with 25 per cent in 1995), against 24 per cent for tax relief (compared with 30 per cent in 1995) (see Figure 10.1).

Despite the growing importance of housing benefits, familialisation has been the main path chosen in order to deal with young people. However, this familialisation almost exclusively concerns young people in higher education. In fact, the state supports the family to help young people only because they are still students; these young people do not have any income, and as a result they are considered to be 'dependent'. Yet, because of the increase of youth unemployment since the 1970s and the growing difficulties in entering the labour market, a growing share of young people does not earn any income from work and is not enrolled in higher education. For these youth, increasingly specific employment policies have been developed, creating a second layer of social policies for the (low-skilled) young.

10.3   The introduction of active labour market policies (ALMPs) for low-skilled young people

The French social protection system has been shaped along the industrialist tripartition of the life-course: after the time of childhood and education, citizens are expected to work, and social citizenship is organised around position and status in employment (Castel, 1999; Harris, 1989; Marshall, 1950). The fact that an increasing number of individuals are unable to find jobs after leaving school is particularly challenging for this kind of system (Palier, 2010). In France, as well as in many other parts of Europe, very few benefits are available for young people out of work, training or education. The increase of youth unemployment has led to the development of active labour market policies (ALMPs) directed specifically at young people. In this respect, social benefits still remain rather rare, and are supposed to be 'active': in France, these policies take place within the so-called employment policy towards young people (*politique d'insertion des jeunes*).

10.3.1   The institutionalisation of a secondary labour market for new entrants

Labour market policies towards young people were implemented when youth unemployment rose steadily during the 1970s (see Figure 10.2). Overall, more than 80 different schemes specifically directed towards young people have been set up since then. Still, a common trend can be found in these numerous policies: they aim at creating non-standard,

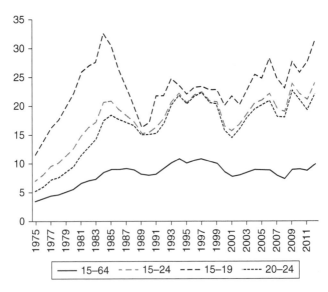

Figure 10.2   Unemployment rate by age, 1975–2012 (per cent)
Source: INSEE (2013a).

often subsidised, jobs, both in the private and in the public sectors (Lefresne, 2012).

Raymond Barre, who was prime minister from 1976 to 1981, identified the gap between youth education and actual jobs as the main cause of youth unemployment (Askenazy, 2011, p. 75). In order to address this issue, he launched three 'Pacts for Employment' (*Pactes pour l'emploi*) starting from 1977, which marked the political fight against youth unemployment, as well as the beginning of a restructuring of the labour market.

The strategy of these Pacts was structured along two objectives. On the one hand, the labour cost of people under 25 years old was lowered, with social contribution exemptions for employers who proposed a contract for more than six months to the young unemployed. On the other hand, the pacts tried to improve training by fostering employment training contracts, internships and apprenticeships (Aeberhardt et al., 2011, p. 155). The period was marked by the multiplication of supply-side measures for young people instead of a comprehensive reform of the labour market or the educational system. Thus, 'instead of fighting against this exceptional increase of the precariousness of young people in their access to employment, the first Pact of 1977–1978 institutionaliz[ed] it' (Askenazy, 2011, pp. 78–9), in the sense that with the development of these policies, more and more young people entered the labour market through (subsidised) low-paid, low-quality jobs. These jobs were supposed to be stepping stones whose function was to adjust the skills of the young and the needs of the employers. After the first Pact was adopted in 1977, many more measures were taken to combat youth unemployment using these two strategies (to lower youth labour cost/to upgrade their skills). A third strategy emerged shortly afterwards, with the development of jobs heavily subsidised by the state in non-market activities, starting from the 'Collective Utility Jobs'[6] and including 'Youth Jobs'[7] in 1997 (Aeberhardt et al., 2011, p. 158), or the more recent 'Contracts for a future'.[8] All these jobs are called 'subsidised jobs' (*emplois aidés*) in the sense that the state has developed and partly financed these kinds of contracts in order to foster youth employment.

These policies have had the effect of gradually restructuring the labour market, leading to a polarisation between a primary labour market reserved for prime age workers, and a secondary labour market reserved for new entrants, such as young people with low skill levels. The transition to a post-industrial economy has stressed the importance of skills in the labour market, which has brought greater difficulties for young people who do not go into higher education. This process of polarisation of skills owing to deindustrialisation (Esping-Andersen, 1999) is part of a broader process of dualisation (Emmenegger et al., 2012). The activation policies that are mainly directed to the most vulnerable young people contribute to a double process of dualisation. On the one hand, there is a dualisation of the labour market mentioned above, with the low-skilled young people stuck in the secondary labour market; and on the other hand, there is a dualisation of young people themselves, through a dualisation of youth policies, with family (and housing) policies taking care of the students and specific ALMPs taking care of the low-skilled young people. These labour market policies have thus progressively institutionalised a second labour market for young people, composed of non-standard jobs (see Figure 10.3).

In France, young people are over-represented in part-time and temporary contracts. In the private sector and public companies, 26 per cent of young people are in short-term contracts, against 10 per cent for the whole active population (DARES, 2011a, p. 26). Another survey shows that '86 per cent of the beneficiaries of subsidised contracts in the private sector are young people' (Gineste, 2010, p. 7). Figure 10.4 also underlines the fact that young people are over-represented in part-time

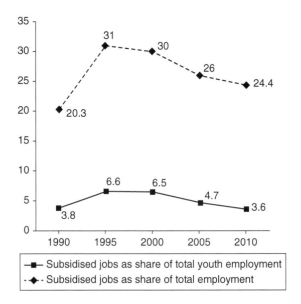

Figure 10.3   Young people in subsidised non-standard jobs, 1990–2010 (per cent)
Source: DARES (mesures pour l'emploi), INSEE (enquête Emploi) in Aeberhardt et al. (2011).

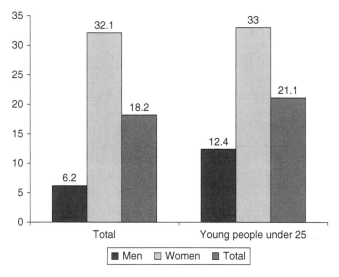

Figure 10.4   Part-time jobs (civil service excluded) by age and sex in 2011 (per cent)
Source: INSEE in Pak (2013).

jobs compared with the overall population, especially young men. And when young people are in part-time jobs, it is more often involuntary: 45.8 per cent of part-time work is involuntary for young people, against 33.4 per cent in the overall population in 2011 (Pak, 2013, p. 33).

It could be argued, though, that these jobs can operate as stepping stones towards further integration into the primary labour market. Yet these non-standard jobs do not necessarily lead to such integration: some studies have shown that low-skilled young people can actually be trapped in that secondary labour market (Arrighi, 2012; Gazier and Petit, 2007). The institutionalisation of a dual labour market because specific employment policies have expanded the prevalence of atypical job contracts in France (Palier and Thelen, 2010) has therefore changed the entry of young people into the labour market, especially the low skilled.

10.3.2   The institutionalisation of employment policy towards young people

At the beginning of the 1980s, policymakers tried to give some coherence to these increasingly important employment policies targeted at young people. In 1981, a report by Bertrand Schwartz proposed a general policy framework called the 'occupational and social integration policy for young people' (*politique d'insertion professionnelle et sociale des jeunes*). It tried to address the problem of early school-leavers in a comprehensive way and with reinforced individual support (DARES, 2003, p. 38). Accordingly, the 'Interdepartmental Commission on the Occupational and Social Policy for Vulnerable Young People' (*Délégation interministérielle à l'insertion professionnelle et sociale des jeunes en difficulté*) was established in 1981. Specific local agencies were created in March 1982 to serve as the youth public employment service (for 16–25-year-olds). This strongly institutionalised the specific entry into the labour market of vulnerable young people through the systematisation of individual support (Lima, 2008, p. 64). By 2004, seven out of ten low-skilled young people conducted their first job search through specific agencies (Mas, 2004, p. 2).

The problem for the most vulnerable young people is assumed to be their low level of skills. The specific employment policies targeted at young people should therefore enhance their skills, and their so-called 'employability' (Nicole-Drancourt and Roulleau-Berger, 2006). However, most of the schemes targeted at them do not propose any education or training. Although apprenticeships have been progressively fostered to ease the entry into the labour market (Verdier, 1995, 1996), the principal action has been to expand social contribution exemptions for employers who hire young people in general (or the most vulnerable in particular in some schemes), without any educational conditions (Lefresne, 2012). This has notably contributed to the development of low-quality jobs and the downgrading of the job structure in France (Askénazy, 2011; Lefresne, 2012; Lizé, 2006).

10.3.3   The activation of social benefits

These activation policies put young people under pressure to accept a job or training. At least, they need to present a professional project to receive support from the state. This active turn towards the young has been criticised for providing 'activation without protection' (Lima, 2012b). On the one hand, recipients must commit to some positive actions to find employment in order to receive benefits; if they do not, they lose their entitlement. On the other hand, being under 25 years old, they cannot claim for most social benefits that constitute social citizenship (see above).

This is why more recently, governments have tried to associate some very limited social benefits with specific activity contracts. Some new specific schemes introduced an allowance to support young people while they are actively in search of a job. A new 'social inclusion contract' named CIVIS (*Contrat d'insertion dans la vie sociale*), created in 2005 (282,000 young people concerned in 2010, see DARES, 2012), provides such an allowance, which depends on the parental income (hence still reflecting some kind of familialisation). Besides the CIVIS, the new 'Autonomy Contract' (*contrat d'autonomie*, created in 2008) is targeted at low-skilled young people specifically in geographic areas with the highest youth unemployment. It provides personal support and offers a small allowance, independent of parental income (benefits around €300 a month) for those actively seeking jobs or participating in training activities. Still, this programme remains underdeveloped: from July 2008 to March 2010, 25,000 contracts were signed, with over 45,000 planned for the end of 2011 (DARES, 2011b). The new 'contract income for autonomy' (*revenu contractualisé d'autonomie*) (still being tested), launched in early 2011 for 5,500 young people, reinforces this logic of giving an allowance to the young while they are in search of a job (Aeberhardt et al., 2011, p. 164). The opening of the RSA in 2010 for young people who have been in full-time work for two years out of the past three is part of the same logic, which is to provide a benefit only to young people who are actively seeking a job.

In December 2012, the new socialist government decided to launch (experimentally) a 'youth guarantee' (*garantie jeune*) for those aged 18–25 who are not in education, employment or training (NEETs): it provides intensive personal support for all young people in these categories, as well as an allowance equivalent to the RSA (€483) for the period of enrolment. The programme is provided for one year, but is renewable. It ends either when young people find a place in employment, education or training, or when they reach the age of 26 (Wargon and Gurgand, 2013).

Hence, ALMPs have been steadily developed to deal with youth unemployment since the 1970s. They have progressively restructured the labour market through the institutionalisation of a second labour market for new entrants. Activation policy has been considered as the main way to tackle the specific problem of the low skilled. As a result, some social benefits have been linked to these activation programmes and designed not to provide any disincentive to work or to search for work, reflecting the process of activation of social benefits: not only is the amount of such benefits very low, but these benefits remain residualist and tightly linked to participation in specific labour market schemes. These kinds of policies constitute the other part of the dualisation of youth social policies, which is directed to a specific group of young people: the low skilled, as opposed to those pursuing higher education who benefit from family-related benefits.

10.4   Conclusion

In this chapter, we have shown that there has been a progressive dualisation of social policies towards young people in France. On the one hand, a familialisation of social policies has occurred regarding young people in higher education. This familialisation means that the state helps the family to take care of its children, but does not provide any direct support to young people themselves. Three characteristics constitute this familialisation: benefits are directed to parents since young people are considered as dependent; parental income is taken into account when calculating the amount of benefits; and finally, most of the benefits enjoyed by young people are in the form of benefits and tax relief to families.

On the other hand, in response to the rise of youth unemployment, there has been a progressive implementation of ALMPs towards young people, and especially towards the low skilled. For this specific group of young people, the so-called employment policy towards young people (*politiques d'insertion des jeunes*) has developed hugely. The policy consists of many different programmes aimed at pushing young people towards employment, or at least towards education and training. The state has created plenty of subsidised jobs, both in the private and in the public sectors, institutionalising a secondary labour market for lower-skilled youth.

As far as social citizenship is concerned, it is interesting to note that, even though different social policies are used to deal with different groups of young people, they still reflect a rather similar image and place of young people in the welfare state; that is, young people are still conceived of as 'dependent' persons. Young people can be considered as dependent on their parents because they are in education or as dependent on the state because they are unemployed (but are not entitled to unemployment insurance since they do not have the contributions history to create their own right to unemployment allowance). This situation of 'dependency' means that they do not have full access to social citizenship. They cannot claim the same social benefits as 'normal' citizens, who can either rely on social insurance (after they have paid enough social contribution) or on assistance benefits.

In terms of intragenerational inequalities, this kind of dualisation does reinforce inequalities among young people. At the bottom, as we saw, no safety net prevents them from falling into poverty. This explains why the youth poverty rate (between 18 and 24) was as high as 21.9 per cent (against 12.6 per cent for the whole population over 18) in 2010 (INSEE, 2013b). At the top, on the other hand, the importance of tax relief for parents who have children in higher education favours young people coming from the most privileged families. In fact, first, this kind of aid benefits those families who already pay income tax, as the poorest households do not pay income tax in France. Second, the richer you are, the more tax you pay, and the bigger the tax relief is (even though some ceilings to this tax relief have been implemented). That is why this dualisation is particularly anti-redistributive and contributes to increasing inequalities.

As a result, although there is a common image of 'dependency' for young people, this 'dependency' status does not mean the same thing for them, according to their situation and their social background. On the one hand, the acceptance of dependency on the family, as long as young people are in education, leads to extra help for those who are less in need. On the other hand, the resistance towards welfare dependency leaves the most deprived young persons with almost no public help at all. They must rely on their families or provide for themselves, but without any job, they face the increasing risk of falling into poverty and social exclusion (especially if they come from an already deprived family). Hence, we can see how the welfare state, far from reducing inequalities, can sometimes produce and even reinforce them.

Nevertheless, the political discourse regarding these policies is always about social inclusion and access to autonomy. It is assumed that these specific policies towards young people will allow them to find their independence. Yet international comparisons (for instance, Van de Velde, 2008) show that access to autonomy is more easily achieved by integrating young people into the common law scheme, for instance by repealing the age limitations concerning the access to social benefits, rather than keeping young people in specific benefit programmes. Yet in the current political climate, three obstacles impede such an improvement. First, the cost of this extension of social benefits, at least in the short run, can be seen as a problem for policymakers in the context of budgetary constraint. Second, as we have underlined particularly in the French debate, providing young people with access to the general income-tested assistance benefits would appear to be favouring welfare dependency rather than creating necessary conditions for autonomy, and would create a political risk for policymakers. Third, on the contrary, creating specific schemes for young people (as long as they are linked to specific activity or behaviour) may be positively accounted by policymakers. Youth is a politically symbolic category of the population, and a significant amount of credit-claiming is at stake here. Policymakers may have more interest in adopting schemes that target a specific and 'problematic' section of the population, and this with higher visibility, than in widening general and already existing schemes.

Notes

1. The French family policies refer to the notion of *'enfant à charge'*.
2. Student loans have always been and remain marginal in France. They only concern around 3,000 young people (Ministère de l'Education Nationale Ministère de l'Enseignement Supérieur et de la Recherche, 2012).
3. The Civil Code, created by Napoleon, is made to codify relations between individuals. It incorporates a strong commitment to family members' obligation to support each other.
4. Authors' translation.
5. Their child is therefore considered as an independent fiscal household and must declare his/her income. However, if s/he has no other income than the maintenance allowance, s/he would not be taxable.
6. *travaux d'utilité collective – TUC*.
7. *emplois jeunes*.
8. *contrats d'avenir*.

References

Abrassart, A. (2011). *Cognitive Skills Matter. The Employment Disadvantage of the Low-Educated in International Comparison* (Edinburgh: RECWOWE Publication).

Aeberhardt, R., Crusson, L. and Pommier, P. (2011). 'Les politiques d'accès à l'emploi en faveur des jeunes: qualifier et accompagner', in *France, Portrait social* (Paris: INSEE Références), pp. 153–72.

Arnett, J.J. (2000). 'Emerging Adulthood: A Theory of Development from the Late Teens through the Twenties'. *American Psychologist* 53, 469–80.

Askenazy, P. (2011). *Les décennies aveugles, emploi et croissance (1970–2010)* (Paris: Le Seuil).

Blaug, M. and Woodhall, M. (1978). 'Patterns of Subsidies to Higher Education in Europe'. *Higher Education* 7, 331–61.

Breen, R. and Buchmann, M. (2002). 'Institutional Variation and the Position of Young People: A Comparative Perspective'. *The Annals of the American Academy of Political and Social Science* 580, 288–305.

Busemeyer, M.R. (2009). 'Asset Specificity, Institutional Complementarities and the Variety of Skill Regimes in Coordinated Market Economies'. *Socio-Economic Review* 7, 375–406.

Castel, R. (1999). *Les Métamorphoses de la question sociale* (Paris: Gallimard-Jeunesse).

Ceccaldi, D. (2005). *Histoire des prestations familiales en France* (Paris: Comité d'histoire de la Sécurité sociale).

Arrighi, J-J. (2012). *Quand l'école est finie...Premiers pas dans la vie active d'une génération. Enquête 2010* (Céreq).

Chevalier, T. (2012). *L'Etat-providence et les jeunes* (Paris: L'Harmattan).

CNAF [national fund for family allowances] (2012). *Prestations familiales 2011. Statistiques nationales.*

Damon, J. (2006). *Les politiques familiales* (Paris: PUF).

DARES (2003). *Les politiques de l'emploi et du marché du travail* (Paris: La Découverte).

DARES (2011a). 'Emploi des jeunes. Synthèse des principales données relatives à l'emploi des jeunes et à leur insertion'. Document d'études No. 166.

DARES (2011b). 'Le contrat d'autonomie: mise en oeuvre par les opérateurs et profils des bénéficiaires'. DARES Analyses.

DARES (2012). 'Le contrat d'insertion dans la vie sociale (CIVIS): moins d'emplois à la sortie du Civis en 2009 et 2010'. DARES Analyses.

De Foucauld, J.-B. and Roth, N. (2002). *Pour une autonomie responsable et solidaire. Rapport au Premier Ministre* (Paris: Commissariat général au Plan).

Emmenegger, P., Häusermann, S., Palier, B. and Seeleib-Kaiser, M. (eds.) (2012). *The Age of Dualization: The Changing Face of Inequality in Deindustrializing Societies* (Oxford: Oxford University Press).

Esping-Andersen, G. (1990). *The Three Worlds of Welfare Capitalism* (Cambridge: Polity Press).

Esping-Andersen, G. (1999) *Social Foundations of Postindustrial Economies* (Oxford: Oxford University Press).

Eurydice (2009). *L'aide aux étudiants de l'enseignement supérieur en Europe* (Bruxelles: Commission Européenne).

Ferrera, M. (1996). 'The "Southern Model" of Welfare in Social Europe'. *Journal of European Social Policy* 6, 17–37.

Galand, O. (1993). 'Qu'est-ce que la jeunesse?' in Cavalli, A. and Galand, O. (eds.) *L'allongement de la jeunesse* (Arles-Poitiers: Actes Sud).

Galland, O. (2012). 'Préambule. Les deux jeunesses', in Labadie, F. (ed.) *Inégalités Des Jeunes Sur Fond de Crise. Rapport de L'observatoire de La Jeunesse* (Paris: La Documentation française), pp. 58–61.

Galland, O. and Oberti, M. (1996). *Les Etudiants* (Paris: La Découverte).

Gallie, D. and Paugam, S. (2000) *Welfare Regimes and the Experience of Unemployment in Europe* (Oxford: Oxford University Press).

Gazier, B. and Petit, H. (2007). 'French Labour Market Segmentation and French Labour Market Policies since the Seventies: Connecting Changes'. *Economies et Sociétés*, 28, 1027–56.

Gineste, S. (2010). *Youth Employment Measures 2010. France* (Brussels: European Employment Observatory).

Harris, N.S. (1989). *Social Security for Young People* (Hants: Avebury).

INSEE [National Institute for Statistics and Economic Studies] (2013a). *Enquêtes Emploi 1975–2012.*

INSEE [National Institute for Statistics and Economic Studies] (2013b). *Les revenus et le patrimoine des ménages, édition 2013.*

Kesteman, N. (2010). 'Le logement des jeunes: synthèse des études statistiques récentes'. *Politiques sociales et familiales*, 99, 113–20.

Labadie, F. (ed.) (2012). *Inégalités entre jeunes sur fond de crise. Rapport de l'Observatoire de la jeunesse 2012* (Paris: La Documentation française).

Lefresne, F. (2012). 'Trente-cinq ans de politique d'insertion professionnelle des jeunes: un bilan en demie-teinte', in *Politiques de Jeunesse: Le Grand Malentendu* (Nîmes: Champ social), pp. 106–25.

Lenoir, R. (1991). 'Family Policy in France since 1938', in Ambler, J.S. (ed.) *The French Welfare State: Surviving Social and Ideological Change* (New York: New York University Press), pp. 144–86.

Lima, L. (2004). 'L'âge de l'État social: une comparaison France-Québec des systèmes d'assistance-jeunesse'. Presented at the MATISSE *L'accès inégal à l'emploi et à la protection sociale*, Paris.

Lima, L. (2008). 'Le temps de la prime insertion professionnelle: un nouvel âge de la vie', in Guillemard, A.-M. (ed.) *Où Va La Protection Sociale?* (Paris: PUF).

Lima, L. (2012a). 'Les jeunes vulnérables: laboratoire de l'Etat social actif?' in *Inégalités Des Jeunes Sur Fond de Crise. Rapport de L'observatoire de La Jeunesse* (Paris: La Documentation française).

Lima, L. (2012b). 'Politiques d'insertion et citoyenneté sociale des jeunes', in *Politiques de Jeunesse: Le Grand Malentendu* (Nîmes: Champ social), pp. 126–37.

Lizé, L. (2006). 'Facettes du déclassement, quel rôle pour les politiques de l'emploi?' *Travail et Emploi* 107, 33–45.

Marshall, T.H. (1950). *Citizenship and Social Class and Other Essays* (Cambridge: Cambridge University Press).

Mas, S. (2004). 'Le réseau des missions locales et permanences d'accueil, d'information et d'orientation: un intermédiaire important pour les jeunes peu qualifiés'. *Premières informations. Premières synthèses*, 1(46), 1–46.

Ministère de l'Education Nationale, Ministère de l'Enseignement Supérieur et de la Recherche (2012). 'Repères et références statistiques sur les enseignements, la formation et la recherche'.

Nicolas, M. (2010). 'La politique familiale destinée aux jeunes'. *Politiques sociales et familiales*, 102, 113–19.

Nicole-Drancourt, C. and Roulleau-Berger, L. (2001). *Les jeunes et le travail. 1950–2000.* (Paris: PUF).

Nicole-Drancourt, C. and Roulleau-Berger, L. (2006). *L'insertion des jeunes en France* (Paris: PUF).

Orivel, F. (1975). *L'aide aux étudiants en France: faits et critiques* (Dijon: IREDU).

Pak, M. (2013). 'Le travail à temps partiel'.*Synthèse.Stat'* (DARES).

Palier, B. (2005). *Gouverner la sécurité sociale?: Les réformes du système français de protection sociale depuis 1945* (Paris: PUF).

Palier, B. (ed.) (2010). *A Long Good Bye to Bismarck? The Politics of Welfare Reforms in Continental Europe* (Amsterdam: Amsterdam University Press).

Palier, B. and Thelen, K. (2010). 'Institutionalizing Dualism: Complementarities and Change in France and Germany'. *Politics & Society* 38, 119–48.

Prost, A. (1984). 'L'évolution de la politique familiale en France de 1938 à 1981'. *Le mouvement social*, 129, 7–28.

Sayn, I. (2005). 'Les obligations alimentaires (droit civil et droit de la protection sociale)'. *Revue Française des Affaires Sociales* 4, 11–33.

Vallat, J.-P. (2002). *La politique familiale en France (1945–2001): construction des intérêts sociaux et transformations de l'Etat-providence* (Paris: Institut d'études politiques).

Van de Velde, C. (2007). 'La dépendance familiale des jeunes adultes en France. Traitement politique et enjeux normatifs', in Paugam, S. (ed.) *Repenser La Solidarité. L'apport Des Sciences Sociales* (Paris: PUF).

Van de Velde, C. (2008). *Devenir Adulte: Sociologie comparée de la jeunesse en Europe.* (Paris: PUF).

Verdier, E. (1995). 'Politiques de formation des jeunes et marché du travail'. *Formation Emploi*, 50, 19–40.

Verdier, E. (1996). 'L'insertion des jeunes "à la française": vers un ajustement structurel?' *Travail et Emploi*, 69, 37–54.

Wallace, C. and Bendit, R. (2009). 'Youth Policies in Europe: Towards a Classification of Different Tendencies in Youth Policies in the European Union'. *Perspectives on European Politics and Society* 10, 441–58.

Walther, A. (2006). 'Regimes of Youth Transitions: Choice, Flexibility and Security in Young People's Experiences across Different European Contexts'. *Young* 14, 119–39.

Wargon, E. and Gurgand, M. (2013). 'Garantie Jeunes'. Synthèse des travaux du groupe ad hoc – DGEFP.

11
Young Adults' Transitions to Residential Independence in the UK: The Role of Social and Housing Policy

Ann Berrington and Juliet Stone[1]

11.1 Introduction

This chapter examines UK young adults' housing transitions, particularly leaving the parental home, and explores the ways in which these may have been shaped by government social and housing policies. Housing remains an important welfare service in the UK, but is distinctive in the coexistence of a large and enduring private housing market (Malpass, 2004). Housing has arguably moved further away from the core welfare state as a result of the mass privatisation of council housing which began in the early 1980s and a lack of sufficient new social housing (Forrest and Murie, 1983; Malpass, 2004). Access to social housing is increasingly difficult for young, particularly single, adults (Anderson, 1999), who increasingly look to the private rented sector (PRS) for accommodation during the early phases of the life-course. The role of the welfare state has thus shifted from the provision of council housing to the subsidisation of private rents via welfare benefits (Murie, 2012).

For the past three decades, UK governments have tried to reduce the welfare benefits bill by transferring responsibility for young adults from the state back onto families, for example by withdrawing unemployment benefits to most 16–17-year-olds, and restricting housing benefits for single people (Rugg, 1999; Rugg et al., 2011). Recently, the Conservative/Liberal Democrat Coalition government, citing burgeoning costs, has cut expenditure on housing, making access to housing benefits more difficult for young adults. Recent political and media debates in the UK about whether housing benefit should be withdrawn from the majority of those aged under 25 (Chapman, 2013; *The Telegraph*, 2012) echo a discourse in the 1980s – also under a Conservative government and post-recession – of young unemployed adults funding 'holidays on the dole' through board and lodging payments paid to hotels and bed and breakfast providers in British seaside towns (Rugg, 1999).

Given the context described above, achieving residential independence from the parental home is increasingly linked to successful labour market participation and/or parental financial support (Heath and Calvert, 2013). Recent academic research has focused on the impact of recession, increased unemployment and economic precariousness on the ability of young adults to leave home and maintain residential independence (Coles et al., 1999; Mandic, 2008; Stone et al., 2011, 2013). Young adults' housing transitions are also influenced by broader shifts in society, such as economic restructuring, educational expansion and changing aspirations for family formation (Beer and Faulkner, 2011), and we discuss potential impacts of social and housing policy within this broader context.

Increasingly, transitions to residential independence are becoming non-linear. Recent UK research has drawn attention to the way in which partnership dissolution can precipitate a return to the parental home, particularly for men (Stone et al., 2013). Since low-income non-resident fathers are not awarded priority status in social housing, they often cannot afford family housing and so are prevented from offering their child a second home (Speak, 1999; Rugg et al., 2011). Given the potential impact of recent policy changes for these young fathers, we provide some of the first estimates of the size and living arrangements of this group in our empirical analysis.

This chapter sets out to answer a number of research questions. How have the living arrangements of UK young adults been changing? Has the prevalence of adult child/parent co-residence increased during the great recession? How does housing tenure vary according to young adults' living arrangements? How many young men are not living in the same household as at least one of their children? What are the living arrangements of young, non-resident fathers?

We first review recent evidence relating to young adults' living arrangements in the UK and highlight some of the key socio-economic changes which have affected young adults' housing transitions, including the expansion of higher education (HE), increased economic precariousness and the decline in affordable housing. We then review changes since the 1980s in the extent to which young adults are supported in making transitions away from the parental home by welfare state policies. Of particular interest is the likely impact on non-resident fathers of two changes introduced by the Coalition government: the extension of the shared accommodation rate of housing benefit to all single adults under the age of 35,[2] and the removal of the 'Housing Benefit Spare Room Subsidy in the Social Rented Sector' (often referred to by critics as 'the bedroom tax').[3] Finally, we provide new empirical evidence to address our research questions and discuss the policy implications of these findings.

11.2   Background

11.2.1   Leaving home and the living arrangements of UK young adults

In Britain during the 1970s and 1980s young adults tended to leave home relatively early for both positive reasons, such as to attend HE or for marriage, or for negative reasons, such as friction in the parental home (Furlong and Cooney, 1990; Jones, 1995). This early transition was facilitated by relatively generous welfare benefits (for example, supplementary benefits for school leavers and grants to attend HE) and a supply of cheap private rented housing in hostels and shared houses (Furlong and Cooney, 1990). Although co-residence with parents in young adulthood has become more prevalent in the UK since the 1980s (Berrington et al., 2009), currently far fewer UK young adults remain living with their parents in their late twenties and early thirties as compared with many eastern and southern European countries (Figure 11.1).

The living arrangements of young adults in the UK have changed considerably over past decades, with a delay in family formation (both partnership and parenthood) a key underlying factor. Fewer adults are leaving the parental home to live with a partner and more are leaving to attend university or for employment. Consequently living arrangements upon leaving the parental home have also changed, with more young adults living outside a family unit. During the 1980s, much of the increase in non-family living was associated with increased solo living among young adults (Berrington and Murphy, 1994), whilst the 1990s and 2000s saw a significant increase in levels of sharing among non-related young adults (Berrington et al., 2009). Shared accommodation with non-relatives is more common for ex-students, especially those in their twenties. For some, shared living would appear to be a living arrangement of choice, with a cultural expectation for shared living

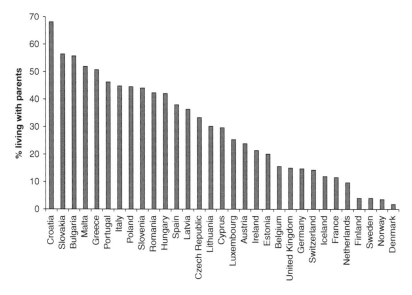

Figure 11.1   Percentage of young adults aged 25–34 living with their parents, 2011
Source: EU-SILC (Eurostat).

(Ford et al., 2002; Heath, 2004), but for others it is the result of necessity or is a preferred alternative to living alone (Roberts, 2013).

There are significant differences in the timing and linearity of leaving the parental home in the UK according to gender, class and ethnicity. Some researchers have referred to a 'fast track' to adulthood among disadvantaged young adults, who tend to form partnerships, enter the labour market and obtain residential independence earlier than their more advantaged peers, whose attendance at HE contributes to their 'slow track' to adulthood (Bynner et al., 2002). However, these differentials are strongly dependent on age and gender. Moreover, constraints arising from labour market instability mean that an increasing proportion of disadvantaged young adults are not following the 'fast track' to adulthood but are remaining in or returning to the parental home, delaying or precluding partnership and parenthood (Stone et al., 2011).

11.2.2   The changing socio-economic context

11.2.2.1   *The expansion of higher education (HE)*

In the UK most young adults leave home (or at least 'live away from home') when they start university, although there are important differences, for example, by geographical locality and ethnicity

(Patiniotis and Holdsworth, 2005). Increasing HE enrolment rates have therefore placed downward pressure on the median age of leaving home in the UK. Evidence from the Labour Force Survey showed that between 1988 and 1998, early leaving at ages 18 and 19 became increasingly common (Berrington et al., 2009). There was less change in patterns of leaving home in the subsequent decade 1999–2008 – consistent with the idea that the cause of this change in behaviour was the rapid expansion in HE which followed the 1988 Education Reform Act and the Further and Higher Education Act of 1992 (Boliver, 2011) – (see Figure 11.2).

Although enrolment rates continued to increase between 2008 and 2010, this may not have translated into even more young adults leaving home earlier. First, there has been a move to widen HE participation in groups who are generally less likely to leave home to attend (Holdsworth, 2009). Second, over the 2000s there has been a decreasing amount of support given to students, for example with student loans replacing grants for many and the introduction of university tuition fees, with a cost of up to £9,000 per year for entrants in 2012/13 (Callender and Jackson, 2008). It also seems likely that rising levels of student debt and a weak graduate job market will encourage returns to the parental home among young graduates who have previously moved away.

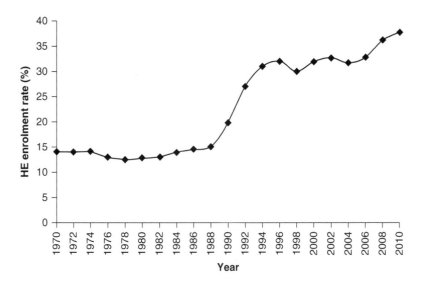

Figure 11.2   UK HE enrolment rate, 1970–2010
Source: Department for Business and Innovation (2012).

11.2.2.2 *Increasing youth unemployment and economic insecurity*

Youth unemployment rose during and immediately after each of the last three recessions. In the last quarter of 2011, there were 1.04 million unemployed young people aged 16–24 in the UK, compared with peaks of 924,000 in 1993 and 1.2 million in 1984 (Office for National Statistics, 2012). Although youth unemployment fell slightly during 2012, levels remained high during the first quarter of 2013, at 958,000 (Office for National Statistics, 2013). Labour market precariousness makes it very difficult for many young adults to achieve the level and stability of income required for a rental or mortgage deposit (Clapham et al., 2012; McKee, 2012). Remaining in the parental home into the late twenties and early thirties is increasingly concentrated among students, the unemployed and those in insecure employment. Young men in insecure employment – defined as being either in part-time work or in temporary jobs[4] – are significantly more likely to remain at home compared with those in full-time employment, and the gap increased over the decade 1998–2008 (Stone et al., 2011).

11.2.2.3 *Increasing house prices and lack of mortgage credit*

House prices increased dramatically during the late 1990s and the 2000s, with average 'house price to individual income' ratios increasing from around 3.0 to greater than 5.0 (Wilcox, 2005). From late 2007, first-time buyers were further affected by more restrictive loan-to-value requirements. According to the Council of Mortgage Lenders (CML), the average size of deposit increased from 10 per cent to 25 per cent of the purchase price of the property between 2007 and 2009. The average deposit for a first-time buyer is over £26,000 (representing 79 per cent of the average annual income from which the mortgage is paid). As a consequence, young adults increasingly negotiate with older generations in order to buy a property (Heath and Calvert, 2013). According to CML estimates in 2005, half of first-time buyers aged under 25 were able to buy without assistance from their families. In 2011 this had fallen to less than one in ten (Council of Mortgage Lenders, 2011).

11.3   Welfare and housing policies

11.3.1   The decreasing availability of social housing

At the same time as young adults are being priced out of owner occupation, we have seen a continued contraction in the availability of social housing as a result of the sale of social housing stock to sitting tenants under 'Right to Buy' policies and a lack of new build of social housing. The proportion of all households renting from a social landlord declined from 32 per cent in 1981 to 23 per cent in 1991 and only 17 per cent in 2009/10 (Kemp, 2011). Access to social housing in the UK has in recent decades become increasingly restricted by a needs-based allocation (Kennett et al., 2012). The current statutory framework prescribes a series of 'reasonable preference' categories for council house allocations, including: families with dependent children and pregnant women; people occupying temporary/insecure accommodation; persons with a particular need for settled accommodation on medical or welfare grounds; and statutorily homeless households (Fitzpatrick and Pawson, 2007).

As the size of the social rented housing stock has declined over the past decades, the PRS has increased significantly (with the proportion of households renting from the PRS increasing from 9 per cent in 1991 to 16 per cent in 2009/10 (Kemp, 2011)). However, increasing rents and declining government support with rents means that it is often difficult for low-income young adults to attain and maintain a private rented tenancy.

11.3.2   Welfare support: From provision of council housing to the subsidisation of private rents

The residualisation of social housing and the consequent reliance on the increasingly expensive PRS for those in need of welfare support can be seen clearly in Figure 11.3. The number of households renting in the private sector increased dramatically from 2000, whilst the number of housing benefit recipients increased slowly from 2000 to 2007 but more rapidly since 2008. The Coalition government argues that their reforms to reduce the burgeoning housing benefit bill are also necessary because social security benefits have distorted housing markets, including pushing up rents, and eroded incentives to work (Chapman, 2013; Murie, 2012). Some of these reforms, for example Local Housing Allowances, affect all age groups but others, such as the Shared Accommodation Rate of Housing Benefit, are targeted towards young adults.

11.3.2.1   *Local housing allowances*

Local Housing Allowances (LHA) were implemented across Great Britain in 2008. The aim of the policy is to ensure that those claiming housing benefit cannot afford better housing than those not claiming benefits by capping the amount of housing benefit based on the number of

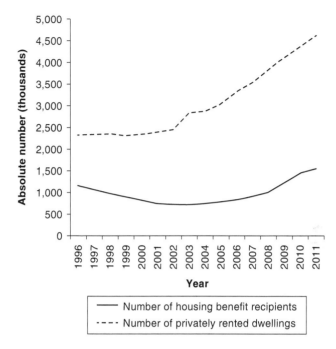

Figure 11.3   Number of dwellings that are privately rented dwellings and number of housing benefit recipients, 1996–2011, Great Britain

Sources: Pawson and Wilcox, Tables 17c and 116a in Housing Review 2013 (Chartered Institute of Housing). Estimated data for 2008 from Housing Benefit and Council Tax Benefit Caseload Statistics: November 2008 to February 2013, DWP.

people in the household and local rents. In 2011, the maximum benefit available was changed from the median to the 30th percentile of local rents for a property of the required size. Although the LHA will tend to have less impact on young adults overall than for older people, those with families who require larger properties will be particularly affected, especially given that the LHA only allows for a maximum of four bedrooms.

11.3.2.2   *Housing benefit restrictions for single young adults*

Housing benefit policies also impact upon the ability of young adults to sustain residential independence, in particular to live alone in a self-contained property. Whilst most benefit recipients are seeing a reduction in the generosity of their housing benefit under recent welfare reform (Kennett et al., 2012), young adults have been hit particularly hard through the restriction of housing benefit for those aged under 35, to the level of a room in a shared house. The Shared Accommodation Rate (SAR) was originally introduced as the Single Room Rate, capping housing benefit for those aged under 25 (Kemp and Rugg, 1998), but was extended to those aged under 35 in April 2012 (Rugg et al., 2011). For housing benefit purposes, a shared room is accommodation where the tenant has exclusive use of only one bedroom, and where the tenancy provides for shared use of one or more of a kitchen, a bathroom, a toilet or a living room (Rugg et al., 2011). The government's stated objectives for this extension to age 35 are: to ensure that those receiving housing benefit do not have an advantage over those who are not on benefit, but have to make similar choices about what they can afford; to help contain growing housing benefit expenditure; and to remove a potential work disincentive (DWP, 2011). The SAR thus discourages young adults from leaving home and makes it more difficult to maintain independence, especially in geographical areas where houses in multiple occupation (HMOs) are less available.[5]

11.3.2.3   *The removal of spare room subsidy from housing benefit for social renters – 'the bedroom tax'*

The 2012 Welfare Reform Bill, implemented in April 2013, states that housing benefit claimants in social housing who are occupying a larger property than their household requires must either downsize or make up the shortfall in rent (DWP, 2012). The policy has been controversial, with one criticism being that although there is a need to make more effective use of available housing, the lack of appropriately sized and located residences in the social rented sector will be a major obstacle to downsizing (Kelly, 2013). This means that many residents will be at risk of rent arrears if they are unable to find a suitable alternative to their 'under-occupied' property. Among those living with dependent children, sharing a bedroom is expected for children aged under ten regardless of gender, and under 16 for those of the same gender. However, although the government has allocated emergency funds to help those judged to require an 'extra' room, for example disabled residents who require an overnight carer, this policy does not adequately take account of the needs to provide a 'part-time' family home for non-resident children.

11.3.3   The impact on non-resident fathers

Rules for housing entitlement and housing benefit are based on the assumption that, following partnership breakdown, one parent has primary care of the child. Following separation, the majority of UK children remain primarily resident with their mother (Office for National Statistics, 2011). However, this obfuscates often complex parenting arrangements. Shared parenting has attracted much debate from lobby groups, academics and policymakers (see, for example, Fehlberg et al., 2011; Smart, 2004). The UK government has declared support for the view that the vast majority of children 'benefit from a continuing relationship with both parents, and that shared parenting should be encouraged where this is in the child's best interests and is safe' (Ministry for Justice and Department for Education, 2012). However, the government, through its recent cuts to housing benefit, makes it difficult for low-income non-resident parents to participate fully in the caring of their children. Many non-resident fathers aged under 35 will be classed as single with no dependent children, will not be a priority for social housing and will only qualify for housing benefit in the PRS at the Shared Accommodation Rate. Living in a bedsit or sharing a house, particularly with strangers, may not be ideal conditions for permitting children to visit or stay overnight. A study by Crisis found evidence that some non-resident parents reported difficulties in maintaining their relationship with their children owing to problems with shared accommodation, including 'noise levels, cleanliness of communal areas, and doubts about the backgrounds of other residents' (Rugg et al., 2011).

Young non-resident fathers renting in the social sector will be disproportionately affected by the introduction of the 'bedroom tax'. Since the children cannot be registered as being co-resident twice (in the father's household as well as the mother's household), any bedroom kept for the use of non-resident children when they come to visit will be deemed as a 'spare room'. This applies to young fathers who are living alone or sharing, as well as those who have formed a new family. Thus, recent welfare reforms do not adequately support young men in their shared parenting responsibilities.

11.4   Empirical findings

We use data from the autumn quarters of the 1998, 2008 and 2012 Labour Force Survey (LFS) to examine changes in the living arrangements and housing tenure of young adults aged 20–34, both over the longer term and focusing on the change since 2008 (before the recession). The LFS comprises a nationally representative sample of households living at private addresses in the UK.[6] Using information collected within a 'relationship grid' we identify the relationship between all members of the household and thus categorise young adults as to whether they are living with a parent, living away from the parental home as a couple, or as a lone parent, or living outside a family (either alone or sharing with unrelated individuals).

First, in Section 11.4.1 we discuss overall changes in living arrangements. Next, we examine the relative importance of private and social renting among those aged 20–34 and the likelihood of being in receipt of housing benefit among those sharing or living alone. Section 11.4.3 provides new insight into the numbers and living arrangements of young non-resident fathers.

11.4.1   Changes in living arrangements

Tables 11.1a and 11.1b show the distribution of living arrangements among young men and women in 1998, 2008 and 2012. Men are consistently more likely to be living in the parental home than women, with more women living as a couple or as a lone parent. The proportion of young adults living with their parents decreases dramatically with age. Changes over time in proportions living in the parental home are most pronounced for the younger groups, although the patterns differ by gender. Young men in their early twenties show a significant decrease in the proportion living with their parents between 1998 and 2008, but this is counteracted by a subsequent increase between 2008 and 2012, following the recent recession. For women aged 20–24, the proportion living with their parents increased in both time periods.

Table 11.1a indicates that young men experienced significant increases in the proportion living in shared accommodation between 1998 and 2008, for example from 19.6 per cent to 25.6 per cent among men aged 20–21. It is possible that this was in part in response to the introduction of the SAR for under-25s in 1996, but given that a significant increase in sharing is also observed for men aged 25–29 (from 9.5 per cent in 1998 to 14.7 per cent in 2008) this is unlikely to be the only explanation. Sharing is much less common among those in their early thirties (around 5 per cent of men and 2.4 per cent of women). Table 11.1b shows that women are much less likely than men to be living in shared accommodation and shows little change over time in the proportion of young women in such living arrangements. Overall, there is little significant change in the prevalence of sharing following the changes to the SAR at the beginning of 2012, but a decline is consistently observed in men and women of all ages, and particularly among men in their twenties. Looking at those living outside a family, there is no evidence of a move away from living alone to living in shared accommodation, although it should be remembered that living alone is

Table 11.1a Changing distribution of living arrangements of young men in the UK by age group in 1998, 2008 and 2012

Type of living arrangements by age group	1998		2008		2012		Absolute change	
	(n) %	95% confidence interval	(n) %	95% confidence interval	(n) %	95% confidence interval	1998–2008	2008–2012
20–21	(n = 1,345)		(n = 1,167)		(n = 961)			
With parent(s)	68.6	(66.2, 71.1)	62.9	(60.0, 65.7)	69.1	(65.9, 72.0)	−5.7	6.2
In a couple	7.8	(6.5, 9.4)	8.8	(7.3, 10.6)	5.4	(4.1, 7.0)	1.0	**−3.4**
As a lone parent	0	(0.0, 0.0)	0.1	(0.0, 0.6)	0.0	(0.0, 0.0)	0.1	−0.1
Alone	3.9	(3.0, 5.1)	2.6	(1.9, 3.7)	5.0	(3.8, 6.6)	−1.3	2.4
Sharing	19.6	(17.5, 21.9)	25.6	(23.0, 28.3)	20.5	(17.9, 23.4)	5.9	5.0
22–24	(n = 2,098)		(n = 1,695)		(n = 1,425)			
With parent(s)	53.3	(51.1, 55.4)	50.1	(47.7, 52.5)	56.8	(54.2, 59.5)	−3.2	−6.7
In a couple	24.1	(22.3, 26.0)	24.5	(22.5, 26.6)	21.5	(19.4, 23.8)	0.4	**−3.0**
As a lone parent	0	(0.0, 0.3)	0.1	(0.0, 0.4)	0.2	(0.1, 0.6)	0.1	0.1
Alone	7.8	(6.8, 9.1)	7.1	(6.0, 8.4)	6.8	(5.5, 8.3)	−0.8	−0.3
Sharing	14.8	(13.3, 16.5)	18.2	(16.4, 20.2)	14.6	(12.8, 16.7)	3.4	−3.6
25–29	(n = 4,461)		(n = 3,077)		(n = 2,440)			
With parent(s)	24.3	(23.0, 25.5)	24.5	(23.0, 26.1)	26.9	(25.2, 28.7)	0.2	**2.4**
In a couple	52.6	(51.2, 54.1)	47.7	(45.9, 49.5)	50.8	(48.8, 52.8)	**−4.9**	3.1
As a lone parent	0.3	(0.2, 0.5)	0.3	(0.2, 0.6)	0.4	(0.2, 0.7)	0.0	0.1
Alone	13.4	(12.4, 14.4)	12.8	(11.6, 14.0)	11.6	(10.4, 13.0)	−0.6	−1.2
Sharing	9.5	(8.7, 10.5)	14.7	(13.4, 16.1)	10.3	(9.1, 11.7)	5.2	**−4.4**
30–34	(n = 5,375)		(n = 3,122)		(n = 2,953)			
With parent(s)	10.2	(9.4, 11.0)	10.3	(9.3, 11.4)	9.7	(8.7, 10.8)	0.1	−0.6
In a couple	70.9	(69.6, 72.1)	69.9	(68.2, 71.5)	71.1	(69.4, 72.8)	−1.0	1.2
As a lone parent	0.9	(0.7, 1.0)	0.7	(0.5, 1.1)	0.4	(0.3, 0.8)	−0.2	−0.3
Alone	13.7	(12.8, 14.7)	13.4	(12.2, 14.6)	13.7	(12.4, 15.1)	−0.4	0.3
Sharing	4.4	(3.8, 5.0)	5.7	(4.9, 6.7)	5.1	(4.3, 6.1)	1.4	−0.7

Notes: Unweighted *n* and weighted percentage.
Absolute changes over time where confidence intervals for individual years do not overlap are shown in bold.
Source: Author's analysis of LFS Quarterly Household dataset, September–November 1998, October–December 2008 and October–December 2012.

Table 11.1b Changing distribution of living arrangements of young women in the UK by age group in 1998, 2008 and 2012

Type of living arrangements by age group	1998		2008		2012		Absolute change	
	(n) %	95% confidence interval	(n) %	95% confidence interval	(n) %	95% confidence interval	1998–2008	2008–2012
20–21	(n=1,410)		(n=1,206)		(n=1,052)			
With parent(s)	43.0	(40.4, 45.6)	46.4	(43.6, 49.3)	55.6	(52.5, 58.7)	3.4	9.2
In a couple	24.0	(21.8, 26.3)	21.7	(19.4, 24.2)	15.3	(13.0, 17.9)	-2.3	-6.4
As a lone parent	8.0	(6.8, 9.5)	7.3	(6.0, 8.8)	6.0	(4.7, 7.6)	-0.7	-1.3
Alone	5.3	(4.2, 6.6)	3.3	(2.4, 4.4)	3.8	(2.8, 5.1)	-2.0	0.5
Sharing	19.7	(17.7, 22.0)	21.3	(19.0, 23.8)	19.3	(16.9, 21.9)	1.6	-2.0
22–24	(n=2,385)		(n=1,824)		(n=1,636)			
With parent(s)	30.0	(28.3 32.0)	34	(31.8, 36.2)	38.5	(36.1, 40.9)	4.0	4.5
In a couple	40.3	(38.3, 42.3)	39.5	(37.2, 41.8)	35.5	(33.1, 38.0)	-0.8	-4.0
As a lone parent	10.2	(9.1, 11.4)	11.2	(9.9, 12.7)	11.2	(9.8, 12.7)	1.0	0.0
Alone	6.5	(5.6, 7.5)	4.7	(3.8, 5.7)	5.4	(4.4, 6.6)	-1.8	0.7
Sharing	12.9	(11.6, 14.4)	10.6	(9.2, 12.2)	9.4	(7.9, 11.2)	-2.3	-1.2

	(n=5,100)		(n=3,562)		(n=3,139)			
25–29								
With parent(s)	10.7	(9.9, 11.6)	12.8	(11.7, 13.9)	13.3	(12.2, 14.5)	**2.1**	0.5
In a couple	61.6	(60.2, 62.9)	62.5	(60.9, 64.0)	63.6	(61.9, 65.3)	0.9	1.1
As a lone parent	12.5	(11.7, 13.4)	11	(10.1, 12.0)	10.9	(9.9, 11.9)	-1.5	-0.1
Alone	8.6	(7.9, 9.4)	7.2	(6.4, 8.0)	6.5	(5.7, 7.5)	-1.5	-0.6
Sharing	6.6	(5.9, 7.3)	6.6	(5.8, 7.5)	5.7	(4.9, 6.7)	0.0	-0.9
30–34	(n=5,866)		(n=3,540)		(n=3,382)			
With parent(s)	4.1	(3.6, 4.6)	4.9	(4.2, 5.6)	5.7	(5.0, 6.5)	0.8	**0.8**
In a couple	73.0	(71.9, 74.1)	72.6	(71.2, 74.1)	72.8	(71.3, 74.3)	-0.4	0.2
As a lone parent	13.9	(13.1, 14.8)	11.9	(10.9, 12.9)	12.2	(11.2, 13.2)	**-2.0**	0.3
Alone	7.1	(6.5, 7.8)	7.4	(6.6, 8.4)	7.0	(6.1, 7.9)	0.3	-0.5
Sharing	1.9	(1.6, 2.3)	3.2	(2.6, 3.9)	2.4	(1.9, 3.1)	**1.3**	-0.8

Notes: Unweighted *n* and weighted percentage.
Absolute changes over time where confidence intervals for individual years do not overlap are shown in bold.
Source: Author's analysis of LFS Quarterly Household dataset, September–November 1998, October–December 2008 and October–December 2012.

heterogeneous and may include some houses in multiple occupation. Taken together with the observed increase in co-residence with parents, this apparent move away from living outside a family, in particular in shared accommodation, suggests that living independently may have become a less realistic or attractive prospect for young adults in the context of the recent recession.

11.4.2   Housing tenure of young adults living outside the parental home

Table 11.2 shows the housing tenure of young men and women living outside the parental home according to their living arrangements in 2012, by age group. Owner-occupation increases with age and is most common among men and women who are living with a partner. Social renting is relatively uncommon among couples, with the exception of the youngest age group (20–24), where 24.1 per cent of men and 18.7 per cent of women are in council or housing association accommodation. This reflects the fact that these younger couples are likely to be relatively disadvantaged in socio-economic terms, perhaps having left education at the earliest opportunity and taken a 'fast track' to adulthood (Bynner et al., 2002). This emerges even more strongly when looking at lone parents, who are the group most likely to be living in social rented housing. This applies to both male and female lone parents, but the rarity of lone fathers necessarily focuses our discussion on lone mothers. The prevalence of social renting among young lone mothers, which remains high at 42.9 per cent even among those in their early thirties, is a clear reflection of the prioritisation of social housing as discussed above. In contrast, young adults who are not living with dependent children receive far less state support in making housing transitions.

It might appear counter-intuitive that a third group often living in socially rented housing is those living alone, especially at younger ages. At age 20–24, 31.3 per cent of men and 27.9 per cent of women living alone are in social rented housing. However, the LFS data presented in Table 11.2 do not allow us to distinguish between different types of housing so may mask a somewhat heterogeneous living arrangement. Indeed, a proportion of these young adults are likely to be living in bedsits that in other circumstances might be classified as 'shared' accommodation, even if residents are not strictly part of the same 'household'. In Table 11.2, the definition of 'sharing' is based on relationships between all members of a household defined as follows: 'A household comprises of a single person, or a group of people living at the same

Table 11.2 Housing tenure of young adults living outside the parental home by age group, sex and living arrangements, UK, 2012

Age group	Living arrangements	n	Owner occupier %	Private rent %	Social rent %
				Housing tenure	
Men 20–24	With partner	359	20.1	55.7	24.1
	Lone parent	3	–	–	–
	Alone	144	21.1	47.6	31.3
	Sharing	342	5.3	90.7	4.0
25–29	With partner	1,263	41.8	43.4	14.7
	Lone parent	10	–	–	–
	Alone	275	41.8	38.2	19.9
	Sharing	219	17.6	78.0	4.4
30–34	With partner	2,173	56.1	33.9	10.0
	Lone parent	13	–	–	–
	Alone	367	41.2	40.8	18.0
	Sharing	117	24.1	71.5	4.4
Women 20–24	With partner	641	25.6	55.6	18.7
	Lone parent	302	0.3	43.7	55.9
	Alone	138	17.1	55.1	27.9
	Sharing	311	4.7	89.7	5.6
25–29	With partner	1,835	45.0	41.6	13.4
	Lone parent	449	5.2	40.0	54.8
	Alone	218	33.8	49.2	17.0
	Sharing	164	10.1	83.5	6.4
30–34	With partner	2,357	61.7	27.6	10.7
	Lone parent	500	17.4	39.7	42.9
	Alone	242	48.9	34.5	16.6
	Sharing	66	21.9	72.3	5.8

Note that the number of lone fathers in the sample is too small to make inference.
Source: Authors' analysis of LFS Quarterly Household dataset, October–December 2012.

address who have the address as their only or main home. They also share one main meal a day or share the living accommodation (or both)' (Office for National Statistics, 2008, p. 4). In our analyses, young adults are classified as sharing if they are recorded as living in the same household as at least one other person who is not their parent or child. Therefore, sharing will encompass a wide range of circumstances including those who choose to share with friends, those who are sharing (perhaps with strangers) out of necessity and those who are living with family members other than their parent or child (such as a sibling or aunt/uncle). What consistently emerges from Table 11.2, however, is that social renting is very uncommon among young adults living in shared accommodation.

The findings in Tables 11.1a and 11.1b suggest that the SAR has not had any substantial impact on the numbers of young adults sharing in the social rented sector and is more likely to have had an effect on the numbers living in the parental home. Private renting is the majority tenure among sharers in all age groups, although it does decrease with age as owner-occupation increases. Figure 11.4 shows the proportions of

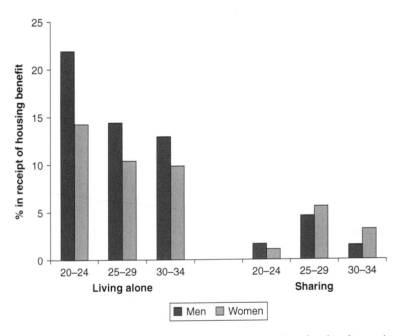

Figure 11.4   Percentage of men and women living outside a family who are in receipt of housing benefit, by living arrangements and age group, 2012
Source: Author's analysis of LFS Quarterly Household dataset, October–December 2012.

young adults living outside a family who are in receipt of housing benefit. The proportions among sharers are very low, peaking at only around 5 per cent for those aged 25–29. Instead, among those living outside a family, young men and women living alone in their early twenties are the groups most likely to be in receipt of housing benefit (22 per cent of men and 14 per cent of women living alone in this age group). This suggests that for single young adults who are reliant on housing benefit, whether in social housing or, more likely, in the private sector, sharing is not a commonplace practice. Furthermore, sharing may not be a practical option for certain groups of young adults, such as non-resident fathers (Rugg et al., 2011), who are the focus of the next section.

11.4.3   Non-resident fathers

In order to judge how widespread the impact of changes in housing benefit policy might be on young fathers, it is useful to first describe the prevalence of non-resident fatherhood at these ages. Table 11.3 shows, for the UK and by age group, the percentage of men and the percentage of fathers who report having at least one non-resident, dependent child. Overall, around 5 per cent of all men and a quarter of fathers are non-resident fathers; this rises to 10 per cent among those in their early thirties (Table 11.3). Expressed as a percentage of fathers, over a third of men in their early twenties who have a child are non-resident with at least one of their children, declining to about one in five of fathers in their early thirties.

Figure 11.5 shows the living arrangements of non-resident fathers by age group. A large proportion (around 60 per cent) of non-resident fathers in their early twenties are living with their parent(s), around one-fifth are in a co-residential partnership whilst less than one-fifth are living alone or sharing with others. In contrast, those men in their

Table 11.3   Prevalence of non-resident fatherhood in the UK

Age group	Non-resident fathers	
	% of all men	% of fathers
20–24	3.1	37.2
25–29	7.7	26.3
30–34	9.5	19.5
Total (20–34)	5.4	24.2

Source: Authors' analyses of UKHLS 2009/10.

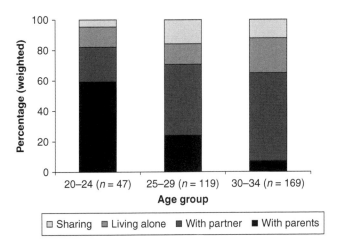

Figure 11.5   Distribution of living arrangements among UK non-resident fathers by age group
Source: Authors' analyses of UKHLS 2009/10.

early thirties who report living apart from at least one of their children are predominantly living outside the parental home. The majority are living in a partnership but over one-third are living alone or sharing. These substantial differences by age group highlight how young fathers in their twenties are restricted in their residential transitions, particularly in the face of unexpected life events such as union dissolution. Furthermore, their status as parents is a key factor, with young fathers significantly more likely to return to their parental home following union dissolution than those without children (Stone et al., 2013).

11.5   Conclusions

This chapter has brought together an overview of the social and housing policies that have been implemented in the UK in recent years, with new empirical findings on young adults' living arrangements and housing tenures. This work broadens the analysis of youth transitions beyond the school to work transition to additionally consider living arrangements and housing trajectories (as advocated by some scholars, such as MacDonald (1998)). By analysing men and women separately we also address concerns put forward by feminist critiques of youth studies (for example, Griffin, 1993) who suggest that women's transitions have been marginalised as a result of too much focus on school to employment transitions.

Our empirical findings are consistent with the suggestion that recent changes to welfare provision for young adults have encouraged more young adults to co-reside with their parent(s), particularly in their early twenties. However, policies that limit young adults' access to independent housing have likely worked in tandem with wider effects of the economic recession, such as persistently high youth unemployment and the rise of 'precarious' work (Clapham et al., 2012; McKee, 2012; Roberts, 2011; Stone et al., 2011).

In such a context, limited support from the state means that young adults must be increasingly reliant on family resources as a 'safety net' in times of hardship; however, this assumes that such resources are available. Evidence from existing quantitative research in the UK (Coles et al., 1999; Jones, 1995) suggests, for example, that parental family type is related to the timing of leaving home and the propensity to return, with co-residence less common among those from 'blended' families. Whether for practical, financial or emotional reasons, living in the parental home will not be feasible for all young adults. Welfare restrictions could be particularly damaging for this subgroup of young men and women.

Recent media and political discourse (Chapman, 2013; *The Telegraph*, 2012) has questioned whether unemployed youth are better able to afford independent living (as a result of welfare subsidies) than those employed in low paid work. The introduction in 1996 of the SAR, and its extension to all single young adults up to the age of 35 in 2012 is based on the rationale that young adults who are supported by the state should not expect to be able to afford self-contained accommodation (since this is often unaffordable to those in paid work). We have shown that sharing with unrelated others is common at younger ages, especially those in their early twenties. Sharing tends to be associated with recent experience of HE and living in 'student houses' (Stone et al., 2011). However, by their early thirties, only 5 per cent of men and 2 per cent of women are sharing with unrelated others. Thus sharing accommodation with unrelated others at these older ages is *not normative*. Living alone (some of which encompasses living in houses in multiple occupation) is more common among those in their early thirties (especially among men). Indeed, social renting and being in receipt of housing benefits are much more strongly associated with living alone than with sharing. This suggests that, despite restrictions on housing benefit for young people via the SAR, this has not resulted in a move to shared living. Instead, sharing is dominated by young people who are not receiving housing benefit and are living in the PRS.

This raises some questions about the stated objective of the SAR and its extension to the age of 35, that it is promoting 'fairness' in access to housing such that those who are on benefit do not have an advantage over those who are not (DWP, 2011). Although, as we have previously described, sharing is becoming more prevalent among certain groups of young adults (Berrington et al., 2009), this is a complex trend that is linked to the expansion of HE, immigration of young adults to the UK and the more general postponing of transitions to adulthood (Stone et al., 2011). Sharing is likely to be a very different experience for more advantaged young adults – often graduates – who choose to live with a group of friends, compared with those for whom sharing is a financial necessity, who may be living with strangers (Ford et al., 2002; Heath, 2004; Kemp and Rugg, 1998). It is perhaps unsurprising, therefore, that increasing welfare restrictions do not appear to have had the effect of encouraging sharing among young adults who are reliant on housing benefit, who are less likely to have had the experience of 'supported' sharing in, for example, university halls of residence.

Instead, our results show that a substantial proportion of young adults living alone are in receipt of housing benefit. However, experiences of living alone are not uniform and can range from people residing in low-quality bedsits in a deprived inner-city area, to those in luxury city-centre apartments (Rugg and Rhodes, 2008). Given the restrictions on housing benefit for single people under the age of 35, we must question the quality of accommodation that those in receipt of benefits would be able to afford.

It could be argued, then, that rather than promoting 'fairness', the recent changes in welfare support for young adults have in fact served to reinforce inequalities in housing among different groups of young adults. Less-advantaged young adults are less likely to benefit from supported transitional housing (for example, in halls of residence), and do not have the experience gained by sharing student housing (Ford et al., 2002). Furthermore, low-income young adults, especially those on benefits, often face fierce competition for low-cost housing with students, and there is evidence to suggest that private landlords often prefer students to those on welfare benefits (Rugg, 1999). Young adults on low incomes will be severely limited in their options for accommodation, particularly if they do not have access to family support. Socio-economic disadvantage and housing disadvantage are, therefore, strongly linked

(Beer and Faulkner, 2011), with certain groups 'consistently more likely than others to be in the worst parts of the stock, and in the worst [...] locations' (Clapham et al., 1990, p. 60).

In this chapter, we have highlighted young, non-resident fathers who rely on state support for housing as a particularly vulnerable group. For many of them, returning to the parental home is likely to be the most financially viable option following union dissolution, at least in the short term. However, this course of action will not be available to all young fathers, depending on their parental family circumstances. Low-income, non-resident fathers living alone or sharing will be limited in the level of housing benefit that they are eligible for as a result of the cap to housing benefit under the SAR. Non-resident fathers living in social housing will be affected by the 'bedroom tax' – the removal of the housing benefit spare room subsidy. For both these groups recent welfare reform could make it more difficult to co-parent.

More generally, young adults now and in the future face increasing uncertainty in the economy, the labour market and in the housing market, while also living in a context of increasingly diverse family structures. All these things combine to make transitions to residential independence problematic for many young adults. The required policy response needs to be practical and, importantly, facilitate the narrowing of housing inequalities between subgroups of young adults. Possible measures might include increasing availability of transitional or supported housing (the equivalent of halls of residence for non-graduates); increasing the level of benefits paid to young adults; allowing those aged 16 to hold social tenancies in their own right; and changing the rules under which housing benefit is paid, to account for significant levels of shared parenting across households, for example (Anderson, 1999; Smith, 2004). Ultimately, the aim should be to provide a truly 'fair' system that enables all young adults to make a successful transition to residential independence.

Notes

1. This research is funded by ESRC Grants numbers RES-625-28-0001 and ES/K003453/1. The ESRC Centre for Population Change (CPC) is a joint initiative between the University of Southampton and a consortium of Scottish universities in partnership with ONS and GROS. The findings, interpretations and conclusions expressed in this chapter are entirely those of the authors and should not be attributed in any manner to ONS or GROS. *The Labour Force Survey* is conducted by the Office for National Statistics and the Northern Ireland

Statistics and Research Agency. *Understanding Society* (UKHLS) is conducted by the Institute for Social and Economic Research at the University of Essex. Access to all data is provided by the UK Data Service. Thanks are due to Vicki Boliver for helping source historical data on higher education enrolment rates.
2. Introduced from January 2012 for new claimants.
3. Came into force on 1 April 2013 as part of the 2012 Welfare Reform Act http://www.dwp.gov.uk/adviser/updates/size-criteria-social-rented/.
4. We are aware that part-time work is not necessarily temporary or even insecure and may be preferred over full-time work in some cases. However, part-time work may result in an insecure lifestyle for those who want/need more hours.
5. Houses of multiple occupation is a term generally used to describe houses split up into small bedsits where individuals share kitchen or bathroom facilities.
6. It also includes National Health Service hospital accommodation, but excludes communal establishments such as prisons, hostels and halls of residence. UK university students usually move out from halls of residence into private sector accommodation after their first year of study, and so our estimates of living arrangements for those aged 20 and above will be generally unbiased.

References

Anderson, I. (1999). 'Young Single People and Access to Social Housing', in Rugg, J. (ed.) *Young People, Housing and Social Policy* (London: Routledge), pp. 25–49.

Beer, A. and Faulkner, D. (2011). *Housing Transitions through the Life Course: Aspirations, Needs and Policy* (Bristol: The Policy Press).

Berrington, A. and Murphy, M. (1994). 'Changes in the Living Arrangements of Young-Adults in Britain During the 1980s'. *European Sociological Review* 10 (3), 235–57.

Berrington, A., Stone, J. and Falkingham, J. (2009). 'The Changing Living Arrangements of Young Adults in the UK'. *Population Trends* 138, 27–37.

Boliver, V. (2011). 'Expansion, Differentiation, and the Persistence of Social Class Inequalities in British Higher Education'. *Higher Education* 61 (3), 229–42.

Bynner, J., Elias, P., McKnight, A., Pan, H. and Gaelle, P. (2002). *Young People's Changing Routes to Independence* (York: Joseph Rowntree Foundation).

Callender, C. and Jackson, J. (2008). 'Does the Fear of Debt Constrain Choice of University and Subject of Study?' *Studies in Higher Education* 33 (4), 405–29.

Chapman, J. (2013). 'No Benefit for Your Third Child If You're on the Dole: Tories Unveil Controversial Welfare Plan'. *Daily Mail On-Line 16/7/2013*. Available from: http://www.dailymail.co.uk/news/article-2364718/No-benefit-child-youre-dole-Tories-unveil-controversial-welfare-plan.html (accessed on 15 February 2014).

Clapham, D., Buckley, K., Mackie, P., Orford, S. and Stafford, I. (2012). *Young People and Housing in 2020: Identifying Key Drivers for Change* (York: Joseph Rowntree Organisation).

Clapham, D., Kemp, P. and Smith, S. (1990). *Housing and Social Policy* (Basingstoke: Macmillan).

Coles, B., Rugg, J. and Seavers, J. (1999). 'Young Adults Living in the Parental Home. The Implications of Extended Youth Transitions for Housing and Social Policy', in Rugg, J. (ed.) *Young People, Housing and Social Policy* (London: Routledge), pp. 159–81.

Council of Mortgage Lenders (2011). *First-time Buyers and Affordability: A Fresh Perspective* (London: Council of Mortgage Lenders).

DWP (2011). 'Housing Benefit: Equality Impact Assessment. Increasing the Shared Accommodation Rate Age Threshold to 35', Available from: https://www.gov.uk/government/uploads/system/uploads/attachment_data/file/220261/eia-hb-shared-accommodation-age-threshold.pdf (accessed on 15 February 2014).

DWP (2012). 'Housing Benefit: Under Occupation of Social Housing', Available from: https://www.gov.uk/government/uploads/system/uploads/attachment_data/file/214329/social-sector-housing-under-occupation-wr2011-ia.pdf (accessed on 15 February 2014).

Fehlberg, B., Smyth, B., Maclean, M. and Roberts, C. (2011). 'Legislating for Shared Time Parenting after Separation: A Research Review'. *International Journal of Law, Policy and the Family* 25 (3), 318–37.

Fitzpatrick, S. and Pawson, H. (2007). 'Welfare Safety Net or Tenure of Choice? The Dilemma Facing Social Housing Policy in England'. *Housing Studies* 22 (2), 163–82.

Ford, J., Rugg, J. and Burrows, R. (2002). 'Conceptualising the Contemporary Role of Housing in the Transition to Adult Life in England'. *Urban Studies* 39 (13), 2455–67.

Forrest, R. and Murie, A. (1983). 'Residualisation and Council Housing: Aspects of the Changing Social Relations of Housing Tenure'. *Journal of Social Policy* 12 (4), 453–68.

Furlong, A. and Cooney, G.H. (1990). 'Getting on Their Bikes: Teenagers Leaving Home in Scotland in the 1980s'. *Journal of Social Policy* 19 (4), 535–51.

Griffin, C. (1993). *Representations of Youth: The Study of Youth and Adolescence in Britain and America* (Cambridge: Polity Press).

Heath, S. (2004). 'Peer-shared Households, Quasi-Communes and Neo-Tribes'. *Current Sociology* 52, 161–79.

Heath, S. and Calvert, E. (2013). 'Gifts, Loans and Intergenerational Support for Young Adults'. *Sociology* 1–16.

Holdsworth, C. (2009). ' "Going away to uni": Mobility, Modernity, and Independence of English Higher Education Students'. *Environment and Planning* 41 (8), 1849–64.

Jones, G. (1995). *Leaving Home* (Buckingham: Open University Press).

Kelly, K. (2013). 'We Must Balance the Need for New Housing against the Need for Affordable Homes'. JRF Blog Available from: http://www.jrf.org.uk/blog/2013/07/homes-affordable-supply (accessed on 15 February 2014).

Kemp, P. and Rugg, J. (1998). *The Single Room Rent: Its Impact on Young People.* (University of York: Centre for Housing Policy).

Kemp, P.A. (2011). 'Low-Income Tenants in the Private Rental Housing Market'. *Housing Studies* 26 (7/8), 1019–34.

Kennett, P., Forrest, R. and Marsh, A. (2012). 'The Global Economic Crisis and the Reshaping of Housing Opportunities'. *Housing, Theory and Society* 30, 1–19.

MacDonald, R. (1998). 'Youth, Transitions and Social Exclusion: Some Issues for Youth Research in the UK'. *Journal of Youth Studies* 1 (2), 163–76.

Malpass, P. (2004). 'Fifty Years of British Housing Policy: Leaving or leading the Welfare State?' *European Journal of Housing Policy* 4 (2), 209–27.

Mandic, S. (2008). 'Home-Leaving and Its Structural Determinants in Western and Eastern Europe: An Exploratory Study'. *Housing Studies* 23 (4), 615–36.

McKee, K. (2012). 'Young People, Homeownership and Future Welfare'. *Housing Studies* 27 (6), 853–62.

Ministry for Justice and Department for Education (2012). *The Government Response to the Family Justice Review: A System with Children and Families at Its Heart* (London: The Stationery Office).

Murie, A. (2012). 'The Next Blueprint for Housing Policy in England'. *Housing Studies* 27 (7), 1031–47.

Office for National Statistics (2008). 'Labour Force Survey User Guide'. Volume 8: Household and Family Data (London: The Stationery Office).

Office for National Statistics (2011). 'Households and Families', in Beaumont, J. (ed.) *Social Trends 41* (Basingstoke: Palgrave Macmillan).

Office for National Statistics (2012). *Characteristics of Young Unemployed People, 2012.* Office for National Statistics (London: The Stationery Office).

Office for National Statistics (2013). *Labour Market Statistics, June 2013* (London: The Stationery Office).

Patiniotis, J. and Holdsworth, C. (2005). 'Seize That Chance! Leaving Home and Transitions to Higher Education'. *Journal of Youth Studies* 8 (1), 81–95.

Roberts, S. (2011). 'Beyond "NEET" and "Tidy" Pathways: Considering the "Missing Middle" of Youth Transition Studies'. *Journal of Youth Studies* 14 (1), 21–39.

Roberts, S. (2013). 'Youth Studies, Housing Transitions and the "Missing Middle": Time for a Rethink?' *Sociological Research Online* 18 (3), 11.

Rugg, J. (1999). *Young People, Housing, and Social Policy* (New York: Psychology Press).

Rugg, J. and Rhodes, D. (2008). *The Private Rented Sector: Its Contribution and Potential* (University of York: Centre for Housing Policy).

Rugg, J., Rhodes, D. and Wilcox, S. (2011). *Unfair Shares: A Report on the Impact of Extending the Shared Accommodation Rate of Housing Benefit* (York/London: Crisis/Centre for Housing Policy).

Smart, C. (2004). 'Equal Shares: Rights for Fathers or Recognition for Children?' *Critical Social Policy* 24 (4), 484–503.

Smith, J. (2004). 'Risk, Social Change and Strategies of Inclusion for Young Homeless People', in Barry, M. (ed.) *Youth Policy and Social Inclusion: Critical Debates with Young People* (London, Routledge), pp. 131–151.

Speak, S. (1999). 'Housing and Young Single parent Families', in Rugg, J. (ed.) *Young People, Housing and Social Policy* (London: Routledge), pp. 127–144.

Stone, J., Berrington, A. and Falkingham, J. (2011). 'The Changing Determinants of UK Young Adults' Living Arrangements'. *Demographic Research* 25 (20), 629–66.

Stone, J., Berrington, A. and Falkingham, J. (2013). 'Gender, Turning Points and Boomerangs: Returning Home in Young Adulthood in Great Britain'. *Demography* 51 (1), 257–67.

The Telegraph (25 June 2012). David Cameron: 'Questions Need Asking on Welfare', *The Telegraph*. Available from: http://www.telegraph.co.uk/news/politics/david-cameron/9354236/David-Cameron-Questions-need-asking-on-welfare.html (accessed on 15 February 2014).

Wilcox, S. (2005). 'Trends in Housing Affordability,' in Regan, S. (ed.) *The Great Divide: An Analysis of Housing Inequality* (London: Shelter), pp. 117–44.

12
Life-Course Policy and the Transition from School to Work in Germany

Walter R. Heinz

12.1 Introduction

In this chapter, an overview of the life-course policy concerning German young people on the road to adulthood in the last decade is presented, with a focus on Vocational Education and Training (VET) pathways and Integration Measures. Life-course policy refers to the state's regulations, scripts and provisions concerning biographical transitions and social risks. To explain the continuity of Germany's 'dual system' in the context of labour market deregulation and activation policies, the chapter delineates between its structural features – an occupation-centred labour market and social partnership, that is, shared responsibility by state, employers and labour unions to organise and provide vocational training and citizenship education – and the main components of the transition system.

This chapter shows how the transition system is embedded in the welfare state and its provisions for young people at the intersection of education and employment, creating biographical turning points. The reasons for and mechanisms of active labour market policy are highlighted and their consequences for youth transitions illuminated. It is argued that retrenchment of the generous welfare state is shifting the responsibility for managing life-course transitions and employment risks to young people by demanding employability and self-responsibility. This restructuring is deepening the inequality of life chances by creating precarious transitions which tend to primarily harm the youth who are coming from the low ranks of Germany's three-tier

---

I thank John Bynner for helpful comments that improved this article.

school system. However, the experiences of precarious transitions create biographical uncertainty not only for the disadvantaged, but also extend to young adults with a better education. Because of the declining birth rate, however, the number of school leavers who are relegated to vocational integration measures instead of entering an apprenticeship has been declining. Finally, reforms of the institutional arrangements in the transition system in regard to the social heterogeneity of young people are discussed.

12.2   Welfare reform and activation policies

Germany's welfare state rests on a history of more than 120 years of responding to the great transformations of industrial production, international economic exchange and population dynamics. It is characterised by social reform from the top and based on a system of social (unemployment, retirement and health) insurance (paid by workers and employers) as a means to socially integrate the working class and of securing the legitimisation of the power structure.

Germany's welfare regime with its social and liberal elements is based on a strong manufacturing and export industry and is embedded in a system of social partnership facilitating the coordination of education, training, employment and social policies.

The mechanisms of the post-Second World War 'social market economy' are embedded in Germany's tradition of corporatism, which promotes a dynamic continuity of its welfare system and the system of Vocational Education and Training (VET). Social partnership between industrial associations, unions and the state works as a regulative institution that has turned out to be adaptable to political and economic turbulence since the end of the Second World War. Social policy and labour market regulations were adapted after the reunification of Germany in 1989, partly restructured in 2005 by the 'Agenda 2010' (so called 'Hartz-Acts'), and managed to respond quite successfully to the consequences of the global financial crisis in 2008.

The life-course model in Germany in the second part of the 20th century was guided by stable (male) employment, part-time work for women, long-term accumulation of prosperity, saving plans (including for home ownership) and paying back bank loans as building blocks of biographical planning. This model was also the yardstick for transmitting life plans, living standards and lifestyles between generations.

This all radically changed in the first decade of the 21st century, which was characterised by a decline in long-term security. People are now called upon to take care of their living standards by flexible employment and investing in social, retirement and health insurance; they are expected to act as dynamic players in the markets. This means that in the period of flexible capitalism, 'success' is rewarded instead of the recognition of 'achievement', a cultural shift which puts the moral foundations of the work society into question (Lessenich, 2008; Sennett, 2007). The liberalisation of employment regulations has been leading to a weakening of social partners' capacity to shape transitions and employment conditions, to an expansion of the low-wage sector, and of temporary work, together with a shift of costs from the corporations and banks to the taxpayers and the welfare system (Streeck, 2009).

A crucial event that marked this turning point was the joint declaration by the former Labour Party leaders and chiefs of state Tony Blair (UK) and Gerhard Schröder (Social Democratic Party, Germany) in 1999, which prepared the labour market and social policy reforms that were put to work in Germany in 2005 as 'Agenda 2010'. These reforms were rooted in the blueprint for a modern social democracy, called 'Europe: The Third Way', inspired by the British sociologist Anthony Giddens's (1998) concept of 'the third way', beyond the left-socialist and the right-conservative political camps.

Liberty and citizenship for modern social democratic policymaking meant that 'self-determined action' was embedded in the quest for social equality. The message was that there are no rights without obligations. The notion of the New Centre ('Die Neue Mitte'), located between a neo-liberal market economy and social capitalism, brought about an ideological shift of the German Social Democratic Party as a response to the impact of globalisation. The credo was that social and economic policy cannot be clearly separated, as the following quotes from the declaration document: 'Modern social democrats want to transform the safety net of entitlements into a springboard to personal responsibility ... All social policy instruments must improve life chances, encourage self-help and promote personal responsibility' (Blair and Schröder, 1999, p. 10). Therefore, investing in human capital to make individuals and businesses fit for the knowledge-based economy was seen as the 'most important task of modernisation'. This meant that 'standards at all levels of schooling and for all abilities of pupils must be raised' and that all young people should have the opportunity to enter employment 'by means of qualified vocational training' (Blair and Schröder, 1999, p. 8).

In the past decade, for a growing number of school leavers, this activation programme created precarious transitions into employment since not all instruments succeeded in enabling individual initiative or in opening up employment opportunities after vocational education and training. Those who could not take pathways into the labour market such as an apprenticeship or academic studies were directed to integration measures, courses of vocational preparation and episodes of work experience as instruments of improving employability and promoting maturation, at least until the mandatory school-leaving age of 18.

Active labour market policy is intended to promote employability and flexibility of people at risk of unemployment. This is connected with a demand for intensified individual investment in education, training and job search, and the willingness to lower expectations about good work. Since the introduction of the reforms in 2005, the low-wage sector has been expanding, a development that required the state to extend social assistance entitlement to the working poor in order to maintain a decent standard of living. About 1.3 million recipients of social assistance (unemployment benefit II, 'Hartz IV') were employed in the low-wage sector in 2012; half of them had 'mini-jobs' in sales, restaurants, health and social services, most of them women, earning not more than €450 a month (tax-free). Furthermore, the redefinition of the criteria of acceptability for recipients of benefits, that is to take any kind of paid work, meant that a growing number of VET and BA graduates accepted fixed-term, low-income employment, which sometimes required resettlement or long-distance travel between home and the workplace. Such work circumstances contribute to a devaluation of young people's skills, disenchantment among young people and additional pressure on families to take care of their offspring during the transition from school to work.

A decoupling and part restructuring of education, VET and employment occurred in the context of welfare reform. After a period of rising unemployment and increasing welfare expenditures in the 1990s, consequences of the economic recession and the reunification of Germany in 1989, the Labour/Green Federal government passed a massive and controversial social policy reform, the so called 'Hartz-Acts', named after the head of the planning committee, which was implemented in 2005.

A process of deregulation was intended to reduce social expenditure and to increase the flexibility of the labour market. A transformation of the bureaucratic Employment Office by establishing job centres, designed according to the UK model, led to the creation of local service organisations for the unemployed, job seekers and welfare recipients. Furthermore, unemployment benefits and social assistance were combined and benefits from unemployment insurance were fixed at 12 months. Case managers were to instil and to control individual initiative – according to the principle of 'carrot and stick' – by promoting

active job search and placement, requiring unemployed youth to participate in job preparation and skill training in order to make them fit for
entering an apprenticeship. Clients who do not comply face penalties,
including a 10 per cent reduction in their social assistance payments.

The focus of new social policy arrangements was on activation,
incentives and social selectivity. The young persons were defined as
independent actors, who have to account for the results of their actions:
self-responsible and self-sustainable conduct. The job centres' arrangements for promoting training and job search required young people's
visible effort. For navigating interlinked transitions between training,
studying and working, and between different housing arrangements
in the rapidly shifting landscape of skill demands and employment
conditions, young adults must continue to accumulate educational,
social and cultural resources that are needed as a basis for exercising
their agency. In the labour market, they have to come to terms with
deregulation; that is, a decline in standard employment, a growing low-
income sector, fixed-term contracts, short-term employment, episodes
of internship and unemployment. Thus, they must engage in short-term
decision-making, learning to become resilient and how to consolidate
fragmented paths.

The situation of the younger school-leaving cohorts, however, shows
some improvement: because of the declining birth rate they experience less competition on the apprenticeship market, and for the better
educated there are new options to combine VET and college ('dual
studies').

12.3   The welfare regime and its life-course policy

The life-course as a social institution (Kohli, 2007) is more or less structured by the German welfare state, which provides a framework of
security, transition markers and entitlements in the various life phases.
Its social expenditures are financial contributions and benefits to individuals and households in order to provide support in all phases of
the life-course and risk situations. Furthermore, the welfare regime
designs and monitors life scripts as temporal sequences of legitimate
participation in the different spheres of life (for example, compulsory schooling, duration of unemployment benefits and the onset of
retirement benefits). Institutions of education, training and employment provide resources and temporal orientations for passing through
transitions and thus have the power to modify the structure of life-
courses. Hence, the government shapes biographies when it restructures

labour laws, improves the reconciliation of employment and family and changes age-related entitlements, such as tuition fees, duration of schooling and studying. From kindergarten and schools to higher education, employment and retirement, the German life-course policy is focused more on security than on equality (Leisering, 2003), a concept which cannot close the increasing gap between the rich and the poor.

The social structure of Germany has been characterised by an unequal distribution of income and wealth ever since the 'economic miracle' of the 1950s. Recently, the debate about social inequality has again raised the issue of social justice in regard to equal opportunities in education and employment. While the power elite defend and legitimate their status by pointing to the successful operation of economic growth machinery, members of the middle class are exhibiting feelings of uncertainty about being able to maintain their standard of living and are concerned about social downward mobility, and the working class are struggling to make their ends meet. Germany's social structure is characterised by growing inequality in income and property: 36 per cent of wealth was owned by the top 1 per cent of the population in 2010, a number which is getting close to the USA, where 40 per cent of wealth was owned by the top 1 per cent of the population (Hartmann, 2013).

In the second half of the 20th century, the welfare state followed a middle of the road route, in that it provided social security and social assistance to employees and their families by combining elements of a market and a means-tested model, mounting to social expenditures of about one-third of the GDP in 1995. It expanded until the present century, when reforms were implemented as a response to rising unemployment and to the increasing costs of social assistance. A reduction of the high rates of unemployment in the 1990s resulted from the loosening of employment standards, raising the barriers for obtaining social assistance and a limitation of one year for receiving unemployment benefits. A structural weakness of this policy was that unemployment benefits were only available for employees with more or less stable careers who experience episodes of joblessness; workers in the low-wage sector with interrupted careers were less well off.

In the 1990s the unemployment rate was quite high and the proportion of young skilled workers in regular full-time jobs comparatively low. There was a sharp separation between the core labour force and the peripheral workers (between 'insiders' and 'outsiders', see Emmenegger et al., 2012) because job security of the employed was high. This was changed not necessarily to the advantage of young people by the

Agenda 2010, since most of them have to start their work trajectory on a fixed-term contract.

The liberalisation of financial markets, the growing public budget deficits and the debts of private households (in the USA and UK, related to real estate/the housing bubble) since the 1990s affected the welfare system. Moreover, the current Euro crisis, in the wake of international efforts to save the bankrupt states of Greece, Cyprus, Portugal and Ireland, also endangered the German economy and reduced private savings (because of low interest rates). Labour market policy responded with an increase of sub-standard (fixed-term and low-wage) employment, and in the welfare system there were deep cuts in public benefits in favour of consolidating the state budget. Globalisation and monetary crisis have been transferring power relations between the state and the financial markets to the disadvantage of the government and the working population. This became evident in the shift of social and labour market arrangements from job creation and social assistance to workfare, which requires recipients of benefits to accept any kind of paid employment.

Rising pension expenditure and social assistance for poor families reinforced the existing imbalance and led to a policy of shifting from a generous and caring to an activating welfare state: The ominous 'Agenda 2010' brought cuts through a merger of unemployment benefits and social assistance. Preventative and activation mechanisms were combined in order to create, keep and restore employability of young people who were at risk of not succeeding in the labour market.

In the wake of neo-liberal policy strategies, most western welfare states' labour market reforms were implemented to demand and to promote workers' flexibility, accompanied by a shrinking of expenditure on social security. This policy shift extended low-income employment, fixed-term contracts, privatisation and job cuts in the public sector. These were symptoms of the retrenchment of the welfare state and of a growing disparity in life-chances for the younger generation compared with those who had gone before. Austerity measures are supposed to reduce the public debt, but will be harmful for economic growth, social expenditures and investments in education and training (Streeck, 2013).

The labour market impact of the Great Recession, which has been affecting national economies world-wide since 2008, was cushioned in Germany by federal subsidies (for short-term work) for companies which kept their labour force, for promoting more flexible employment, and modernising VET. Second, because of the low birth rate, the demand for apprenticeships has been declining, which contributed to keeping youth unemployment low. Third, the number of school leavers continuing their education at universities of applied sciences and other universities increased, driven by the introduction of the BA (Bologna Process) with a shorter duration for obtaining a first degree than the former Diploma (equivalent to the MA or MSc).

12.4 Transition pathways from school to work

Youth unemployment in Germany was at 7.6 per cent in March 2013 (EUROSTAT), the lowest rate in Europe. This is mainly because of the long-standing transition system that provides pathways into the labour market (see Baethge, 2008; Rauner, 2008).

There were 344 registered occupations in which young people could apply for a three-year firm-based apprenticeship in 2010; half of them had a modernised curriculum and one-fifth were newly designed occupations. The access to apprenticeships is still heavily segregated by gender.

The German education system distributes life chances through its hierarchy of lower (Hauptschule), middle (Realschule) and high schools (Gymnasium, conferring the 'Abitur'), which has been the tripartite education regime for generations, a regime which distributes life chances by reinforcing social origins and creating inequality. According to a comparative study of education arrangements in West Germany, Britain and Sweden by Allmendinger and Hinz (1989), the German education system is highly socially selective (see also OECD; PISA). There are only a few comprehensive schools which are characteristic of the Scandinavian countries, or multi-tracked high schools as in France, the UK and Italy. In the past decade, there has been an increase in high school graduates and a decline in low-level school leavers, without changing the impact of social origin on educational careers, though.

Public expenditures on education have been lower in Germany than in most other European countries: 4.6 per cent of the GDP in 1995, 4.4 per cent in 2006, compared with 5.1 per cent in the EU27, and much lower than in Denmark (8.0 per cent) or in Sweden (6.9 per cent). The most obvious differences, however, concern the VET completion rate, which in 2010 was 55 per cent in Germany, 32 per cent in Sweden and only 8 per cent in Spain, whereas the tertiary completion rate was 27 per cent in Germany, 42 per cent in Sweden and 40 per cent in Spain (OECD, 2013).

Besides the 'dual system' of VET, there are five distinct institutionalised pathways from education to employment:

- Full-time vocational education (school-based)
- Integration Measures (vocational orientation and preparation)

- Dual Studies (combining VET and BA)
- University of Applied Sciences (former Polytechnics)
- University

The latter three pathways require the 'Abitur'.

The mainstream of the German VET is organised as a 'dual system' (firm-based training plus vocational school) – a transition pathway also established in slightly different versions in Austria, Switzerland and Denmark – and is embedded in a corporatist steering system which adapted to the changes in occupational structure from manufacturing to services. It is regulated by federal legislation (1969, modernised in 2005), supervised by the Federal Ministry of Education and Research (BMBF) and administered by the Federal Vocational Education Agency (BIBB).

What is the employers' rationale for training apprentices compared with hiring them after graduation as skilled workers? There are two strategies: recruiting employees who were trained by another firm (traditionally from SME) or to build an internally trained workforce. The larger the company the more apprenticeships tend to be offered. It is mainly the SME in the sectors of restaurant, sales and hotel services which reduce their apprenticeship places because they can hire (and fire) cheap labour according to the liberalised/deregulated labour market. However, crafts, manufacturing and IT services are complaining about the lack of skilled workers and technicians and are campaigning for school leavers to apply for apprenticeships. This signals the rediscovery of a long-term qualification strategy which is combined with hiring skilled workers and technicians from eastern and southern Europe.

The main costs are carried by the training firms (€8 billion; in German: milliards) and the state (€3 billions/milliards for vocational schools) in 2010; quality controls and examinations are conducted by the regional chambers of commerce and crafts. There is a long-term return of investment in training. The training companies' yearly costs per apprentice were €15,000 in 2010, the benefits €11,700, the further gain of employing skilled workers familiar with the firm not included (for these and other figures, see the Federal VET Report, BIBB, 2012).

Training allowances (apprenticeship wages) are about a fourth of adult wages, depend on tariffs and increase in the course of the VET. In 2011 the average allowance was €708 (West Germany), €642 (East Germany).

The wider benefits of VET concern the trainees' development of self-esteem, self-confidence and occupational identity which implies commitment to quality work. The curricula of vocational schools and the occupational communities also contribute to preparing apprentices for civic participation (Rauner, 2008).

The German transition system and its main VET pathway are still an internationally recognised model for a well-regulated and close coupling between a stratified educational system and an occupational labour market. This matching of skills with job profiles and smooth labour market entry depends on employers' willingness to provide training places/apprenticeships, which is contingent on economic growth and training costs.

The dual system is unique in providing portable and certified skill profiles that are sustainable over the work life-course and promote a matching of training and employment. More than half the apprentices are being employed by their training firm after graduation. The others either change their employer or their occupational field, running the risk of becoming employed below their level of competence. A minority with a high level school-leaving certificate ('Abitur') move on to further academic education. Depending on the business outlook of the respective economic sector, the rate of skilled young adults becoming employed by their training firm varies: It increases by company size and varies by economic cycle; it was two-thirds in 2000, 58 per cent in 2005 and 62 per cent in 2010 (BIBB, 2012).

Germany's education and training structure is known and rightly criticised (OECD, 2013) for its persistent relationship between school level and access to the occupational ranks, expressing unequal life chances: Young people who left school without a certificate were almost completely excluded from apprenticeships, whereas 43 per cent of the apprentices came from the middle school, 33 per cent had a low-level school background and 21 per cent the 'Abitur' in 2010. Depending on their education level, they enter VET in different occupational sectors: The university-bound are clearly preferred for the top occupations that can be combined with subsequent academic studies, for example industrial, financial and insurance management, and ICT services, while the low-level graduates are trained in the crafts, manufacturing and sales.

The dual system still mirrors the unequal distribution of men and women in the German occupational structure: women are concentrated in service jobs (62 per cent) and the full-time vocational schools, men in manufacturing and crafts (88 per cent).

The proportion of school leavers with the 'Abitur', the prerequisite to enter the pathways of tertiary education, has been increasing steadily since the 1990s, in parallel with a decline in the numbers of lower and middle level school graduates. Nevertheless, the VET is still the most popular pathway taken, with almost two-thirds (570,000) of all school leavers in 2011. There has been substantial continuity in the preference for the VET over the past decade, with a peak of 68.7 per cent (622,000) in 2000 and a low of 57.8 per cent (550,000) in 2005. The year 2005 was a critical year, because the 'Hartz IV-measures' were introduced and many school leavers who did not get an apprenticeship had to settle for the Integration Measures which put them on a waiting loop.

Despite the declining numbers of school leavers, VET applicants from low-level schools and those with low grades only get a chance if they are able to compensate for their educational and/or ethnic background by adaptability, good manners and visible engagement in the job interview. Migrant youth are confronted with doubts when applying for an apprenticeship: they are still looked at with the expectation that they will not fit into a firm's team (Solga and Kohlrausch, 2012). Germany's population and most of the country's employers have not yet succeeded in shifting from latent racism to a culture of diversity. Thus, low-level school graduates who got the chance to present themselves to the firm during a practical stint were successful.

There are, however, promising signs of improvement: in the wake of the dramatic demographic change in Germany, the disadvantages embedded in the institutional framework of youth transitions are becoming a social policy and labour market issue. The labour administration is moving towards joint and preventative transition management by communities, schools, firms, vocational counselling and the employment agency, an approach which indicates 'biographical sensitivity' towards the disadvantaged.

Despite the popular laments about a shrinking German population, the figures suggest that the 'cunning of reason' is at work: whereas the share of 20–24-year-olds increased by only 1.8 per cent since 2005, the share of 15–19-year-olds has declined by 15 per cent. This drop in the number of candidates for an apprenticeship will motivate employers to become less socially selective and also to give low achievers and migrant youth a chance.

12.5 The institutional context of transitions

The transitions from school to work are embedded in the institutional fabrics of education, training, labour market and social policy. These institutions are interconnected and show continuity across historical periods; that is, they provide social mechanisms for maintaining and adapting path-dependent routes to employment in changing economic circumstances. This also means that they are difficult to transfer to other societies which have different education and employment structures.

The triad of free education and VET, employment standards and social policy in Germany rests on the coordination of social partners. It is embedded in a model of life-course policy that social security is to be provided for all stages and mishaps of life, based on a system of workers' and employers' contributions to social insurance. The impact of rising tensions between economic growth, capital gain (stakeholder values) and social protection for young people tends to be cushioned in the German welfare state by providing several alternative education to employment pathways. Integration measures intend to prepare the less well educated to move on to regular skill training and contribute to reducing social disparities and individual disadvantage. Offering access to public education and transition systems is still the aim of coordinated planning by government, employers' associations and the labour unions (see Allmendinger and Leibfried, 2003).

The growing scarcity of young skilled employees, caused by Germany's declining birth rate, calls for an investment in occupational guidance and transition management, which is supposed to start with new pilot programmes in grade seven (when pupils are aged 13) of the 'Hauptschule'. This concerns the question of employability, competence and citizenship in a life-course perspective: not just for job entrance, but also for risks at biographical turning points; that is, the ability to make a living in the different phases and spheres of life until retirement. This cannot be left to the employers' business plans, which require flexibility and low wages, but must be embedded in a combination of the states' education, labour market and social policy with the goal of preventing unemployment, of creating bridges to employment for disadvantaged school leavers and subsidising work creation and benefits alike in periods of recession.

This problem affects the 77,000 applicants who were registered as not having found an apprenticeship in 2011 – when at the same time a rising number of employers complained that they could not find any suitable applicants. This disparity between demand and supply has been a weak point in Germany's life-course policy for quite some time: Despite the popularity of the dual system and the full-time vocational schools, there were 2.15 million young adults between the age of 20 and 34 without a vocational certification (Statistisches Bundesamt, 2012).

In the past, these deficits were due to the impact of recessions on firms' willingness to offer training places. Today, the reasons for the same problems are obvious: there is a general decline in the size of the school-leaving cohorts, more are continuing with academic education, and applicants from the low-level school, many of them with Turkish or Arabian background, are not yet regarded as trainable and employable by many firms. The major reason is, however, that the number of firms which offer apprenticeships has been declining, to 22.5 per cent in 2010, the lowest figure since 1999. According to the BIBB (2012), 56 per cent of all firms were recognised as training providers and under half of them actually participated.

For low achievers and teenagers, who are regarded as not being fit ('mature') for an apprenticeship, there are the short-term (up to one year) school-based and work experience integration programmes. The transition sector 'Integration into the VET' includes several pathways; the most important are courses of occupational preparation and of compensating for lack of a secondary school diploma. Educational experts and employers see such pathways as inefficient and leading into 'waiting-loops', instead of into an apprenticeship, because the German VET culture puts a premium on a firm-based process of occupational socialisation (Heinz, 2008). On the other hand, educational policymakers see these measures, if they start before young people graduate from school, as best practice for promoting the competence needed for a reasonable occupational choice and for improving the odds of landing an apprenticeship. The target groups are socially disadvantaged youth, mainly migrants and applicants who did not succeed in the year(s) before ('Altbewerber').

The educational backgrounds of the participants in integration measures differ: half of them have a secondary school certificate, a quarter have a middle school diploma, and one-fifth no certificate. These measures mop up those whose education biography did not sufficiently prepare them for firm- or school-based occupational training.

Recent data from the integrated VET reporting system (iABE; BIBB, 2012) document that 14.3 per cent (almost 300,000) of all entrants into the transition system in 2011 had no other choice than to be channelled into integration measures. The fact that the number of new entrants into this sector has been declining steadily, by 36 per cent since 2005, leads the authors of the VET Report (BIBB, 2012, p. 379) to conclude: 'the development of the integration sector has less to do with a lack of "training maturity" than with the classical market laws'. This is a remarkable conclusion, because it lifts the blame placed on the low achievers and highlights the economic context of the employers' hiring strategy.

There are two reasons, however, to maintain this transition route: besides the self-sustaining interest of education providers in this sector, young people at risk of becoming excluded because of schooling deficits and a lack of parental support will need such a remedial pathway for gaining self-confidence by participating in a chain of education and work experience. This strategy could prevent a situation comparable to the young people in England who are not in employment, education or training (NEETs) (Bynner and Parsons, 2002; Yates and Payne, 2006). It is focused on vocational training as a prerequisite of employability and thus differs from employment-enhancing measures in England, where employment with on-the-job training is viewed as a better alternative.

Quite a number of young adults do not manage to complete their apprenticeship after three years of firm-based and school-related learning. A severe problem is the increasing proportion of young people who drop out of an apprenticeship (most in the first year); 23 per cent gave up their contract in 2010, most frequently in stressful and low-income work contexts such as restaurants, hotels and security services. Encouragingly, however, is that half of this group signed up for a new apprenticeship in another firm or occupation a year later.

Dropping out of an apprenticeship may also be caused by bad employment prospects. Not all VET graduates find a job right away: in 2012, 61 per cent got a job offer from their training firm, one-third were unemployed. As documented by the IAB company-panel study, for most of the unemployed the situation improved after three years: 81 per cent were employed in the West (70 per cent on a permanent contract), and 71 per cent in the East of Germany (only 58 per cent with a permanent contract) (BIBB, 2012).

12.6 Biographical uncertainty and unequal life chances

The above figures document that up to 40 per cent of skilled workers are not in stable employment, which indicates a precarious process of entering employment after VET for a substantial number of young adults.

The transition to adulthood implies risks for all cohorts of school leavers, because they are at a turning point which is determined by the state of the economy and the state's life-course policy. Today, biographical uncertainty dominates and the inequality of life chances is spreading, despite young people's increased efforts and achievements in the education system (Heinz, 2009).

The challenges and risks facing young people in Germany differ by social origin, level of education, age, cohort and gender: adolescents must come to terms with the consequences of being allocated to one of the three streams of secondary schooling, only one of them leading to higher education. Depending on their school-leaving certificate, young adults are faced with a hierarchy of vocational and academic pathways: VET, integration measures, dual studies, university of applied sciences, and university (BA/MA). These pathways mirror and deepen the selection processes in the preceding education system and create social inequalities of life chances and influence employment conditions that may be reached.

Does the spreading of precarious, open-ended transitions translate into a feeling of uncertainty? Which life phases, pathways and social classes are most affected? What can life-course policy do about it?

For a better understanding of the biographical impact of transitions with uncertain destinations and the decoupling of young people from the prospect of stable employment which may be leading to situations of social exclusion and poverty, the notion of 'precarity' is useful (Castel and Dörre, 2009; Gallie and Paudam, 2002; Standing, 2011).

Precarious employment means that people drop below the standard level of income, job security and social integration which characterise decent work conditions in welfare states. 'Precarisation' refers to a social process that feeds back to the integrated majority via the erosion of employment standards and social security. It reaches young people who are in training and higher education pathways by predicting difficult times ahead when they are attempting to enter the labour market.

The transformation of the industrial-capitalist to a financial-capitalist service economy with an ever thinner net of social security is at the roots of precarity. It affects not only the life planning of the educationally and socially disadvantaged but also the VET and university graduates, who are more and more confronted with a risky biographical openness concerning their work life-course. Discontinuous employment, low-income jobs, fixed-term contracts, episodes of joblessness and retraining put them at an increasing distance from standard employment, not to mention from a career (Heinz, 2003).

While there is little longitudinal research, recent case studies (see Castel and Dörre, 2009), however, indicate that precarity refers to a heterogeneous social category, there are different social and economic constellations that influence how young adults are dealing with uncertainty. The following examples document the social heterogeneity of this transition zone.

Well-educated young people living in Berlin and working in the media, in web design and the arts, who are used to irregular employment, are attempting to transform the lack of stable employment into a subjective orientation away from the burden of paid work to an alternative communal lifestyle. They live a sort of 'creative precarity' which may turn into a self-employed start-up one day. However, for the time being non-standard work is likely to become an accepted way of earning and of social participation and integration, by identifying with the content of work. This arrangement differs from the traditional 'gap year' taken by Oxbridge graduates because it combines work with a flexible lifestyle.

Managing precarious transitions also concerns the average university graduate. A third of the university graduates in Germany were temporarily employed in 2011 and 80 per cent of the 25–29-year-olds employed in teaching and research had a fixed-term contract, whereas only 17 per cent in this age group overall were on such a contract (Statistisches Bundesamt, 2013).

Changing life-course policy is creating fragmented transitions such as these into academic positions. They have been spreading in the context of public institutions' declining budgets: a step-wise, highly competitive progression is offered with sequences of fellowships, stipends, unemployment spells, part-time work and fixed-term contracts (for example, research grants). With active survival strategies and high achievement motivation young academics respond to the prospect of getting more stable positions by staying in the academic system.

At the lowest level of the social structure, life-course policy has not managed to prevent social exclusion of young women who are caught in the precarious transition from early motherhood to employment. There is an extreme contrast of opportunities between the better educated and disadvantaged young single mothers who dropped out of school and did not have any qualifications. They live in a social context which offers few prospects when they look for work after the three years of parenting and welfare benefits, and they cannot rely on child care. Most still live in their parental home and depend on social welfare. Forty per cent of all single mothers with children under the age of 18 receive benefits, and half of the unemployed do not have a vocational qualification (Bundesagentur für Arbeit, 2010). This puts them into a situation of long-term social marginality, hopeless waiting and idleness.

From a biographical perspective, the institutional regulations connected with the labour agency's activation strategy may – contrary to the goal of promoting a turning point with prospects – reinforce a precarisation process for young people, because it requires job-seekers on benefits to accept non-standard employment often below their skill level. This may set a vicious circle into motion that takes the person away from standard work and traps them in the low-income sector.

In the institutional framework of activation, fitness training for the labour market is meant to improve employability, with a focus on the young person's motivation and goal orientation; this does not create work opportunities, though. The message is to act like a self-made man or self-made woman if you want to get ahead and prevent social exclusion; a self-directed life script requires that you make a living by paid work. Most parents and young adults located around the poverty line in the zone of precarity want to remain participants in the workforce despite restrictive and disappointing labour market experiences. This also creates conflict with parents who rarely experienced unemployment themselves and confront their sons and daughters with the notion of a 'normal' work biography.

Increasingly young people worry about their future life in comparison with their parents because careers after graduation are becoming unlikely. In a representative survey (Bertelsmann-Foundation, 2011) three-quarters of the respondents stated that economic insecurity has increased in the last decade and only a third believed that all people had the same opportunity to get ahead. A study comparing Germany and Sweden (Bild der Frau, 2012) found that in Germany 44 per cent agreed that people who try hard will get ahead; in Sweden, however, two-thirds did. There is a remarkable difference for respondents under 30: whereas only 18 per cent of German lower-class young people believed in the validity of the achievement principle, 68 per cent of the young Swedes did.

Reducing biographical uncertainty in a context of structural and felt precarity by an active shaping of possibilities requires the competence and self-reliance to deal with contingent transitions, which hinge on a life-course policy that not only promotes the acquisition of knowledge and certified skills but also creates opportunities for decent work.

12.7   Policy targets: Preventing instead of mending

There are three fields of life-course policy that deserve attention because they indicate a biographically sensitive life-course policy.

In the recent years of low youth unemployment and shrinking school-leaving cohorts, there has been a shift among German policymakers from blaming the low achievers for their job entry problems to pointing at the transition contexts that create diverse learning biographies and the failures of the integration measures. One example is what one could call 'Operation Vocational Head Start', a new programme which starts in grade seven with an analysis of the young people's interests and learning potential, followed by work experience stints in several occupational fields. The aim is to promote self-reflection, forming realistic impressions about work and connecting with potential training firms. It is crucial is to pave the road to adulthood for the disadvantaged by learning and training in the real world of firms.

Another issue is to encourage employers' active response to the shrinking birth rate. In view of the declining number of applicants, training firms are beginning to eye potential apprentices who come from the integration pathways, though they express doubts with regard to their goal orientation. In regard to Germany's immigrant population of 12 million, social and ethnic diversity can be perceived as a challenge.

This should also be accomplished by improving the matching of applicants and the requirements of SME. Both the less well-educated and the well-prepared apprentices are trained in specialised occupational skill profiles which tend to be difficult to transfer between occupational spheres, for example from manufacturing to IT services. Here the development of integrated technical and service occupations, together with further learning timetables will increase the workers' capacity to adapt to changing markets and job requirements. Such a reconstruction will also help to reduce the drop-out rate from the VET.

Third, there is an urgent and long overdue reform issue to increase permeability between vocational and academic education. These two transition routes are still characterised by a social closure that makes it extremely difficult to move from an occupation to a profession that demands an academic degree. On the other hand, it was recently suggested by the Federal Minister of Education and Research (BMBF, 2013) that for university drop-outs who opt for an apprenticeship the theoretical components of the VET should be recognised, which would shorten the duration of training. A more encompassing life-course policy would be to certify skills accumulated outside the VET and to recognise achievements of unskilled young adults by offering qualification modules for accumulating credits that step by step lead to a VET certification.

References

Allmendinger, J. and Hinz, T. (1989). 'Occupational Careers under Different Welfare Regimes: West Germany, Great Britain, and Sweden', in Leisering, L. and Walker, R. (eds.) *The Dynamics of Modern Society* (Bristol: Policy Press), pp. 63–84.

Allmendinger, J. and Leibfried, S. (2003). 'Education and the Welfare State: The Four Worlds of Competence Production'. *Journal of European Social Policy* 13, 63–81.

Baethge, M. (2008). 'Das berufliche Bildungswesen in Deutschland am Beginn des 21. Jahrhunderts', in Cortina, K.S., Leschinsky, A., Baumert, J., Mayer, K-U. and Trommer, L. (eds.) *Das Bildungswesen in der Bundesrepublik Deutschland; Strukturen und Entwicklungen im Überblick.* 2nd ed. (Reinbek: Rowohlt), pp. 525–80.

Bertelsmann Foundation (2011). *Gerechter Arbeitsmarkt* (Gütersloh: Bertelsmann).

BIBB (Bundesinstitut für Berufsbildung) (2012). *Datenreport zum Berufsbildungsbericht* (Bonn: BIBB).

Bild der Frau (2012). *Chancengerechtigkeit durch Förderung von Kindern. Ein deutsch-schwedischer Vergleich* (Hamburg: Bild der Frau).

BMBF (Bundesministerium für Bildung und Forschung) (2013). *Bundesbildungsbericht* (Berlin: BMBF).

Blair, T. and Schröder, G. (1999). *Declaration: Europe: The Third Way* (Berlin: Friederich-Ebert-Foundation).

Bundesagentur für Arbeit (2010). *Statistik zum Ausbildungsstellenmarkt* (Nürnberg).

Bynner, J. and Parsons, S. (2002). 'Social Exclusion and the Transition from School to Work: The Case of Young People Not in Education, Employment or Training (NEET)'. *Journal of Vocational Behavior* 60, 289–309.

Castel, R. and Dörre, K. (eds.) (2009). *Prekarität, Abstieg, Ausgrenzung* (Frankfurt/Main: Campus).

Emmenegger, P., Häusermann, S. and Palier, B. (eds.) (2012). *The Age of Dualisation: The Changing Face of Inequality in Deindustrialising Societies* (Oxford: Oxford University Press).

Gallie, D. and Paudam, S. (2002). *Social Precarity and Social Integration* (Luxemburg: European Commission).

Giddens, A. (1998). *The Third Way* (Cambridge: Polity Press).

Hartmann, M. (2013). *Soziale Ungleichheit. Kein Thema für Eliten?* (Frankfurt/New York: Campus Verlag).

Heinz, W.R. (2003). 'From Work Trajectories to Negotiated Careers: The Contingent Work Life Course', in Mortimer, J.T. and Shanahan, M.J. (eds.) *Handbook of the Life Course* (York: Kluwer/Plenum), pp. 185–204.

Heinz, W.R. (2008). 'Occupational Socialization', in Rauner, F. and MacLean, R. (eds.) *Handbook of Technical and Vocational Education and Training Research* (New York: Springer), pp. 481–89.

Heinz, W.R. (2009). 'Youth Transitions in an Age of Uncertainty', in Furlong, A. (ed.) *Handbook of Youth and Young Adulthood* (London: Routledge), pp. 3–13.

Kohli, M. (2007). 'The Institutionalization of the Life Course: Looking Back to Look Ahead'. *Research in Human Development* 4, 253–71.

Leisering, L. (2003). 'Government and the Life Course', in Mortimer, T.J. and Shanahan, M.J. (eds.) *Handbook of the Life Course* (New York: Kluwer/Plenum), pp. 205–25.

Lessenich, S. (2008). *Die Neuerfindung des Sozialen: Der Sozialstaat im flexiblen Kapitalismus*. (Bielefeld: Transcript).

OECD (2013). *Employment Outlook* (Paris).

Rauner, F. (2008). 'On the Genesis of TVET Research in Germany', in Rauner, F. and MacLean, R. (eds.) *Handbook of Technical and Vocational Education and Training Research* (New York: Springer), pp. 48–56.

Sennett, R. (2007). *The Culture of the New Capitalism* (New Haven: Yale University Press).

Solga, H. and Kohlrausch, B. (2012). 'How Low-Achieving German Youth Beat the Odds and Gain Access to VET'. *European Sociological Review*, 1–15.

Standing, G. (2011). *The Precariat: The New Dangerous Class* (London: Bloomsbury).

Statistisches Bundesamt (2012). Bildung und Kultur – berufliche Bildung (Wiesbaden).

Statistisches Bundesamt (2013). Integrierte Ausbildungsberichterstattung (Wiebaden).

Streeck, W. (2009). *Re-forming Capitalism: Institutional Change in the German Political Economy* (Oxford: Oxford University Press).

Streeck, W. (2013). *Gekaufte Zeit. Die vertagte Krise des demokratischen Kapitalsmus* (Berlin: Suhrkamp).

Yates, S. and Payne, M. (2006). 'Not so NEET? A Critique of the Use of "NEET" in Setting Targets for Interventions with Young people'. *Journal of Youth Studies* 9, 329–34.

13

Youth Transitions, Precarity and Inequality and the Future of Social Policy in Europe

Lorenza Antonucci and Myra Hamilton

The chapters in this book present research conducted during the current European economic crisis and offer a timely contribution to the analysis of the conditions facing young people in Europe. The emerging risks have to be understood, as we argued in Chapter 1, not only as an effect of the economic crisis but also as a consequence of longer-term patterns in youth transitions. Furthermore, as we pointed out in Chapter 1, a consensus is emerging on the detrimental combined effects of the economic crisis and of European austerity on youth transitions. For the most part, analyses of the effects of risk on young people's lives in this new policy environment have been confined to youth studies, and social policy theory has important insights to offer to this debate. Drawing on new research by social policy scholars, this book shed light on the nature of inequality affecting young people and the relevance of welfare structures in mitigating contemporary risks. In particular, this book has offered both a major contribution to understanding risk and precarity facing young people in the crisis (in the contributions of Part I) and to analysing social policies and welfare mixes (in the contributions of Part II). Making sense of contemporary youth transitions requires efforts to describe both the evolution of individual experiences and an explanation of how these experiences are shaped by structural factors.

13.1 Understanding risk and precarity of young people in the crisis

The first part, 'Precarity, social exclusion and youth policy in Europe', has improved our understanding of risk and young people by clarifying the contours of precarity and disadvantage experienced by young Europeans in the Great Recession. Several conclusions emerge from the cross-national and national case studies presented in this part of the book.

The first element concerns the patterns in the distribution of poverty, social exclusion and risk across Europe. The research in Chapter 3 suggested that there are still substantial variations in the levels of poverty and deprivation across countries. For example, young people from northern European countries experience high levels of poverty compared with other age groups in these states, as a consequence of early transitions to independent housing, but they also show relatively lower levels of deprivation, which could be a consequence of having more generous welfare state interventions. Fahmy's cross-national comparison in Chapter 3 points to the mitigating effects of welfare state interventions in northern countries in limiting the protracted phase of poverty experienced by young people. On the contrary, the experience of long-term deprivation found in eastern and southern Europe suggests a somewhat 'weaker' role of welfare states in those areas in mitigating social risks. While the role of the welfare state emerges as central in mitigating social risk and poverty, the study concludes that differences in poverty levels across countries cannot be explained by the welfare regime division, highlighting the limitations of a welfare regime analysis applied to young people. In addition to this, as emerged in the analysis of socially excluded young people in the UK in Chapter 5, social policy interventions have the risk of reproducing, rather than limiting, patterns of exclusion if they do not challenge old structural patterns of inequality. The 'thick' analysis of social exclusion provided by Sealey suggests that individualised policies in the UK clash with the reality of persistent structural constraints, reinforced by the local labour market and family circumstances.

The contributions in this book have also shed light on the changing nature of risk affecting young people. One important change has been the increasing number of highly skilled or highly educated young people experiencing labour market precarity. The cross-national research in Chapter 4 suggests that the experience of precarity by highly qualified young people is a common feature of youth transitions across a number of different welfare regimes, including Italy, Spain and the UK. While social policies in Europe have focused on improving the number of graduates and highly skilled workers, the analysis by Murgia and Poggio in Chapter 4 shows that this group of young people faces significant challenges in entry into the labour market and in accessing social protection, which are affecting their life-course paths. The comparative findings in Chapter 4 are supported by the case study of Spain in Chapter 7, which shows how graduate young people constitute an important part of the precariat identified by Standing (2011). Overall, these findings challenge the current mantra of European policymaking – that access to tertiary education and skills formation will unquestionably lead to secure labour market outcomes – which, as rightly put by Andy Furlong in the Foreword, is being confronted with the reality of a 'mismatch' between education supply and labour market demands. This draws attention to the needs of this growing group of young people – capturing what has been labelled the 'missing middle' in youth studies (MacDonald, 2011; Roberts and MacDonald, 2013) – that has hitherto been overlooked in policy.

The case studies of Greece and Spain (Chapter 6 and Chapter 7) suggest that the distribution of social risks across European countries is linked to the changing shape of 'welfare mixes', or a reconfiguration in the balance between family, state and labour market as sources of welfare, particularly in southern Europe. This has included a retrenchment of the welfare state and an increasing reliance on family as a source of support for young people. In his chapter, Kretsos linked the current crisis to longer-term processes of labour market deregulation in Greece, including increasingly insecure work accompanied by a decreasing role for the state in guaranteeing labour market protection. The policy responses to the crisis have effectively exacerbated these processes by creating a special employment regime for young people characterised by lower wages and benefits. In his analysis of the *mileuristas* (highly skilled young people with low wages) in Spain, Gentile in Chapter 7 reveals heterogeneity in the experiences of precarity, even among this subgroup of young people. For him, precarity can be either a 'trampoline' or a challenge, depending on young people's contextual situation. The role of family in supporting young people in Spain financially and through housing emerges as a crucial factor in managing instability and social risks.

The findings from the case studies in Greece, Spain and the UK all remark upon how the distribution of risk among young people is dependent both on their socio-economic background and the welfare state apparatus in which they find themselves. The notion of the precariat formulated by Standing (2011), still relatively under-explored in empirical terms, has to be understood as the product of the structural conditions in which young people live and is not irrespective of welfare state models, as Standing seems to suggest. The empirical contributions from this research suggest the presence of a 'structural precariat' in southern and liberal countries framed by their specific welfare mix. They show how the process of dismantling welfare state protection in Greece reinforced the precarious nature of the labour market and how the reliance on family sources to sustain precarious transitions in Spain and the UK reproduces inequalities in young precarious lives. Therefore, we are witnessing several effects of the current crisis on the welfare mix of European countries: on the one hand, we see an increasingly precarious labour market fuelled by state deregulation; on the other hand, the winding back of the state's role in social protection in the name of 'austerity' and a concomitant increase in the role of family as a central source of welfare. The shift in welfare mixes is explored in more detail in the second part of the book.

13.2   Analysing social policies and welfare mixes

The second part of our publication moved onto the analysis of the different sets of welfare state interventions in Europe and the effects of the different sources of welfare in mitigating contemporary risks. It contained a series of contributions that discussed the role of welfare sources (the state, the labour market and the family) and social policies in addressing some of the issues identified in Part I, and how they respond to changing youth transitions.

In a policy context that emphasises the responsibility of the individual in managing his or her labour market risk, by becoming 'active', 'flexible' and 'employable', the contributions in this part emphasise the importance of considering 'structures' in contemporary youth transitions. The chapters reveal the extent to which individual pathways are effectively conditioned by structural conditions around young people. They also draw attention to the changing welfare mixes, and therefore the comparative relevance of family, state and labour market sources of welfare, in sustaining the risky transitions of young people.

In Chapter 8, Maestripieri and Sabatinelli provide an empirical exploration of this process in a comparative analysis of poorly educated and precariously employed young people in ten European countries. The chapter finds that work instability results in various degrees of vulnerability depending both on individual factors and structural factors, such as whether they rely on the state, the labour market, or other informal or quasi-formal networks as their sources of welfare. The findings of this study challenge the narrow focus on employability and underline the importance of considering structural factors in the construction of policies that address precarious transitions. The case studies from France by Chevalier and Palier (Chapter 10) and the UK by Berrington and Stone (Chapter 11) focus on different 'structural transitions', such as education and housing transitions, and the policies concerning them. Both chapters suggest that policy plays an important role in shaping youth transitions, underpinned by normative assumptions about the sources of welfare a young person should be relying on at different stages of the transition to adulthood. In particular they reveal that, where there is an assumption that the family is the most appropriate source of welfare for young people in certain circumstances, policies in both countries can leave young people with no option but to rely on their families (through financial support or housing), or encourage families to support their young members. The two chapters also reveal that at times policy can treat different groups of young people differently, depending on the extent to which they conform to normative expectations of youth transitions, promoting different welfare mixes for different groups of young people.

In relation to this, a further major contribution of this book is to challenge the idea of smooth transitions in certain parts of Europe, in particular in Germany (Chapter 12) and in northern Europe (Chapter 9). While these countries show comparatively better outcomes in terms of deprivation among young people, the contributions in this book show that young people in these countries are also affected by challenges in youth transitions, and are subject to considerable inequalities. The first main 'myth' in the comparative analysis of social policy for young people is that education to work transitions in the German model represent the 'gold standard' of youth transitions in Europe. The contribution by Heinz in Chapter 12 offers a different assessment of the evolution of school to work transitions and identifies several problems in the system, in particular in its capacity for reinforcing social inequalities.

Furthermore, the comparative research across Nordic welfare regimes in Chapter 9 illustrates how social protection for young adults in Nordic countries, in particular in Sweden and Finland, has evolved in a direction that is not in line with the features of the Nordic model. By analysing both the policy evolutions and the outcomes, the chapter indicates that, against what we might expect from our general understanding of social policy in those countries, poverty risk is determined both by socio-economic background and life-course changes. This finding is an important contribution to the overall literature on welfare state recalibration and recasting which, apart from identifying young people as a group affected by new social risks (Taylor-Gooby,

2004), has not yet explored the effects of different welfare state policies on young people. While this analysis shows that there are no welfare regime-types in Europe that are authentically 'young people-friendly', other contributions in the area are needed to understand the degree of convergence across welfare states in relation to youth social policies, in addition to the convergence of the risks that young people face that we identified in the first part of this book.

13.3   Structure, agency and the role of welfare mixes in shaping youth transitions

In sum, the findings above can be interpreted by using the theoretical framework we set out in Chapter 2, where we argued that changes to welfare states in relation to young people need to be analysed by looking at the 'welfare mixes' (the contribution of family, labour market and state sources), without limiting our analysis to welfare regime differences. We also stated that by exploring welfare sources as structures around young people it is possible to understand the processes that generate inequalities in youth transitions. By highlighting the normative assumptions underpinning youth policies in the areas of education and skills acquisition, labour market entry, residential emancipation and family formation, the chapters in this volume help us to understand the way in which different welfare mixes operate in different European countries.

The labour market is the central welfare source that young people draw on to achieve 'semi-dependence' (or 'semi-independence'). However, previous research has suggested that contemporary conditions have generated increasing labour market segmentation, exacerbated by the global economic crisis, between 'insiders' or those with secure work protected by state benefits, and 'outsiders' or those in precarious work that has few occupational benefits and builds no entitlements to social protection (Emmenegger et al., 2012). The research in this book suggests that young people are bearing the brunt of this segmentation, often relegated to 'outsider' status. The chapters in this volume reveal the extent to which states are reinforcing this polarisation of the labour market and further trapping young people in its periphery. States are introducing policies that are designed to support young people's workforce entry, such as promoting internships or apprenticeships or incentivising employers to develop special positions earmarked for young people. However, these forms of work are often insecure and low paid (or not paid) and have become additional forms of precarity, further entrenching young people's exclusion from the 'secure' labour market and deepening labour market segmentation. Policies introduced in the name of austerity, such as strict activation measures, are forcing young people to accept any position in the labour market, those that are often insecure, low paid and incommensurate with their skills, further damaging their labour market prospects.

While young people are spending more time looking for work, the chapters in this book reveal that social protection systems are failing to shield them from increasing labour market precarity. Unemployment protection schemes were based on assumptions of relatively unproblematic transitions into the workforce so that young people would have time to accumulate entitlement to benefits before they experienced labour market contingencies. However, the contemporary context in which many young people experience long spells of unemployment before they enter the labour market, or fluctuate between unemployment and periods of insecure work that do not accrue entitlements to unemployment benefits, challenges the design of traditional social insurance-based measures of social protection. At the same time, cuts to welfare state spending directed to young people and affecting several areas of their transitions (student support, housing benefits and so on) change the balance of welfare sources in the 'welfare mix', by reducing the protection provided by welfare states. If the most important function of the welfare state is to protect people from social risks (Hacker, 2004; Powell and Barrientos, 2004), the challenge facing European welfare states is not only to limit welfare state cuts in those areas where young people benefit the most, but also to adapt, update and recalibrate their policies to offer comprehensive protection against the new social risks that young people face.

The chapters reveal the way that different welfare states are underpinned by normative assumptions about how young people should manage risks as they transition to adulthood. Welfare states stipulate when young people should rely on their families, when they can rely on the state and when they should enter the labour market. The chapters also reveal that even within a welfare state, these normative assumptions do not apply to all young people equally. In particular, the 'familisation' of youth social policies implies an increasing reliance of family sources, which reinforces and reproduces socio-economic differences across the youth population. Many contributions of this book show that, despite the emphasis on young people's independent status in the labour market, family sources are becoming central in sustaining youth transitions.

The individualisation discourse in current policy encourages young people to 'take charge of their biography', build their employability through improving or consolidating their skills, and creating 'successful' trajectories to adulthood. However, conditions in which young people are forced to accept jobs that are low paid or outside their expertise just to make ends meet, with little safety net to protect them should they become unemployed, do not foster longer-term investment by young people in their skills, careers and futures. The chapters in this volume reveal that, as a result, supply-side policies that have dominated the policy environment since the global economic crisis (and leading up to the crisis) are not up to meeting the challenges associated with the new world of work.

The chapters on highly skilled young people's experience of precarious work show that not even highly educated young people are inoculated from the effects of the recession, adding weight to the argument that 'we are all precarious now'. However, many of the chapters in this book reveal that, as a result of structural inequalities, young people experience precarity differently. There is great heterogeneity across and within different groups of young people based on socio-demographic factors such as socio-economic background and gender, based on the social and cultural capital they possess, and based on their capacity to draw on support from informal networks. Importantly, the analysis of current policies for young people shows that policies are not reducing, but are increasing inequality in transitions to adulthood in several areas, in particular as a consequence of the 'dualisation' in youth social policies and of the increasing familisation of youth policies.

Finally, research suggests that precarity among young people is not a new phenomenon – it is the result of longer-term trends that have been exacerbated by the recession, creating new forms of insecurity. While the causes of contemporary risks are both long and short term, so could be the effects. The chapters in this volume suggest that, while young people are struggling to manage these risks in the present, they might face longer-term consequences, not just in the opportunity costs associated with precarious labour market attachment, such as the inability to develop career trajectories and consolidate skills, but in their entitlement to social protection and their plans for family formation. The chapters reveal that young people develop strategies for managing risk in the short term, and are flexible, resourceful and persistent in managing those risks, but the current context forces them to focus on the present and makes it difficult for them to plan for the future. More effective social shock absorbers would create greater biographical certainty for young people to enable them to 'construct their own biographies', or plan for the future.

13.4   Towards a European social policy strategy for young people?

The findings above also suggest some points relevant to European policymaking in this area. First of all, the research set out in this book builds a compelling case for an integrated approach to youth policy, as it crosscuts many different policy areas. The existence of a 'Ministry of Youth' in several European countries signals the priority that youth policies are assuming across Europe, but can be perceived as a limited approach to the challenges described in this book. While European policymaking has effectively incorporated 'gender mainstreaming' as a tool of promoting gender equality in different sets of policies, youth policies are still confined in specific areas and sectors. Furthermore, as we pointed out in Chapter 1, the focus of policies seems to be on youth unemployment, rather than on the complex sets of policies that influence youth transitions. For this reason, there is an urgent need to promote the idea of 'youth mainstreaming' in European social policies, in order to tackle the multiple sets of risks faced by young people.

There is also a specific contribution to be made to the potential content of such 'mainstreamed' policies. The precise effects of European institutions on youth policies are not clear: aside from the pressures of European austerity and its effect on young people, there have been a number of European initiatives formulated to address the contemporary risks facing young people. The most relevant initiative, the European Youth Guarantee 2013, aims to tackle the problems faced by young people following the same old paradigm. This scheme targets young people who are not in work or in education. It provides assistance in the form of individualised support to improve employability, skills upgrading, and in seeking and obtaining work. The assumption underpinning the scheme is, therefore, that improving skills and gaining work experience will enable young people to overcome the challenges they face in finding secure work and building a coherent career trajectory. However, the findings in this publication show that the challenge is more complex than this. Highly educated and highly skilled young people also face precarious transitions into the workforce, and these have a detrimental effect on their lives. At the same time, a 'work-first' approach to policy that channels young people into low paid, insecure work that is often incommensurate with their skills and qualifications does not always improve labour market prospects and can in fact entrench labour market insecurity and disadvantage.

In addition to the need for effective policies that reverse the focus on supply-side policies, the findings from this book suggest that an over-reliance on the family as a source of support for young people can reproduce inequalities and create a dualisation of youth transitions, between those whose families have the means to cushion the effects of contemporary risks on young people's transitions, and those whose families cannot. This challenges the effectiveness of European policy instruments that place a focus on the role of family as a source of welfare to the exclusion of the role of the state. The studies in this book show that state sources of welfare can effectively limit the consequences of labour market risk and ameliorate the inequalities that are reproduced by a reliance on families.

References

Emmenegger, P., Hausermann, S., Palier, B. and Seeleib-Kaiser, M. (2012). *The Age of Dualization* (Oxford: Oxford University Press).

Hacker, J.S. (2004). 'Privatizing Risk without Privatizing the Welfare State: The Hidden Politics of Social Policy Retrenchment in the United States'. *American Political Science Review* 98 (2), 243–60.

MacDonald, R. (2011). 'Youth Transitions, Unemployment and Underemployment: Plus ça change, plus c'est la même chose?' *Journal of Sociology* 47 (4), 427–44.

Powell, M. and Barrientos, A. (2004). 'Welfare Regimes and the Welfare Mix'. *European Journal of Political Research* 43 (1), 83–105.

Roberts, S. and MacDonald, R. (2013). 'Introduction for Special Section of Sociological Research Online: The Marginalised Mainstream: Making Sense of the "Missing Middle" of Youth Studies'. *Sociological Research Online* 18 (1), 1–21.

Standing, G. (2011). *The Precariat: The New Dangerous Class* (London: Bloomsbury Academic).

Taylor-Gooby, P. (2004). *New Risks, New Welfare: The Transformation of the European Welfare State* (Oxford: Oxford University Press).

Index

activation policies, 18, 147–8, 163,
    171–2, 203–4, 236, 237–40, 259
  critique of, 147–8, 163–4, 202–3,
    239, 252
agency, 18, 21–3, 29, 90, 101
  compare welfare structures
anxiety and frustration, 75, 76, 96, 97,
    100, 162–3, 203
  see also labour market youth
    frustration and discontent
austerity, 1, 19, 90, 106, 115–16, 120
  youth resistance, 120

biographies, 14, 17–18, 76–8, 100,
    106–7, 151, 152–9, 236–7,
    249–50, 263
  choice biographies, 28–9, 80, *see
    also* individualization
  traditional/standard, 15, 17, 126

capitalism, 64, 238
Croatia, 49

deprivation, *see* poverty

economic crisis, *see* recession
education
  debt, 15, 74–5
  expansion, 15, 189, 191–3, 213–14
  over-qualification, *see* labour market
    skills mismatch
  system stratification, 243–4, 250
  see also skills, university, vocational
    training
employment, 112–13, 127
  brain drain, 118
  contract, temporary or casual, 62,
    67, 69–70, 198–201
  fragmented transitions between
    jobs, 72, 93–5
  full time, 62, 116–17
  and identity, 15, 129–30, 162, 244

insecure work, 106–7, 108–9,
    116–18, 125, 129–32, 143,
    152–60, *see also* contract,
    temporary or casual
  internships, unpaid, 15–16, 70, 73–4
  minimum wage, 4, 70–1, 96, 116,
    118–19
  pay/earning, low, 74, 96, 101, 114,
    135, 154
  self-employment, 71, 114, 251
  see also labour market
European Union
  Europe 2020 Strategy, 41, 42
  European Commission – Youth
    Guarantee Strategy, 41
  European Communities Household
    Panel Survey, 38–9
  EU Survey of Income & Living
    Conditions 2009, 42–5
  EU Youth Strategy 2010–18, 41

family
  cohabitation, 77, 220, 229
  formation delay and parenthood,
    77–8, 212–13, 261, 263
  as a source of welfare, 24, 76–7, 89,
    101, 110–11, 120, 125, 128–9,
    133–4, 136, 137–8, 141–2,
    161–2, 191–3, 193–5, 210–11,
    215, 229
  strain, 97–8, 161
Finland, 171–2, 174–5,
    179–82
flexicurity, 68
France, 149, 189–206
  social policies (e.g. FAJ, RMI, RSA,
    CIVIS, ALMP), 194–5, 203–4

gender, 152–3
  female caring responsibilities &
    motherhood, 16, 20, 251
  female temporary workers, 77

housing policy impact on
non-resident fathers, 218–19,
227–8, 231
Germany, 150, 162, 236–53
Hartz Acts, 239
Greece, 106–20

higher education, *see* university
housing
cost, increase, 215
housing benefit/subsidy, 196–7,
210, 216–17, 218,
226–7, 229–30
shared accommodation, 212–23,
217–18, 220–4, 229
social housing, 215–16, 224–6

income, *see* employment pay
income support, *see* social assistance
individualization/responsibilisation,
14, 17–19, 24, 88–91, 100, 126–7,
236–7, 240, 263
critique of, 99–102, 242
inequality, 114–15, 241, 246,
249–50, 257
globalisation, exacerbating
inequality, 40
inter-generational & structural, 19,
21–2, 205
policy, exacerbating inequality, 190,
200–1, 230–1, 245
insecurity, *see* risk
intergenerational solidarity,
110–11, 120
Italy, 67, 68–9, 70, 73–4, 76–8, 81–2,
150, 153, 156

labour market
deregulation & flexibilisation
reforms, 64, 68–9, 78, 108,
114–15, 154, 236, 237–8,
239–40, 242, 258, *see also*
employment insecure work
de-skilling, 76
precarity for highly-skilled workers,
16, 20–1, 64, 68–70, 72–6, 80,
106–7, 125–6, 199, 249–50, 252,
see also labour market skills

mismatch and
over-qualification
secondary labour market policies,
trapping youth, 65–6, 198–9,
201–2
segmentation and polarisation, 4,
21, 62, 69–70, 78–9, 82, 114,
127, 199–201, 241–2, *see also*
inequality
skills mismatch and
over-qualification, 15–16, 20–1,
62–3, 67, 75–6, 80, 121, 133–4,
143, 155–7, 257–8
weak integration, 150–1, *see also*
employment insecure work
youth frustration and discontent,
72–3, 75–6, 95–6, 98, 111,
134–6, 137–8, 155, 158
see also employment
life-course perspective, 3–4, 14–18,
179, 197–8, 252–3
policy, 236, 237, 240–1, 247
see also biographies
lost generation, x, 115–16

marketization, *see* labour market
deregulation and flexibilisation
reforms
minimum wage, *see* employment
minimum wage
missing middle, 3, 258

NEET (Not in Education, Employment
or Training), 2, 91, 158, 165, 203
neoliberalism, *see* labour market
deregulation and flexibilisation
Netherlands, 149, 150, 154, 157, 158
Nordic welfare states, 169–85, 260–1
see also individual countries
Norway, 171–2, 175–6, 179–82

Poland, 149
polarisation, *see* labour market
segmentation and polarisation
poverty
cross-national differences attributed
to welfare regimes, 38–9, 45–7,
48–9, 49–50, 52–4, 56, 169

poverty – *continued*
  income poverty, 38, 43–4, 53, 170–1
  material & social deprivation, 44,
    53, 54–5
  measures of poverty, 37–8, 52–3,
    55–6
  subjective poverty, 44, 54–5
  and transition, 50, 52
  youth and adult comparison, 47,
    49–50, 56, 108–9, 118

recession
  effects, long term, 41, 76–8, 80–1,
    119, 162, 256, 263
  effects, short term, 76–8, 162, 256
risk
  heightened sense of, 14, 263
  labour market risk, 17, 139–40, 184
  new risks, 2, 14–15, 22,
    40, 126

school, *see* education
semi-dependence, 19, 26, 27–8, 30, 88,
    147–8, 152–9, 261–2
  social citizenship incomplete,
    194, 204
skills
  acquisition, 135–6, 155–7
  high skilled/qualified, 73, 80, 118,
    126, 137, 142, 190, 247,
    257–8
  low skilled, 150–1, 157, 158, 165,
    190, 198, 247
  over-qualification, *see* labour market
    skills mismatch
  specialised skills, demand for, 15
social assistance or benefits, 153,
    178–80, 190, 194–5, 203–4
  agencies critiqued, 98, 100
  benefits trap, 96
  means-tested, 19, 170, 172–3,
    183–5, 241
social division, 18, 138–40, 179–80
  class, 19–20, 128–9, 129–40, 178–82,
    213, 246
social exclusion and marginalisation,
    89, 99–100, 102, 109, 163,
    172, 199

social inclusion/integration policy
  and paid work, 41–2, 127, 139, 171,
    248–9, 261–2
  post WWII, 88–9
social insurance, 16, 70–1, 170, 172,
    174–8, 204, 262
social policy theory, 3–5, 13–14, 256
social protection, inadequate, 68–70,
    78–9, 154, 262
  suggested reform, 81–2, 164–6
  see also social assistance or benefits
social vulnerability, 148–60
sociology of youth, *see* youth studies
Southern Europe, *see individual
    countries*
Spain, 67, 68–70, 71, 72–80, 81–2,
    125–42, 149, 161, 163
  Mileuristas, 125–6, 127–8, *see also*
    labour market precarity
stratification
  in education, *see* education system
    stratification
  in the labour market, *see* labour
    market segmentation and
    polarisation
structured individualism, 22–3
Sweden, 149, 171–2, 176–8,
    179–82
Switzerland, 149, 163

transitions to adulthood, 4, 129–42,
    179, 189, 250–1, 260
  de-standardised/non-linear changes,
    14–16, 28, 72, 126,
    148, 211
  feminist critique, 228–9
  fluctuating or reversible or yo-yo
    transitions, 16–17, 138,
    183, 214
  moving out of the family
    home/residential
    independence, 137–8, 211,
    212, 215
  policy, impact of, 17–18, 142
  protracted, 4, 17, 133–4, 160–1,
    170–1
  school-to-work, 70, 150–60, 165,
    185, 228, 246–7

structural impediments, 96–7, 99–101, *see also* social division
transition regimes, 7, 39, 52, 188

underemployment, 27, 80, 119, 128, 220
unemployment, 58, 65, 73, 106–7, 117, 127, 152, 215, 243
policy, *see* activation
structural disadvantage, 109–14, 119–20
see also poverty
unemployment insurance, *see* social insurance
United Kingdom, 7, 67–8, 72, 74–6, 78–80, 81–2, 87–102, 149, 163
university, 19–21, 127, 133, 142, 189–94, 204–5, 214, 250

vocational training/education and apprenticeships, 67, 69–70, 90, 150, 157, 192, 199, 202, 237, 243–6, 248–9, 251–3

welfare mix, 7–8, 24–8, 30, 261
welfare regimes/typologies, 6–7, 23–4, 149, 189–90, 262
corporatist welfare regimes, 6, 237, *see also individual countries*
critique, 25–6, 29–30
liberal welfare regimes, 6, 24, *see also individual countries*
social democratic or universalist welfare regimes, 6, 169–85, *see also individual countries*
welfare structures, 8–9, 13, 17–18, 24–6, 29, 67–8, 125, 257, 258–9
compare agency
welfare theory, *see* social policy theory or welfare regimes/typologies

youth studies, 5, 13–14, 28–9, 256, 264–5
youth transitions, *see* transitions to adulthood